DEVELOPING JAVABEANS™ USING VISUALAGE® FOR JAVA™

DEVELOPING JAVABEANS™ USING VISUALAGE® FOR JAVA™

DALE R. NILSSON
PETER M. JAKAB

WILEY COMPUTER PUBLISHING

John Wiley & Sons, Inc.
New York • Chichester • Weinheim • Brisbane • Singapore • Toronto

Publisher: Robert Ipsen
Editor: Theresa Hudson
Managing Editor: Angela Murphy
Electronic Products, Associate Editor: Mike Sosa
Text Design & Composition: Benchmark Productions, Inc.

Designations used by companies to distinguish their products are often claimed as trademarks. In all instances where John Wiley & Sons, Inc., is aware of a claim, the product names appear in initial capital or ALL CAPITAL LETTERS. Readers, however, should contact the appropriate companies for more complete information regarding trademarks and registration.

This book is printed on acid-free paper. ⊗

This publication is designed to provide accurate and authoritative information in regard to the subject matter covered. It is sold with the understanding that the publisher is not engaged in professional services. If professional advice or other expert assistance is required, the services of a competent professional person should be sought.

Library of Congress Cataloging-in-Publication Data:
Nilsson, Dale R.
    Developing JavaBeans Using VisualAge for Java / Dale R. Nilsson and Peter M. Jakab
      p.   cm.
    "Wiley Computer Publishing."
    Includes index.
    ISBN 0–471–29788–7 (pbk./CD-ROM)
    1. Java (Computer program language) 2. JavaBeans. 3. VisualAge.
    I. Jakab, Peter M. II. Title.
    IN PROCESS
    005.13'3--dc21   98–13043

Printed in the United States of America.
10 9 8 7 6 5 4 3 2 1

To my three energetic sons Karl, Erik, and Nikolaus, who are growing up too fast, and to my loving wife, Jacqueline, for her patience, understanding, and endless support. Also for my mother, Patricia, who told me as a youth: *You are judged by what you do, not what you say you will do.*

— Dale R. Nilsson

To my wife Mabel, my daughter Jessie, and my son Justin. Without their support and encouragement this book would not have been written. And lastly, to Goldie, our Golden Retriever, who always kept me company during the long days and nights writing this book.

— Peter M. Jakab

Contents

FOREWORD   xiii

ACKNOWLEDGMENTS   xv

INTRODUCTION   xvii

ABOUT THE AUTHORS   xxiii

CHAPTER 1 BREAKING OPEN THE BOX   1

What Hardware and Software Do You Need?   1
     Hardware Requirements   2
     Development versus Run-time Requirements   5
Installing the Necessary Software   5
     What's in the VisualAge for Java Folder?   6
     Using VisualAge Java Documentation   7
     Starting VisualAge for Java   8
The Integrated Development Environment   8
     IDE Windows   8
     IDE Views   9
How the IDE Stores Data   11
     Repository   11
     Workspace   11
     Loading Java Classes into the Workspace   11
     Running an Applet   15
Summary   25

CHAPTER 2 BUILDING THE HELLO WORLD APPLET   27

Workbench Options   27
Your First Applet   32
Creating Projects and Packages   32
     Projects   33
     Packages   33
Making a New GUI Bean   36
     Getting Acquainted with the Visual
     Composition Editor   38
     Making an Applet   41
     Adding More Function to Hello World   51
     Saving and Testing the Improved
     Hello World Applet   57
     Viewing the Generated Code   58
Summary   60

CHAPTER 3 MAKING AN ADDING MACHINE   61
  JavaBeans Basics   62
    Deprecated Methods   62
  Types of Beans   63
    GUI Beans   63
    Invisible Beans   64
  Building an Adding Machine   65
    Creating a New Package   67
    Creating a New Class   68
    Layout Managers   71
    Adding GUI Beans to a GridLayout   75
    Editing Buttons   77
    Naming Beans   78
    Read-only TextFields   79
    Testing an Applet   79
    Naming Conventions   79
    What Are Tab Stops?   80
    Running the Updated Adding Machine   83
  Summary   84

CHAPTER 4 MAKING INVISIBLE BEANS   85
  Understanding JavaBeans Features   86
    Java Types   86
    What Are Properties?   86
    What Are Methods?   87
    What Are Events?   87
    The BeanInfo Class   87
    Finishing the Adding Machine   88
    Defining Properties   95
    Defining Methods   104
    Using JavaBeans in the Visual Composition Editor 105
  Types of Connections   105
    Property-to-Property Connections   107
    Testing the Calculator   109
    Testing the Calculator Again   113
    Generating Javadoc   114
  Summary   115

CHAPTER 5 DEBUGGING BEANS   117
  Introduction to Debugging   117
    Using System.out.println()   118
    Debugging Connections   118
    The handleException() Method   121
  Introduction to the Scrapbook   122
    Execution Context   123
    Using the Scrapbook   124

The uvm.tools.debugger Package   127
Introduction to the Debugger   128
    Importing the Switcher Package   128
    Debugging the Switcher Program   132
Summary   140

**CHAPTER 6 BUILDING THE ADVANCED
CALCULATOR GUI   141**
Your Next Applet   141
    Packages   141
    Copying Beans   142
Improving the CalculatorView   147
    GridBagLayout   148
    Using GridBagLayout   149
Test Iteration One   151
    Setting TextField Properties   151
    Label Alignment   152
    Setting GridBagConstraints Properties   153
Building a Sub-Panel   155
    Adding a Panel to a Container   158
Test Iteration Two   160
The GridBag Code   160
    Naming the GUI Beans   163
    Using the init() Method   164
Test Iteration Three   166
Summary   166

**CHAPTER 7 BUILDING THE ADVANCED
CALCULATOR LOGIC   167**
Extending an Invisible Bean   167
    Adding the GUI Bean to the Visual Composition Editor   170
Advanced Calculator Connections   173
    Moving Connections   173
    Testing the Add Function   176
    More Connections   177
    Adding a Clear Function   178
    Testing the Math Functions   181
Exception Handling   182
    Using Exceptions   183
    Importing a Bean   183
    Testing Exception Handling   186
    How Does the Exception Work?   188
Modifying the Bean Palette   191
Making a Numeric Only TextField   192
    Importing More Java Files   192

Using a Filtered TextField   193
Testing the IntTextFields   197
How Does the IntTextField Work?   198
IntTextField Hierarchy   198
IntTextField Source Code   198
Summary   200

CHAPTER 8 DEPLOYING JAVA   **201**
Exporting from VisualAge   201
Exporting Java Byte-Code (.class Files)   202
Exporting Java Source (.java Files)   204
Java Archives (.jar Files)   209
How VisualAge Uses Resource Files   212
VisualAge Interchange Format (.dat Files)   215
Exporting an Interchange File   215
Publishing Programs   216
Running Applets Outside of the IDE   217
Making HTML Files   219
Running Applications Outside of the IDE   221
Distributing Beans   222
Summary   226

CHAPTER 9 BUILDING THE INTERNET
ADDRESS APPLET   **227**
Creating the InternetAddress Class   229
Adding Bean Properties to the InternetAddress Class   231
InternetUserInfoPanel   234
Making Constructors   234
Adding Constructor Code   236
Creating User Interface Panels   237
InternetUserInfoPanel   237
VisualAge Variables   237
Using the This   239
InternetAdditionalInfoPanel   240
InternetFormattedInfoPanel   242
InternetButtonPanel   246
Testing the InternetAddress Panels   247
Creating InternetAddressFinalApplet   252
CardLayout   252
Testing the InternetAddressFinalApplet   256
Summary   257

CHAPTER 10 THE REMINDER APPLICATION   **259**
Using Embedded Beans   260
Requirements for the Reminder Application   260
Constructing the Reminder Application   261

RadioButtonManager   262
RadioButtonPanel   264
ReminderPanel   267
ReminderApp   273
Adding Persistence   275
Adding Menus   288
Summary   298

CHAPTER 11 ADVANCED TOPICS   **301**
Enterprise Edition   301
Exploring the Data Access Builder   302
Using the Generated Data Access Beans   311
User-Generated Events   318
Types of Events   319
Making Your Own Events   320
How Events Work   326
Summary of Events   327
Visual Design Patterns   327
GUI Connection Pattern   327
Aggregation Pattern   328
Circular Pattern   328
Monolithic Pattern   329
Tight Coupling Pattern   330
Diamond Pattern   331
Visual Patterns Summary   332
A Tour of the Swing Toolkit   332
Combination Box   333
DebugGraphics   333
Tree View   333
Look and Feel   333
Other Swing Enhancements   336
Summary   337
Wrapping Up the Book   338

RELATED PUBLICATIONS   **339**
INDEX   **341**

FOREWORD

JavaBeans is the only component architecture for the Java platform. When you write a JavaBeans component, it runs on any platform that runs the Java Virtual Machine. JavaBeans is a lightweight component architecture that enables a developer to assemble an application that is written only once, runs anywhere, and consists of components that can be reused everywhere. Although JavaBeans is a fairly new technology—it was first released in February 1997—the uptake has been tremendous. Many development tools support the JavaBeans model and a large number of applications and intranet solutions are based upon JavaBeans.

Through a process called *introspection*, JavaBeans applies standard design patterns or style guides to dynamically determine the capabilities and attributes of a Java class. Once a developer becomes familiar with the Java language, turning out JavaBeans components instead of *just* Java classes is a very simple step. Developers can get started very quickly and while their experience grows begin to take advantage of the more sophisticated features of the JavaBeans specification. Or, to put it otherwise, *simple things are easy, complex things are possible.* Because of the dynamic nature of JavaBeans, both experienced developers and non-programmers feel at ease. The visual orientation of tools like VisualAge for Java allow for the easy composition of existing Beans and support source-code level creation and reuse of Beans.

A JavaBeans component can take many forms, from a simple UI control to a robust, full-fledged distributed application. JavaBeans is device-neutral so that JavaBeans components can be deployed on devices ranging from web phones and JavaStations to back-end servers. You can find numerous examples of commercial JavaBeans-based products at http://java.sun.com/beans/directory.

JavaBeans was developed by Sun Microsystems with the help and support of many industry partners. The VisualAge team at IBM played an important role in making JavaBeans such a success by sharing their expertise in object-oriented development and reusability. This book is a great way to get started with JavaBeans using VisualAge for Java.

Onno Kluyt
Senior Product Manager for JavaBeans
Sun Microsystems Inc., JavaSoft

ACKNOWLEDGMENTS

A number of dedicated professionals helped us with this book. Our managers, Peter Spung, Oma Sewhdat, Allan Friedman, and Greg Clark provided their support, encouragement, and most importantly, the permission to write this book. To Skip McGaughey, the Marketing Manager for VisualAge for Java, who gave us permission to use the VisualAge logo and include the CD with the book. Our legal eagle, Ed Duffield, for his wisdom, colorful stories, and contract approval. Thanks to Dave Peterson who helped with the book agreement and the *Write Now* program.

We were very happy to add contributions from Russ Stinehour and Greg Hester of CrossLogic Corporation. The in-depth technical review from Bryon Kataoka of Commercial Solutions helped improve the quality and accuracy of the book. It was great to have some "fresh eyes" to look over the book and ensure the instructions are complete. Appreciation to John Akerley for supplying some JavaBeans used in this book. Stephan Marceau gave some helpful comments as well.

Thanks to Terri Hudson of John Wiley & Sons, who was great to work with as the book's Senior Editor, and Sandy Bontemps and Kathryn A. Malm for their help with the book's production. Sue Carpenter, our copyeditor, was able to fix the grammar, style, and typos that happen from writing in planes and hotels. Also, thanks to the many people in the VisualAge for Java team who assisted us with information and support.

INTRODUCTION

The use of Java has exploded over the last year, and the introduction of VisualAge for Java in July 1997 has helped many developers create state-of-the-art Java applications. This book helps you learn how to use VisualAge for Java with step-by-step instructions for building a variety of sample Java applications along with numerous screen captures of the actual VisualAge for Java product that provide visual feedback on the progress of your Java applications.

Overview of This Book

This book is adapted from a workshop that we developed to help introduce VisualAge for Java into the marketplace. The authors taught this course to customers and IBM developers to jump-start the introduction of VisualAge for Java. The attendees provided feedback each time the course was conducted, and this feedback was used to improve the course content. The course was taught to developers all over the world, including the United States, Canada, Germany, England, China, Australia, Peru, Mexico, Argentina, and Japan.

We had many requests for the course material from people who had heard about the workshop and wanted to learn VisualAge for Java. We decided to convert the workshop to a book that could be used for the course and by individuals for self-study. To make the book, we combined the course presentation material, the lab scripts, lecture content, and experiences with customers.

With the rapidly evolving status of Java and supporting tools, there is always some late-breaking news. With this in mind, we try to describe and use the "stable" parts of Java. This book focuses on using JavaBeans that are new to the Java Development Toolkit (JDK) Version 1.1 and well supported in VisualAge for Java. We also focus on using the common AWT components and defer coverage of the JDK Version 1.2 components, known as Java Foundation Classes (JFC), to other books.

While writing the book, we improved the sample applications from the workshop. We improved their design, used better controls or widgets, and tried different variations in design.

This book helps prepare you for IBM VisualAge for Java certification, which is part of the IBM Object Technology certification. You can get more information at www.software.ibm.com/ad/certify. There are currently two levels of VisualAge for Java certification:

1. **The Certified VisualAge for Java Object-Oriented Associate Developer.**
   This level requires two, timed multiple-choice tests administered by Sylvan Prometrics. The two tests cover knowledge of the Java language as well as the VisualAge for Java tool. The Java language test is the Sun Programmer test. Examples of test questions are available on the Web site.

2. **The Certified VisualAge for Java Object-Oriented Developer.** After you have passed the VisualAge for Java Object-Oriented Associate Developer tests and you acquire some practical experience developing with VisualAge for Java, you must take one more multiple-choice timed test on the subject of object-oriented design. Then, you can enroll in the Java Developer practicum. This one-week test requires you to solve a business problem. The solution includes validating requirements, object-oriented analysis and design, coding, testing, and deployment in a team environment using VisualAge for Java. This is a good test of applying your knowledge of Java and VisualAge for Java to solve a software problem. It's a very intense week, but for those who prepare sufficiently, it is truly rewarding.

This book is the result of a real collaborative effort between the authors. The chapters show the collective knowledge and experience of all the authors and provide the reader with a comprehensive view of JavaBeans development with VisualAge for Java. The authors draw on their experience using VisualAge for Java with customers for the material in this book. Although the author team for this book is separated by many miles, we are connected by email and a common language—Java. The result of this effort is an easy-to-follow, comprehensive handbook for learning VisualAge for Java visual programming. This is the second book we have produced together.

How This Book Is Organized

Each chapter in this book starts with a brief description of what is covered and ends with a summary. The book has a number of small applications to illustrate a broad range of application development topics. This book starts out slowly with quite a bit of detail. As you progress in the book, the instructions become briefer and the amount of function in the applications increases.

Chapter 1: Breaking Open the Box

This chapter gets you started on the right foot. It covers installation considerations, the help system, and starting VisualAge for Java. We introduce you to the integrated development environment (IDE) and the various views, and you can try some IDE customization. This chapter describes the repository and the workspace and shows you how to make bookmarks in the IDE. Finally, you learn how to import Java classes into the IDE and how to run an applet.

Chapter 2: Building the Hello World Applet

Chapter 2 shows you how to build the Java Hello World applet. To do this, you create a project and a package, then define an applet. We also discuss visual builder basics, including the use of categories, a label, how to set properties, and how to test an applet. We show you how to improve the applet with invisible beans and visual connections. You then run the completed applet.

Chapter 3: Making an Adding Machine

In this chapter we cover the basics of JavaBeans including GUI, invisible, and composite beans. We then discuss Layout Managers and develop an applet using a GridBagLayout with TextFields, Labels, and a Button.

Chapter 4: Making Invisible Beans

We continue our discussion of JavaBeans with coverage of properties, events, and methods. This chapter shows you how to create your own invisible JavaBeans using the SmartGuide in VisualAge for Java. You learn how to edit the generated methods and how to use invisible beans in the Visual Builder.

Chapter 5: Debugging Beans

Chapter 5 covers debugging Java programs using the VisualAge for Java integrated Debugger. You see how to debug a Java program by stepping through the code, inspecting objects, and changing code. You also learn how to use the Scrapbook and the Console windows in VisualAge for Java.

Chapter 6: Building the Advanced Calculator GUI

Chapter 6 has information on more advanced user-interface beans in AWT including a good overview of the different types of JavaBeans. You learn how to use the ominous GridBagLayout Manager and GridBag Constraints. You also learn additional functions in the IDE like how to copy beans, set tabs stops, and edit bean properties.

Chapter 7: Building the Advanced Calculator Logic

In this chapter we show you how to extend invisible beans with additional behavior and how to incorporate exception handling for error detection and correction into your Java programs. You learn how to import classes and Java files into the IDE. As you finish the Advanced Calculator applet, you use a message box and add numeric-only TextFields to the applet. You also see how to modify the bean palette in the Visual Builder.

Chapter 8: Deploying Java

Chapter 8 covers the important task of creating the runtime files. You learn how to export and package Java files, class files, and Jar files. You learn the basic HTML tags needed to test a simple applet. You also test Java applets and applications outside the VisualAge for Java IDE.

Chapter 9: Building the Internet Address Applet

We present a comprehensive, sample Java program that uses a CardLayout manager. You also learn how to define constructors in VisualAge for Java and how to use them in the Visual Builder. We show you how to layer in Java and how to use Variables and Factory Objects in the Visual Builder.

Chapter 10: The Reminder Application

Chapter 10 shows you how to use a number of more complex user-interface beans. You develop a Reminder List program and use Menus and Submenus. You create Checkbox Groups with Radio buttons. You also use Event-to-Script connections and add a File dialog to your Java program. Finally, this chapter shows you how to develop user Help for a Java program and then use a Web Browser to display HTML Help.

Chapter 11: Advanced Topics

With this final chapter we cover four important topics. First, we provide an overview of the components in the Enterprise Edition of VisualAge for Java with a detailed example for using the Data Access Builder. Second, you learn how to create user-generated Events and then add them to your Java programs. Third, we cover Visual Design Patterns that help use the Visual Builder. Finally, you learn about improvements to the AWT in JDK 1.2.

Conventions Used in This Book

This book contains many instructions for completing the sample Java applications. These instructions are shown as lists and use a number of conventions to make instructions, tool text, and Java programming information as clear as possible.

The screen captures displayed in the pages of this book are from the Windows version of the VisualAge for Java product. The OS/2 screens are virtually identical with only minor system specific exceptions like the file dialog and the frame window icons.

As we go to press, the Team edition of VisualAge for Java is almost ready for its debut. Also the first patches to Version 1.0 are being made available to customers. Some changes to the user interface are introduced. The screen captures in this book reflect the VisualAge for Java Version 1.0 single-user try-and-buy edition of the product as it exists in the enclosed CD-ROM.

The field names in the VisualAge for Java user interface and information entered are shown in bold to differentiate them from instructions. For example, an instruction in the book may read: Enter **John Smith** in the **Name** entry field.

Bolding is also used throughout the book to improve readability of VisualAge for Java terms and Java language terms. For example, you use the **GridBagLayout** that is part of Java AWT.

The instructions to build the samples frequently tell you to press a button on a VisualAge for Java tool. We refer to these buttons by their name, but most of the buttons are shown with only a graphic image. To make it clearer, we frequently provide a graphic in the margin that gives you a visual cue to the referenced button. For example, you see the instruction: Press the **Test** button, and the test icon appears in the left margin.

When instructions are given in the book for entering information into VisualAge for Java, the words *enter* and *type* are used interchangeably.

A monospaced font is used to show code segments. Anything typed in this font should be taken literally and entered exactly as shown. This font is also used for code listings, because it preserves spacing in the code. When entering code or code segments, be aware that many of the lines of code in the book had to be split into two or more lines. This is because of the line width available in the page. Every effort has been made to split the lines in a way that causes no problems, even if you enter them as shown, in multiple lines. However in some case, for example when we had to split a literal string, you should join the lines in the page into a single line of code.

Terms Used in the Book

A number of terms in this book use Java language statements and AWT terms, and these are not necessarily Standard English words. For example, the AWT library provides the classes **Frame** and **FlowLayout**. The first time this class name is used in the book, it's mentioned by its formal name. In later sections of the book, an informal term is used and is not bolded such as frame or flow layout.

In the VisualAge for Java product documentation, there are some terms that are not commonly used between developers. For example, some online books use the term *Visual Composition Browser*, and in other places *Visual Composition View* is used. For simplicity, instructions in this book use the shorter generic VisualAge term *Visual Builder*.

The Java language gives you the ability to create applets and applications. Applets are usually integrated in a Web page, run in a browser like Netscape Navigator, and are subject to the Java security model. Applications run separately in a frame and are not subject to the Java security model. For example, they can write to your disk drive. Because it's very awkward to constantly refer to *writing Java applets and applications*, this book frequently uses the phrase *writing Java programs* when referring to Java programming. Whenever we specifically mean applets or applications, we say so in the text.

Throughout this book, we refer to Java classes and JavaBeans interchangeably. The user interface of VisualAge for Java refers to both classes and beans, so the appropriate term is used when referring to the user interface.

Disclaimer

Both of the authors are employees of IBM and wrote this book under an agreement with IBM. The agreement between the authors and IBM requires the following disclaimer:

> The opinions expressed herein are those of the authors and do not represent those of their employer.

Who Should Read This Book?

This book is targeted at the reader that is familiar with object-oriented programming and the Java programming language. A general understanding of graphical user interfaces (GUIs) and a familiarity with the Java AWT classes and their functions is very helpful. There are many sources for learning Java and the AWT classes, which include self-study books, interactive CD-ROMs, and formal education. Other books that can help you with these areas are listed in the Related Publications section.

This book is a great help for anyone new to VisualAge for Java. You learn how to use the development environment from the very basics to building complete Java applets and applications, including their deployment. This book has many examples on proper object-oriented implementations using VisualAge-unique visual construction tools. Even people who are familiar with the other VisualAge products will get a lot of valuable information from this book's extensive coverage of the Java AWT classes and the JavaBeans event model.

What's on the CD-ROM

The CD-ROM contains the Entry edition of VisualAge for Java 1.0. With this version, you can complete all of the sample applications and applets in this book. Follow the instructions in Chapter 1 to install VisualAge for Java from the CD-ROM. For more up-to-date information on the installation of the components on the CD-ROM and other late breaking news, please read the READ.ME file on the root directory of the CD-ROM.

The CD-ROM contains the following:

- VisualAge for Java Entry Edition
- VisualAge for Java 1.0 Patch Set 1
- Sun Java Developers Toolkit 1.1.5
- Sun Java Runtime Environment 1.1.5
- All the completed projects in the book

If you already have VisualAge for Java 1.0 installed, you still need to install Patch Set 1 to get some of the projects in the book to work properly.

Getting Support

Support for VisualAge for Java is provided through the Web site for the product at www.software.ibm.com/ad/vajava. This includes a section for frequently asked questions (FAQs), forums for posting questions, and samples. There are also a number of service-and-support, fee-based offerings from IBM. One way to get help on a project is by sending an e-mail note to tecteam@ca.ibm.com with your request.

Summary

VisualAge for Java is a powerful high-end tool set that contains a very tightly integrated development environment (IDE) with lots of features and functions. Many enterprises have adopted VisualAge for Java for mission-critical Java development. Its feature-rich IDE can be a little intimidating if you are accustomed to editors, compilers, and debuggers that work on files as in the Java Development Toolkit (JDK). This book helps you master the VisualAge for Java IDE and utilize it to write your own Java solutions. We hope you enjoy the book.

ABOUT THE AUTHORS

Dale Nilsson received a BS in Computer Science from California State University, Long Beach. He has been programming for over 20 years and has worked for the State of California, McDonnell Douglas Corporation, IBM, and as an independent consultant. Dale has held various development, management, and planning positions in IBM and has worked with customers and vendors throughout the United States, Europe, Asia, and South America. Dale is currently on the VisualAge Services team consulting and mentoring customers that deploy VisualAge Java projects worldwide. As a certified VisualAge for Java and C++ programmer and instructor, he presents to audiences at trade shows, technical interchanges, and customer locations. Dale Nilsson is a regular contributor to the *Eye-on-Objects* Web magazine on www.Hatteras.com, and he works with the VisualAge for Java certification team as an assessor.

Peter Jakab has been working with IBM since 1969. He has spent the last 16 years in software development. In the past nine years, he has held a variety of positions at the Software Solutions Division Laboratory in Toronto, Canada, ranging from developer to team leader and project management. Peter has been involved in developing object-oriented software solutions for the last seven years. He has been working with VisualAge since 1994. Peter is a Sun Certified Java Programmer, IBM Certified VisualAge for Java Developer, and IBM Certified VisualAge for C++ Developer. He is also one of the lead assessors for the VisualAge Practicums. Peter is currently working for SWS, Product Services providing consulting and education to customers that develop real-world Java applications.

Dale Nilsson and Peter Jakab are the co-authors of *VisualAge for C++ Visual Programmer's Handbook* (Prentice Hall, 1997). They are also part of the team that developed and deployed the VisualAge for C++ and Java Certification Program. Their experience from these projects, engagements with customers on software development projects, and background in object-oriented application development form the foundation for this book.

Greg Hester is the founder of CrossLogic Corporation and is the Vice President of Technology. Greg holds a BS in Computer Science from North Carolina State University and has over 14 years of experience in systems programming, applications development, compiler technology, object technology, and consulting. Greg has developed object technology applications for Fortune 500 clients and products in Java, Smalltalk, and

C++ for CrossLogic. Greg has created and taught courses in Java Applications Development, Advanced Java Programming, VisualAge for Java and IBM VisualAge for Java Certification, and Smalltalk Programming. Greg is a Sun Certified Java Programmer, IBM Certified VisualAge for Java Developer, and IBM Certified VisualAge for Smalltalk Developer. As the senior technical person for CrossLogic, Greg contributes to the software, education, and services side of the business, helping CrossLogic to provide solutions for today's problems and tomorrow's needs.

 **Russ Stinehour** is the President and CEO of CrossLogic Corporation and has over 20 years of software development experience including 16 years of project management, product planning, architecture, and applications development with IBM. Russ holds a BS in Systems Science from Michigan State University and an MBA from the University of North Carolina at Chapel Hill. Russ has created and taught courses in Object-Oriented Analysis and Design, Client/Server Technologies, Graphical User Interface Design, Smalltalk Programming, VisualAge for Java, and IBM VisualAge for Java Certification. Russ is a Sun Certified Java Programmer, IBM Certified VisualAge for Java Developer, and IBM Certified VisualAge for Smalltalk Developer. As a technical manager at CrossLogic, Russ contributes to the education and services side of the business, keeping CrossLogic a premier IBM Business Partner and leader in the industry. Greg Hester and Russ Stinehour can be reached at:

CrossLogic Corporation
206 East Chestnut Street, Suite 3
Ashville, NC 28801
(704) 232-1100

 **Bryon Kataoka** provided the technical review of the book. He is the Chief Technical Architect for Commerce Solutions Inc., a technology enabling company specializing in VisualAge for C++ and Java, DB2 Universal Database, MQSeries, and Lotus Domino. Located in San Francisco, Commerce Solutions Inc. has often partnered with the IBM TecTeam and IBM Global Services to assist customers with mentoring, technical enablement, application development, and VisualAge training. Bryon can be contacted at:

Commerce Solutions Inc.
120 Montgomery St. Suite 1430
San Francisco, CA 94104
(415) 398-2424 ext 121
email: bkataoka@CommerceSolutions.com
website: www.CommerceSolutions.com

BREAKING OPEN THE BOX

What's in Chapter 1

The CD-ROM included with this book has evaluation copies of both the OS/2 and Windows versions of VisualAge for Java, the completed applications covered in this book, and the data required for the exercises. This is a lot of software, and this chapter covers some of the considerations when installing all these components. This chapter covers:

- Understanding installation hardware and software considerations
- Using the VisualAge for Java help system
- Starting VisualAge for Java
- Loading classes in the workspace
- Running a Java applet

Welcome to JavaBeans using VisualAge for Java! The instructions for installing the software on the CD-ROM included with this book are in "Installing the Necessary Software." If you have not read this section, you will need to complete it before you start building the sample applications. The sample applications in this book require VisualAge for Java and some sample files on the CD-ROM. The following sections cover specific information on computer environment issues that affect the VisualAge for Java development and run-time system.

What Hardware and Software Do You Need?

When using application development tools, you need to consider the hardware and software requirements of both the development environment and the target run-time environment. This section describes the factors you should consider in the development environment. VisualAge for Java is a robust application development system; you will need sufficient hardware and the required software to be productive while using VisualAge for Java. One of the essential considerations is the fact that VisualAge for Java is repository-based and not file-based (see "How the IDE Stores Data," later in this chapter).

There are many other considerations for the systems that run your applications and applets. Throughout the book, there is information on these considerations as well as a wide number of options available when you build applications and applets. You can usually assume that users of your applications will not have the same level of hardware resources that you use when developing an application.

Tuning applications for increased performance is somewhat of an art. The reason is that most work to improve performance is usually done at the very end of the development cycle. It is fair to say that you should apply different optimization techniques for the special characteristics of each application. Using the iterative development process is a good way to ensure adequate application performance. Throughout this book, you will use iterative development and you should continue to use this process when developing applications.

Hardware Requirements

VisualAge for Java is a comprehensive Java development toolset that requires enough computing power to satisfy a demanding programmer. This section covers the typical hardware needed to run VisualAge for Java.

Java Programming Requirements

The typical Java developer can use a computer with a 486 processor running at a clock speed of 66 megahertz (MHz) with 16 megabytes (MB) of RAM installed. This is because file-based Java development requires only a text editor and the JDK. In a file-based environment, you use some basic libraries, a compiler, and a debugger. The debugger is only needed if you make programming errors.

This is an adequate environment for dabbling in Java, but you really need a better development environment and more computing horsepower to have a truly productive development system. You must have a browser, a local area network connection, and access to an Internet server, all of which take precious computing power.

VisualAge for Java Programming Requirements

VisualAge for Java provides a complete and integrated development environment (IDE) to develop applications and applets in the Java language. VisualAge for Java tests the old adage that software will fill the ever-expanding hardware capacity. There are two key features that cause VisualAge for Java to need a beefy development system. First, it has a repository-based IDE instead of working on files like many other Java development systems. This consumes additional resources, but at the same time provides a much more responsive and coherent development environment. The second feature is the abundance of views, browsers, and windows that are part of the VisualAge for Java IDE. Java development in this environment uses the standard AWT class libraries, vendor-supplied class libraries, the class browser, the debugger, on-line help, visual builders, and other tools. All these tools and services make you more productive and enable you to construct applications with a lot of function. However, these tools and services consume many system resources when used at the same time.

This high-powered development system requires a robust computer consisting of a fast processor, plenty of disk space, and lots of memory. VisualAge for Java can work (or limp along) on a computer with a 486 processor running at a clock speed of 90 MHz with 32MB of RAM installed, but you will see performance improvements with more memory or a faster processor. Strangely enough, adding memory seems to provide better performance improvements than increasing processor speed. The amount of free RAM directly affects the amount of paging the operating system must perform to keep all of the applications running. You should have at least 64MB of RAM (some developers have 128MB) and a 133-MHz Pentium processor with 500MB of fixed disk space to hold the product and the additional virtual memory required at run time.

You need a minimum of 70MB of fixed disk space in order to install the product from the CD-ROM; the single-user Enterprise edition requires 210MB. You will also need sufficient disk space for virtual memory. In Windows NT, the standard size of 50MB of virtual memory is not enough for optimal performance; a minimum of 100MB (or more) is much better. Use the Control Panel, System, Performance settings to increase it. These are fairly large numbers, but the maximum is required only if you install all components, samples, and on-line documentation. The best guideline is to install only the components that you will use most frequently.

All components and tools run on a VGA (640×480) resolution display, but many menus and windows simply do not fit in this resolution. An SVGA (1024×768) or higher (1240×1024) resolution display is recommended, especially when designing graphical user interfaces using the visual builder. For very high resolutions to be usable, you will need a large monitor. Typically, a 17-inch monitor is the minimum size for 1240×1024. When you are using multiple tools like the visual builder, a browser, a console window, and a debugger window, you will be able to use as much screen real estate as these higher resolution displays allow.

Software Requirements

At the time this book went to press, the VisualAge for Java product is available on the following operating environments:

VisualAge for Java for OS/2 Version 1.0 runs on OS/2 Warp Version 4.

VisualAge for Java for Windows Version 1.0 runs on Windows NT Version 4.0 and Windows95.

The VisualAge for Java for Windows development environment does not run on Windows 3.1. But because Java is a write-once, run-anywhere programming language, you can develop applications on OS/2, Windows95 or Windows NT and run the applications on Windows 3.1 or any other operating environment that has a supporting Java 1.1.1 Virtual Machine (VM). You will need to keep in mind that most systems running Windows 3.1 have slower processors and less memory than Windows95 or Windows NT systems. You can get a Windows 3.1

JDK from www.hursley.ibm.com. This site also has information on JDKs and VMs for other operating systems.

The Entry edition of the VisualAge for Java product is included on the CD-ROM with this book. VisualAge for Java Entry provides all features and functions found in VisualAge for Java Professional with the following modifications or limitations:

- Repository is limited to 100 classes.
- Documentation can only be viewed through the support page on the Web.
- No documentation is shipped with the product.
- If installed, the beta code must be uninstalled.
- Product is licensed for non-commercial use.
- No support is provided.

To find out which version of the product you are running, display the About VisualAge box from the Help menu. After you install from the CD-ROM and apply Patch Set 1, the About box should look like Figure 1.1. Note that in addition to the version and patch set, the number of remaining classes you can add to the product is also displayed on this dialog. Remember that you are limited to 100 new types (classes and interfaces) in the Entry edition.

Figure 1.1 About VisualAge.

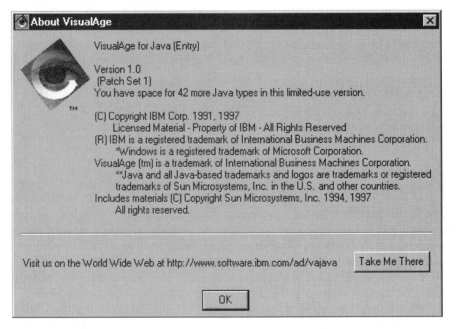

To run the exercises in this book, you must have VisualAge for Java and, at least, the first fix level installed. If you already have the commercial version of the product installed, all you need to do is install the first patch set.

Please note that the exercises in this book have been created and tested using the products at the level found in the CD-ROM. It is very unlikely that the patch set will introduce problems, in fact, each patch set usually fixes a number of problems and can even improve performance. The latest VisualAge for Java patches can be found at www.software.ibm.com/ad/vajava/fixes.htm.

NOTE

Patches for the VisualAge for Java product can be applied to the software in the CD-ROMs. This is either a fluke or a convenient oversight. The patches fix a lot of problems, so they are really worth applying to your system.

Development versus Run-time Requirements

It is important to take into consideration both development and run-time environments when you develop an application. The applications you develop on your 200-MHz Pentium with a 20-inch SVGA display and 64MB of RAM will not show the same performance running on a 33-MHz 486 system with a low-resolution 12-inch VGA display and 4MB of RAM. Throughout this book, there are suggestions and pointers, which cover some of the many design and deployment decisions that need to be made for an application to run well in a given environment. It also covers the trade-offs required to build an application that is flexible enough to run in many environments. Not many books cover this mysterious part of application development.

Installing the Necessary Software

There is a CD-ROM included with this book that includes the Entry editions of VisualAge for Java for OS/2 and for Windows. The Windows version runs on either Windows95 or Windows NT. If you already have VisualAge for Java installed, you must still install the sample applications and solutions to the exercises provided on the CD-ROM in order to successfully complete the samples in this book. For you hard-core command-line programmers, install the contents of the CD-ROM as follows:

1. Place the CD-ROM in the CD-ROM drive.

2. Open a command prompt window.

3. Switch to the root directory of the CD-ROM and in the command prompt window, type **install**.

For you 90s-style typing-challenged programmers, install the contents of the CD-ROM as follows:

4. Place the CD-ROM in the CD-ROM drive.

5. Open the **My Computer** icon.

6. Select the CD-ROM drive.

7. Double-click (open) the Install file.

Please read the information presented in the **Installation and last minute information** window of the installation program. This has detailed instructions on how to install the different components available in the CD-ROM and any other important information that did not make the press deadline for this book. This same information is available for printing in a file called read.me, which is also found in the root directory of the CD-ROM.

What's in the VisualAge for Java Folder?

 After installing VisualAge for Java in either Windows NT or Windows95, an IBM VisualAge for Java for Windows category is added to the Programs folder of the Start menu. You can get to it with the following steps:

On the task bar, select Start, Programs, and then IBM VisualAge for Java.

 If you installed the OS/2 version, you now have a folder on your desktop representing VisualAge for Java for OS/2.

Open VisualAge for Java by double-clicking the mouse on this menu item.

If you have previously installed the Professional or the Enterprise version of the product, you have also installed the full help subsystem. The appropriate entries have been created for you in the IBM VisualAge for Java folder.

Other items in the IBM VisualAge for Java folder are:

• The start icon for the Product

• IDE and Java HTML Help (full editions only)

• Start and Stop icons for the Help (full editions only)

• Product ReadMe (which is really a marketing letter missing all the good stuff that should be in a ReadMe file)

• HTML-based release notes (which includes the ReadMe and an index to the help, including the good ReadMe files with some good readme information)

• The Uninstall icon

The Entry edition in the CD-ROM does not include the on-line help subsystem. Mainly, this is to reduce the time it takes to download this version from the Web. It also reduces the cost of producing the trial version. Do not despair; you can get to all of the available documentation on the Web at www.software.ibm.com/ad/vajava/library/onlinehelp/ide/doc/index.htm.

Using VisualAge Java Documentation

In the full editions of the product, the various help icons start a Web browser, load the HTML-based help system, and start the HTML search engine. In the Entry edition, you start your Web browser manually and load the starting page from www.software.ibm.com/ad/vajava/library/onlinehelp/ide/doc/index.htm.

This page contains reference information and user guides for the VisualAge for Java tools, the AWT class library, and the components currently installed.

Finding Information

From this page, you can browse or search for the information you need on VisualAge for Java, Java, and AWT. The Netscape version has the different types of documentation listed at the top, categories listed on the left, and specific contents in the center main section of the browser. This gives you a convenient way to quickly find the information you need. You can quickly and easily get to any item you choose from this browser.

The on-line documentation is preferred over the hard copy because the search function in the browser is very useful, and it is always available. If you need some information, you can easily get to the search screen, enter the search argument and get a list of all the occurrences of entries containing what you are looking for. You can locate any of the items in the list by selecting it from the list.

You can use the search screen to easy locate a specific class or method you want to review. You can also enter more abstract concepts, for example, if you are interested in learning more about the Remote Method Invocation facility in Java, you could just search for *RMI*.

Sometimes it is better to try to narrow down the search by entering a more specific argument, for example: *RMI Samples*, instead of just *RMI*. If you don't qualify the search, it might take a long time and will probably yield a very long list of unrelated topics.

If you know what you are looking for, you can go directly to that area of the documentation. For example, if you need to look up the AWT **Frame** class in the Reference document:

1. Select the References page of the notebook.

2. Select **JDK1.1** at the bottom of the list on the left.

3. Select **package java.awt** under the JDK 1.1 API list. The main panel displays the reference information for the java.awt package.

4. Scroll down to the Class Index and select **Frame**.

When you are finished with help, you should close all the open Web browser windows to conserve system resources. However, if you have a high-powered system, you may want to keep the browser open for quick access.

Starting VisualAge for Java

Because VisualAge for Java is not just a Java compiler but a fully integrated development environment, the IDE is used to launch all other related tools. You only need to start VisualAge for Java from its icon on the folder or the task bar.

The majority of the exercises you do while using this book are completed inside the IDE. Later in the book, we will cover deploying Java programs and how to make your programs work outside the IDE.

This book does not cover developing an application using the team versioning support VisualAge for Java Enterprise. This is beyond the scope of this book, requires additional installation information, and it is not necessary for you to develop a good understanding of the basics.

Start the VisualAge for Java IDE by locating and double-clicking its icon.

Make sure that VisualAge for Java starts up correctly. Shown in Figure 1.2, the VisualAge for Java splash screen should be displayed for a brief amount of time after starting the program.

After a few seconds, the VisualAge for Java Workbench appears on your screen, as shown in Figure 1.3.

The Integrated Development Environment

VisualAge for Java has a very tight with a ton of unction. This section introduces you to some of the basic features of the IDE. Additional specific features of the IDE are covered throughout the book.

IDE Windows

In this book, we use the terms *IDE* and *Workbench* interchangeably to refer to the main window of VisualAge for Java. The IDE actually has a number of secondary windows, which are selected from the Windows menu in the Workbench. These windows include:

Clone—a useful function that creates another Workbench window

Console—used to view Standard In, Standard Out, and a list of threads needing input

Log—a window for displaying system generated messages

Debugger—a separate multi-paned window with the debugger functions

Figure 1.2 VisualAge for Java splash screen.

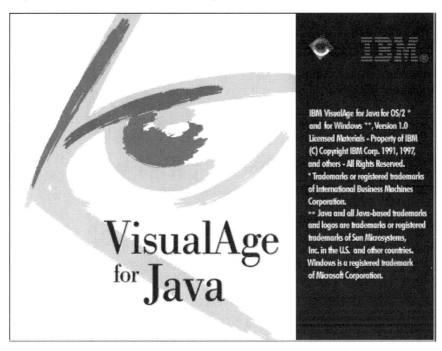

Breakpoints—displays a list of all breakpoints set

Repository Explorer—a read-only view of the classes available in the repository

Scrapbook—a scratch pad where Java code can be tested

IDE Views

The Workbench is command central for the VisualAge for Java IDE. The IDE gives you access to the Java classes you are working with in the VisualAge for Java development environment. There are a number of views in the Workbench; they show the program elements loaded in the workspace.

The Projects view is the default view. It appears initially when you start the Workbench. It appears as an expandable tree view, because projects contain packages, which contain classes, which contain methods.

If you have previous knowledge of the Java language, you are probably familiar with the following terms:

- Package
- Interface

Figure 1.3 Workbench.

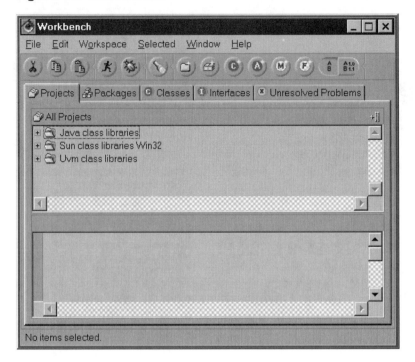

- Class
- Method

You are probably not familiar with the term *project*. This is because a project is not a Java program element. Projects are implemented in VisualAge for Java to help you organize packages. Projects have no significance in the Java programming language. Use projects to group the packages that comprise an application or to group associated packages.

Switch through the pages of the Workbench to get familiar with the other views:

The Packages view lists all packages in the project, classes in the selected package, methods in the selected class, and source code for the selected method.

The Classes view lists all classes, methods in the selected class, and source code for the selected method.

The Interfaces view lists all interfaces, methods in the selected interface, and source code for the selected method.

The Unresolved Problems view lists all problems detected in the classes loaded in the workspace.

How the IDE Stores Data

VisualAge for Java stores all data in two files. The first file, called the repository, can be found in the x:\IBMVJava\Ide\Repository directory; the file name is ivj.dat. The second file, called the workspace or the image, can be found in the x:\IBMVJava\Ide\Program directory; the file name is ide.icx.

These two files should be backed up regularly. In the unlikely case of a corrupted workspace or repository or a system failure, they can be used to recover your work.

Repository

The repository is the central store for all the classes that you use in VisualAge for Java. In the Entry and Professional editions, the repository retains information about all of the program elements ever loaded. This means it grows with time, consuming more and more disk space as new classes and versions of classes are created. The Enterprise edition of VisualAge for Java has a function, which deletes any classes that you have marked for deletion. We will not cover how to use the repository maintenance features that are only available in the Enterprise edition.

Workspace

The workspace holds all classes that you are currently working with, including those that your classes refer to. The workspace is sometimes referred to as the *image*. The following projects must be loaded into the workspace for VisualAge for Java to work properly:

- Java class libraries
- Sun class libraries Win32
- Uvm class libraries

In the next section, you will learn how to load classes into the workspace. Only packages and classes loaded in the workspace can be used to develop new programs. Referring to packages or classes that are not loaded in the image results in errors.

You should delete any projects, packages, or classes that you are no longer using. This improves the performance of the tool and speeds up the initial program load. Remember that deleted program elements are not really deleted but moved from the workspace into the repository.

A good way to explain this concept is to think of the workspace as, essentially, a subset of the contents of the repository. There are some minor exceptions to this, but for now this definition is adequate.

Loading Java Classes into the Workspace

You can work only with Java packages and classes that are loaded in the workspace. Program elements can be brought into the workspace by loading them from the repository or by creating them directly in the workspace. There are a few sample projects in the repository that you can load into the workspace to use as examples or to quickly verify that all is working fine. Let's load the IBM Java Examples project by following these steps:

Select the Projects icon in the Workbench toolbar. You could also display the workbench pop-up menu and select Add Project. As shown in Figure 1.4, the Add Project SmartGuide window appears.

TIP

While in the Workbench, notice that there are often at least two ways to perform an action. Usually, there is a tool bar button and a context-sensitive pop-up menu also. Pop-up menus can be made to appear by pressing and releasing mouse button 2.

Select the **Add project(s)** from the **repository** radio button; then select the Browse button.

The Add Projects from Repository window lists the projects available from the repository. Select from the list to add a project to your workspace. For this example, select **IBM Java Examples,** as shown in Figure 1.5.

Figure 1.4 Adding a project.

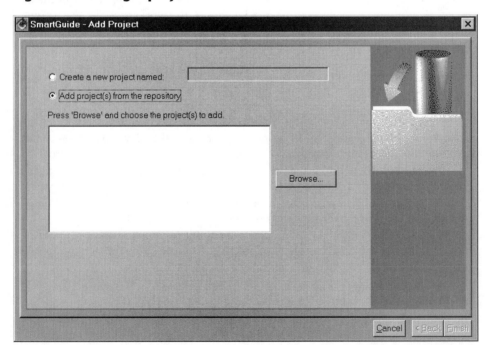

Figure 1.5 Selecting a project.

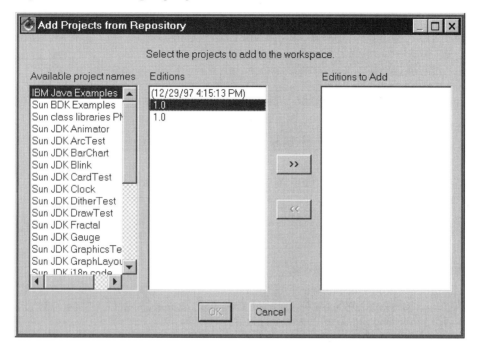

The Editions pane lists all available versions of the project in the repository. Even the Entry edition of VisualAge for Java has a fully functional version-control system. (We cover how to version your program elements in a later chapter.) Select edition 1.0 and press the Add button to add this project to the Editions to Add list. Then select the OK button to close this window.

Select the Finish button to load this project into the workspace.

The loading process takes a little bit of time, because the classes are compiled as they are loaded into the workspace, and there are a lot of classes in this project. Whenever you load a large package, the load takes time. This is a case of "pay me now or pay me later." By compiling classes as they are loaded, you avoid the wait when you run the classes in the IDE later.

While loading this project, pay attention to the progress indicator, shown in Figure 1.6. It provides feedback on the operation being performed.

As the project, packages, and classes are incorporated into the workspace, they are checked against the loaded image to ensure that there are no conflicts.

All prerequisite classes are checked for existence in the image. If any required classes or methods in any classes are missing, errors are posted to the Unresolved Problems page of the Workbench, shown in Figure 1.7. These errors are also reported in the progress indicator.

Figure 1.6 Progress indicator.

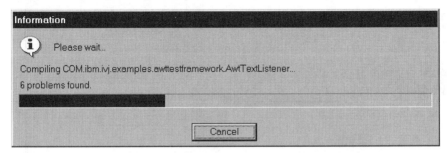

You will notice that as the IBM Java Examples project is being loaded, several errors are reported. This is because one of the samples has a dependency on two other packages in the SUN BDK Examples project, sunw.demo.juggler and sunw.demo.molecule.

Figure 1.7 Unresolved errors.

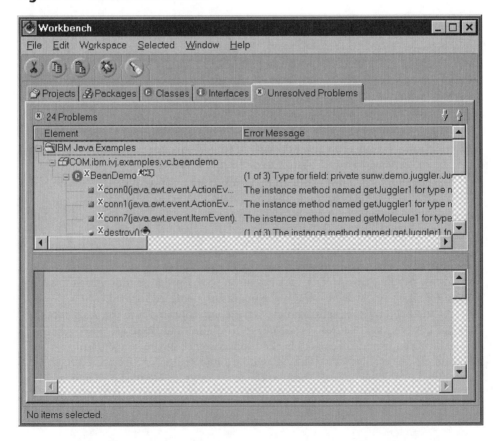

To fix these errors, you have three options:

1. Add the Sun BDK Examples project from the repository.
2. Add the two packages to the IBM Java Examples Project (or any other project).
3. Delete the COM.ivj.examples.vc.beandemo package from the IBM Java Examples project.

The Unresolved Problems view is the only place in which the description of an error appears in its entirety. This is because some error descriptions are very long, and they are displayed in a single line. In this view, you can scroll as far as necessary to see the whole line.

Running an Applet

Running applets or applications in the IDE is very easy. Select a Java class that inherits from Applet and then either press the Run button on the IDE tool bar or select **Run** from the pop-up menu.

Visual cues are displayed throughout the IDE. These cues make it easier to identify the features of program elements in the IDE. The most common ones are shown in Figure 1.8 and Figure 1.9.

Let's try running one of the Java samples that comes with the product as follows:

Open the IBM Java Examples project.

Open the Com.ibm.ivj.examples.hanoi package.

Select the HanoiApplet class. Notice that this class has the executable class icon besides it.

Select the Run button, as shown in Figure 1.10.

The Settings window for the Hanoi applet appears. This window can be used to change parameters passed to the applet at run time; in this case, the numbers of disks in the puzzle could be changed. Shown in Figure 1.11, this window always appears when you run applets in the IDE.

Now let's continue: Select the Run button in the settings window.

An applet viewer automatically starts, and you see the Hanoi applet run, as shown in Figure 1.12. When the applet solves the puzzle, it can be restarted from the Applet menu in the applet viewer.

Before proceeding, close the Hanoi applet by selecting the Close button on the applet viewer.

Congratulations! You have completed running your first Java applet inside the VisualAge for Java development environment.

Let's take a closer look at the HanoiApplet class. By pressing the + sign to the left of the class name you can expand the class and see the methods that make it work. HanoiApplet extends the java.applet.Applet class. Applets do not

Figure 1.8 Visual cues.

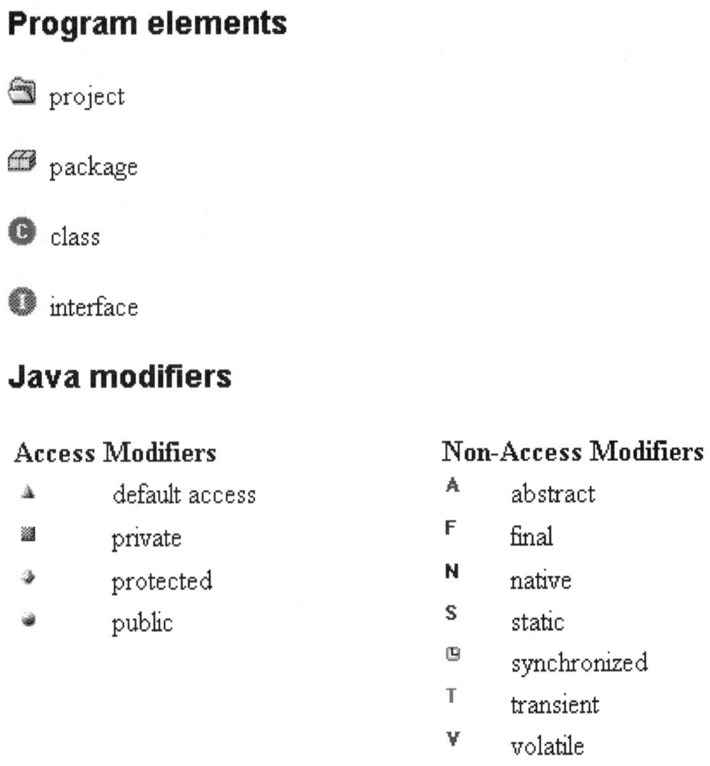

Program elements

project

package

class

interface

Java modifiers

Access Modifiers
▲	default access
▨	private
◆	protected
◕	public

Non-Access Modifiers
A	abstract
F	final
N	native
S	static
◳	synchronized
T	transient
V	volatile

Figure 1.9 More visual cues.

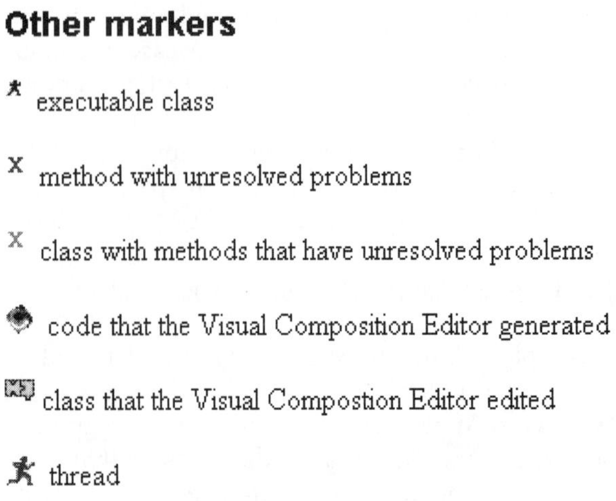

Other markers

✸ executable class

X method with unresolved problems

X class with methods that have unresolved problems

◆ code that the Visual Composition Editor generated

class that the Visual Compostion Editor edited

🏃 thread

Figure 1.10 Running the Hanoi applet.

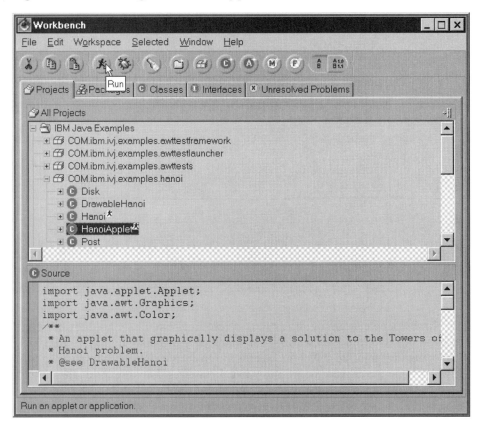

Towers of Hanoi

The puzzle of the Towers of Hanoi is a popular one. Most people are familiar with it. In order to solve the puzzle, all disks have to be moved from the left-hand tower to the right-hand tower. The middle tower is used, as necessary, as a staging area. The only rule is that placing a larger disk on top of a smaller one is not allowed. When all the disks are on the right tower, with the largest disk on the bottom, the puzzle is solved. The larger the number disks, the harder it is to solve the puzzle.

have a frame of their own. That is why they it run either in the applet viewer or, most likely, as part of an HTML page inside of a Web browser.

Applets are subject to the rules of Java applet security. These rules are enforced by code in the Web browser and they vary from browser to browser.

Figure 1.11 Applet parameters.

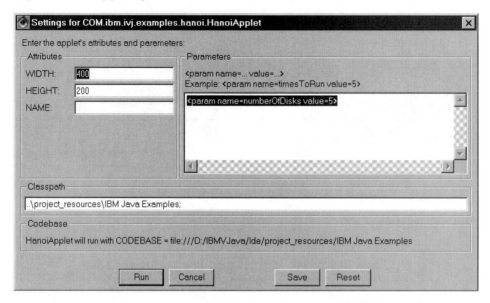

Most notably, applets cannot access system resources like disk files; they can communicate only with the Web server from which they originated.

Because living inside a Web browser is a transitory existence, applets need to know how to initialize, start, stop, and paint themselves. Looking inside the HanoiApplet class, we see such methods. When the applet is first loaded from the Web server, it initializes itself. As a user changes to another page in the browser, the applet is told to stop. When the user returns to this page, the applet is told to start. When the visual contents of the applet change, the applet is told to paint itself.

Selecting each of these methods shows the source code in the bottom pane of the viewer. By far, the most interesting method is **paint**, shown in Figure 1.13.

Figure 1.12 Hanoi applet.

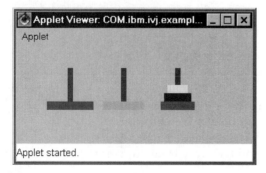

Figure 1.13 Paint method.

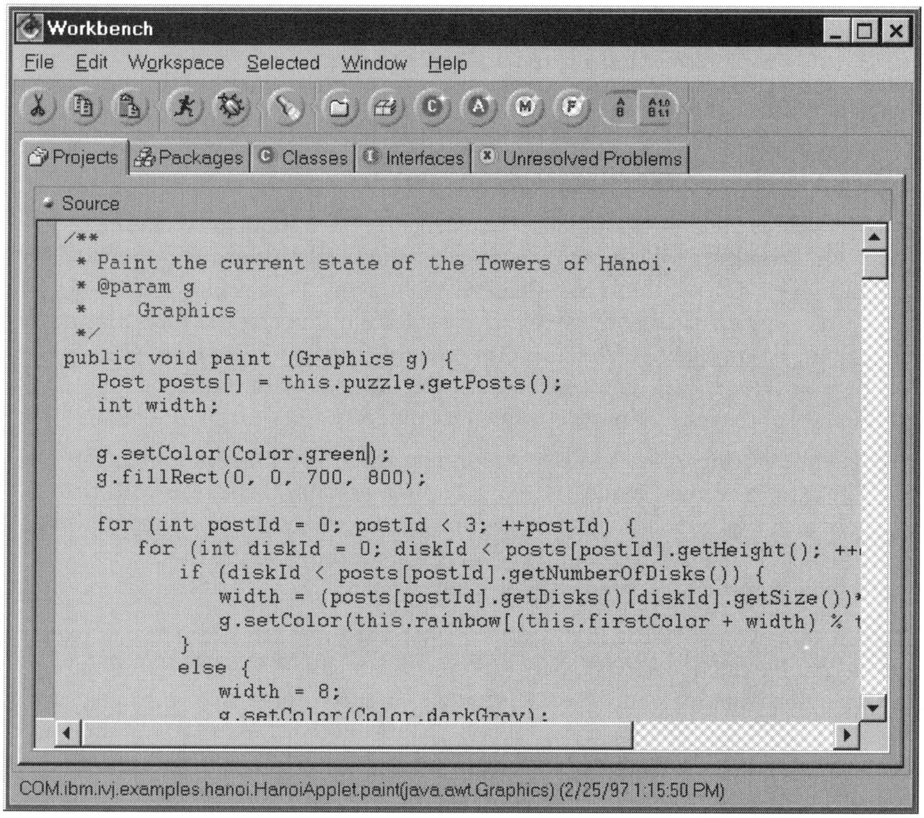

```
Workbench                                          _ □ ×
File  Edit  Workspace  Selected  Window  Help

Projects | Packages | Classes | Interfaces | Unresolved Problems |

Source

/**
 * Paint the current state of the Towers of Hanoi.
 * @param g
 *     Graphics
 */
public void paint (Graphics g) {
    Post posts[] = this.puzzle.getPosts();
    int width;

    g.setColor(Color.green);
    g.fillRect(0, 0, 700, 800);

    for (int postId = 0; postId < 3; ++postId) {
        for (int diskId = 0; diskId < posts[postId].getHeight(); ++
            if (diskId < posts[postId].getNumberOfDisks()) {
                width = (posts[postId].getDisks()[diskId].getSize())
                g.setColor(this.rainbow[(this.firstColor + width) %
            }
            else {
                width = 8;
                g.setColor(Color.darkGray);

COM.ibm.ivj.examples.hanoi.HanoiApplet.paint(java.awt.Graphics) (2/25/97 1:15:50 PM)
```

TIP

Double-clicking the word **Source** maximizes the source pane; double-clicking it again restores it to the original split ratio. This works in most panes in VisualAge for Java.

If the applet viewer is still running, close it. Now start it again, but this time change the parameter **numberOfDisks** to 8. This creates a more complex puzzle, which will take longer to solve and give us time to have some fun.

Once the applet has started, switch back to the Workbench and select the Source pane for the paint method. Locate the statement:

```
g.setColor(background);
```

and change it to:

```
g.setColor(Color.green);
```

Notice that you are changing the code for the paint method while the applet is running in the applet viewer. Save your changes by either pressing Ctrl-S or by pressing mouse button 2 and selecting Save from the pop-up menu.

Saving the paint method started an interesting chain of events:

- The source code was saved.

- A new edition of the paint method was created. An entry in the Log window documented this change.

- The source code was compiled. VisualAge for Java implements an incremental compiler, which compiles each method right after it is modified and saved. Errors, if any, are detected right away. If possible, you should correct any errors before saving. If the nature of the error is such that it cannot be corrected at the time (for example, referencing a class you haven't written yet), you can always save the code with the error. Of course, in that case, the method is not compiled.

- As you remember, the applet was running when you made this change. The next move was made and now it's time to paint the screen with the new disk position. The Java virtual machine accesses the newly compiled code of the paint method and executes it. Not only the next move is shown, but the background color is now green.

As mentioned previously in this section, even the Entry edition of VisualAge for Java has a fully functional version control system in place. When you saved the changes to the paint method, a new *edition* was created. Editions are created every time you modify a method or class. Editions can be modified. At any point in time, usually when you get something working or when you are about to try something daring, you will create a new version of your code. Once you version a program element, it becomes immutable. You can always go back to a previous version and modify it to create a new edition, but the version itself remains unchanged.

You can go back to any version or edition of your code. You can also compare the current edition with any other version or edition of the same program element. Let's compare the two editions of the paint method of HanoiApplet.

In the Workbench, make sure the paint method of HanoiApplet is selected. Bring up the pop-up menu by pressing and releasing mouse button 2. Select **Compare With** and then **Previous Edition** as shown in Figure 1.14.

The current edition is compared with the previous edition, and the Comparing window appears (see Figure 1.15).

The difference between the two editions is displayed. In this case, there is only one difference (if there were more differences, you could use the arrow buttons to traverse through them). Close the window.

Once you see the differences between editions (or versions), you might choose to replace the current edition with one from the repository. From the pop-up menu for the paint method, select **Replace With** and then **Previous Edition** to restore the paint method to the original condition.

Figure 1.14 Comparing with the previous edition.

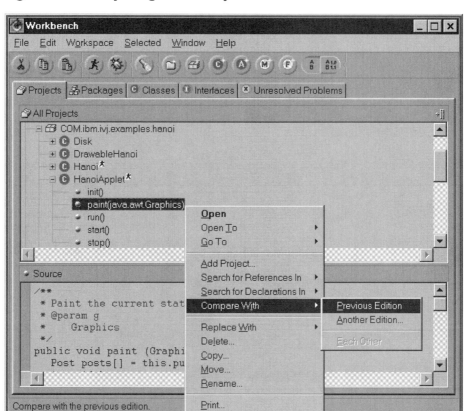

The smallest program element that can be versioned is a class. The versioning process takes the current edition of a project, package, or class and creates a read-only version. Use versioning before you are about to make significant changes to a program element or when you are happy with its behavior and want to take a check point. In the Team edition of VisualAge for Java, you have to version a program element before it can be released to other developers. To version all classes in a package, select the package; to version all the packages in a project, select the project.

Create a new version of HanoiApplet by selecting it in the Workbench. Bring up its pop-up menu and select **Version**.

The Version window appears. The new version of HanoiApplet can be named three ways. These choices appear in Figure 1.16.

Automatic assigns the next version number. For example, if the previous version was 1.0, the new version will be 1.1.

Figure 1.15 Differences between editions.

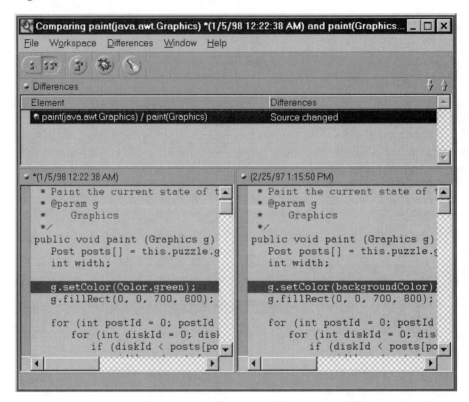

One Name assigns the next version name that you enter to the selected item and all its elements. If you version a package, all the classes in the package will have this name. For example, You can version a package and call it *beta 1* or *This version works*.

Name Each allows you to name the version for the selected item and you can have different names for each of its elements. Additionally, this option gives you a handy list of names already in use.

Select the **Finish** button, and the Workbench will automatically version the selected item. The version is now in the Workbench as seen in Figure 1.17.

TIP

Use the last set of tool bar buttons on the Workbench to display or hide the version numbers that appear at the end of your program element names.

Figure 1.16 Version naming.

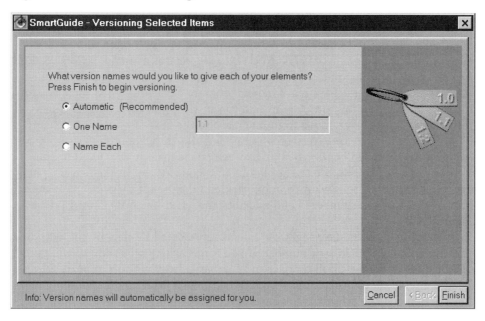

Figure 1.17 HanoiApplet version 1.1.

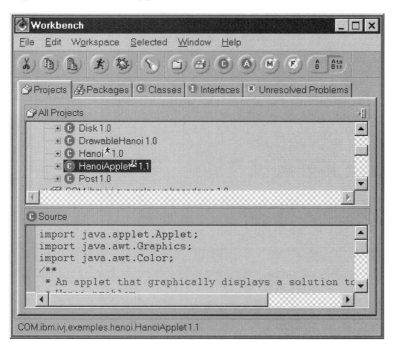

Bookmarks

Once you become familiar with VisualAge for Java, you will use the Projects view of the Workbench more and more. In this view, you have a complete picture of what is loaded in your image. During development, you will often move from package to package and from class to class to see what is available, check method names, check input parameters for the methods, and so on. You will find yourself jumping back and forth between different program elements. When there is a lot loaded in the image, this jumping around can be slow and confusing as you scroll through many screens to move from one place to the next.

VisualAge for Java enables you to set bookmarks throughout the Projects view and then use these bookmarks to jump between points that are of interest to you.

To set a bookmark, use the Set Bookmark icon. Just select the project, package, class or method you want to bookmark and then select the icon. As you add bookmarks, they are numbered and added to the left of the bookmark icon (see Figure 1.18).

To move between the program elements represented by the bookmarks, click the corresponding bookmark number. If you forget where a bookmark will take you, just rest the mouse pointer over the number; a help window appears, identifying the program element it represents. You can also bring up the pop-up menu for a bookmark and select **Go to** or **Remove**.

Figure 1.18 Bookmarks.

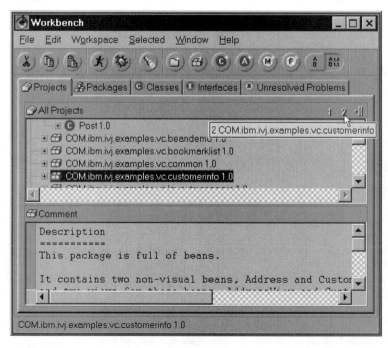

Summary

In this chapter, you prepared your system to continue with the rest of the book. To do this, you:

- Reviewed the hardware and software requirements for running VisualAge for Java.
- Learned how to find information in the on-line documentation. This will be very helpful when using VisualAge for Java and the AWT class library.
- Learned about the IDE and loaded Java classes from the repository.
- Started the Workbench and tested a sample applet. Everything is working properly.

Now that VisualAge Java is installed and working, you are ready to start building Java applications! The instructions in this book rarely require you to look in the documentation for help, but if you ever need more information during development, consult the on-line help.

BUILDING THE HELLO
WORLD APPLET

What's in Chapter 2

Now that you have all the necessary software installed and have tested your setup by bringing up the Workbench and studying its various views and components, you are ready to start visual programming. In this chapter, you build your first VisualAge Java application, which is a simple Hello World window. Building this application covers the basic elements of visual programming that you will continue to use throughout this book.

In this chapter, you will learn how to :

- Set Workbench options
- Create projects and packages
- Work in the Visual Composition Editor
- Use simple Abstract Windowing Toolkit (AWT) beans to design an applet
- Generate Java code
- Build and run an application

If you have closed VisualAge for Java, you need to restart it. The simplest way to start the VisualAge for Java is to double-click its icon. To make it easier to access VisualAge for Java, you may want to create a *shortcut* of its icon. For convenience, you can place the *shortcut* icon directly on the desktop.

As you remember, when you start VisualAge for Java, the workspace is loaded, and any open windows or views that were opened when you last saved the workspace are reopened. Restoring the workspace to the last saved state can take quite a while, especially if there were many opened windows, which need to be reconstructed. One way to avoid this slow startup is to close any unnecessary windows and browsers before the next time you close the Workbench.

Workbench Options

There are a number of options you can set in the Workbench to make it work to your liking. Many of the settings will be unfamiliar to you; you will probably not change them until you become more familiar with VisualAge. Some options change many settings that are familiar to you, for example, the fonts that are used in the different browsers and editor windows.

All customizable options are grouped together in the Options window. To bring it up select Workspace and then Options from the menu bar. The window appears as shown in Figure 2.1. There are seven pages in this window; the following sections cover only those pages that require explanation.

On the Appearance page, you can decide whether you want the Projects and Unresolved Problems views split horizontally or vertically, and the percentage each pane in the view will occupy. You can only set this option for these two views because they are the only ones with two panes. All other views have more than two panes, and their orientation cannot be customized.

When you install VisualAge for Java, the default behavior for double-clicking the left mouse button is to expand the item selected. For example, if you double-click

Figure 2.1 Options.

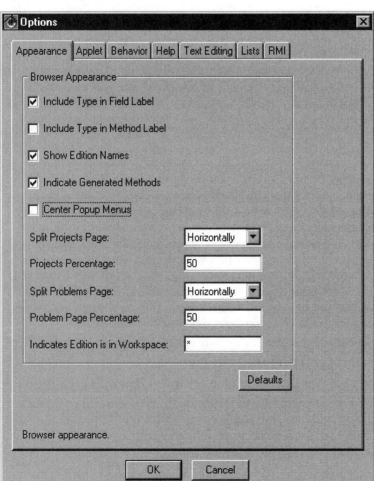

on a class, it will expand to expose its methods. Since the user interface already has the + icon to perform that function, it might be useful to change this behavior to open the class in its own browser.

On the Behavior page, select the Double Click Opens radio button at the bottom of the page as shown in Figure 2.2.

Another interesting option on this page is **Delay Before Lists Pop Out**. Depending on the resolution of the display you have installed in your machine, certain items might not display fully. If you leave the mouse pointer to rest on these items, they pop out over the top of the window boundaries to display more of the text. The number you enter here determines, in milliseconds, how long the cursor must rest on the item before the text expands. You may feel that

Figure 2.2 Behavior options.

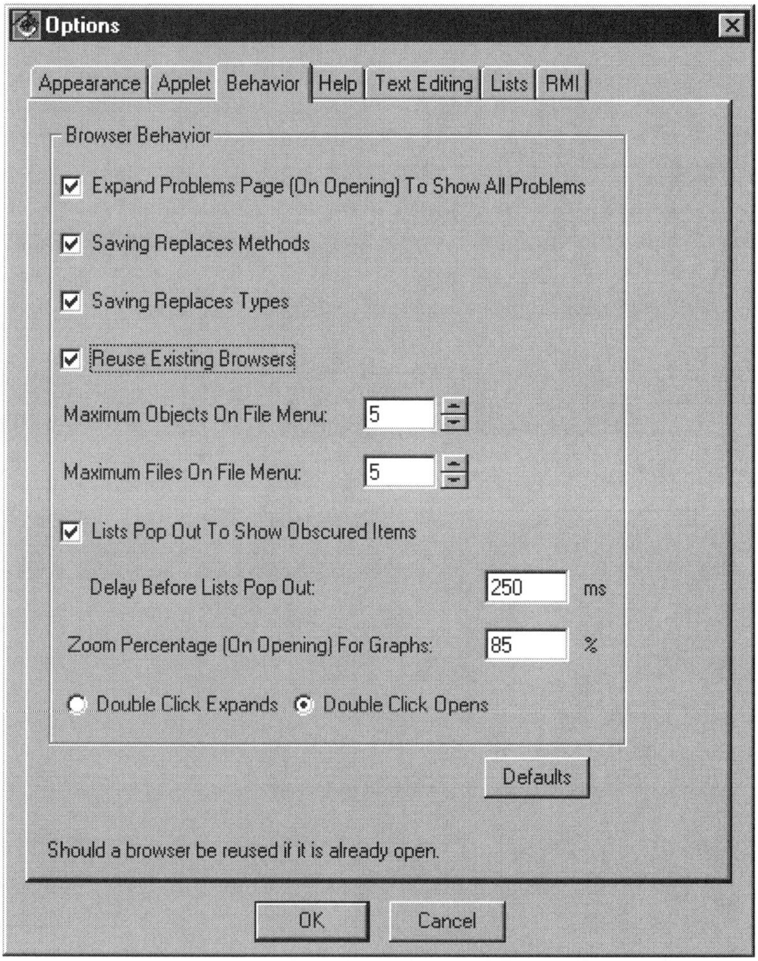

250 milliseconds is too short a time and may want to change this setting to a half second (500 milliseconds).

When you edit a method and save it, the IDE replaces the existing copy. In some cases, you may want to create a similar method, for example, an overloaded version, using the original method as a base for the new one. You can select the original method, change its signature, make the necessary changes and save it. The option **Saving Replaces Methods** determines whether the original method is overwritten or a new one is created.

Changing fonts in the Workbench requires you to set fonts for the different kinds of panes. The font used for the editor and the various colors used for syntax highlighting are set from the Text Editing page shown in Figure 2.3.

Figure 2.3 Changing source editor fonts.

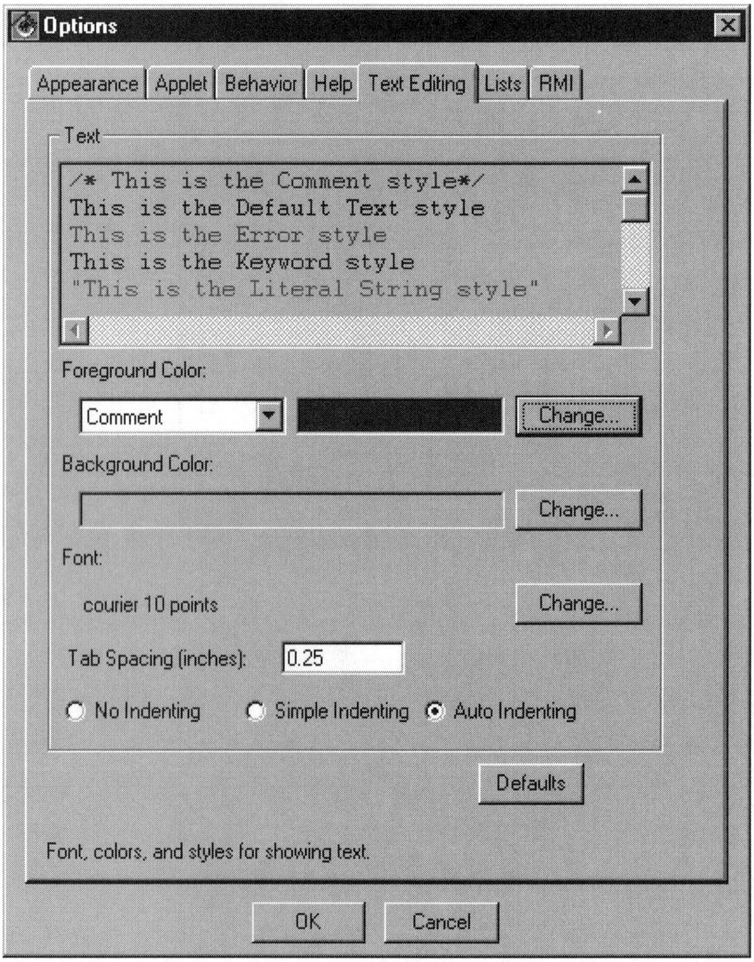

To change the way lists appear in the IDE, such as their font and colors, select the Lists page shown in Figure 2.4.

Other options enable you to set the default size of your applets. If you have the Enterprise edition installed and are developing applets which implement Remote Method Invocation (RMI), you can choose whether to start the RMI registry and what port to use. If you installed either the Enterprise or the Professional editions, you can customize which browser to use for displaying the on-line help.

Select the OK button to save and close the Options window.

The options you changed are saved only when exiting VisualAge or when selecting File and then Save Workspace from the main menu bar of the Workbench.

Figure 2.4 Changing the Lists options.

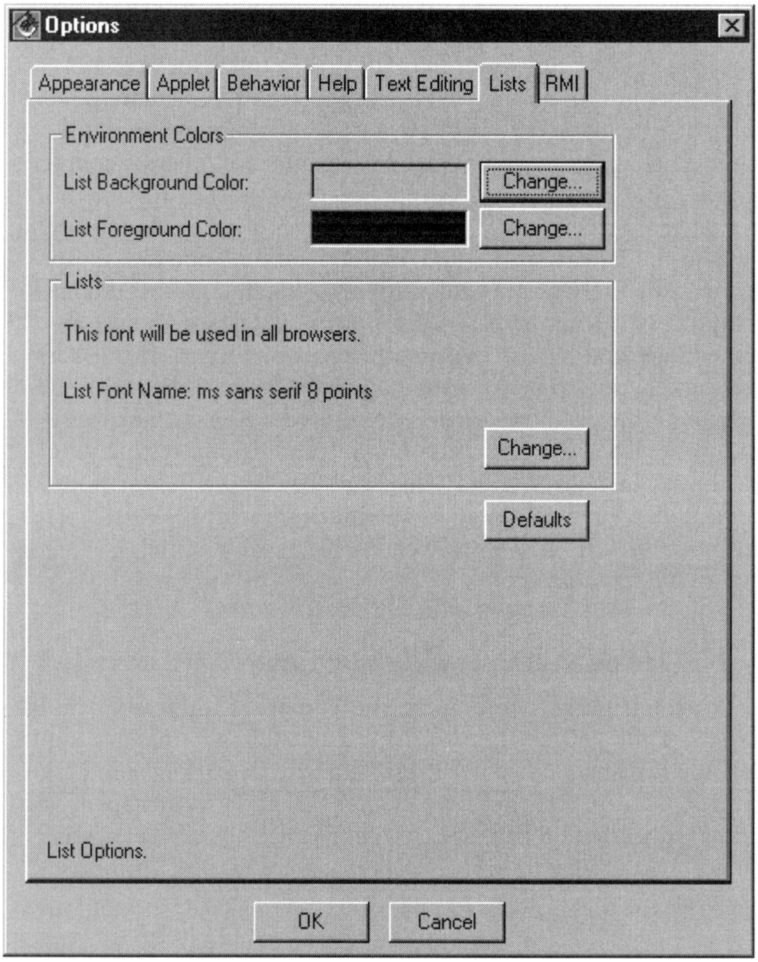

Your First Applet

Let's get started building your first applet with VisualAge for Java using the Visual Builder.

The process for building this applet will use the iterative development method. You develop the applet's user interface first, save your work, and test the Java code by running it in the IDE. You iterate by progressively adding more function and user interface elements, saving, and testing again. Every time you save your work while in the Visual Builder, 100% pure Java code is generated and compiled. The program is automatically run if you press the Test button rather than selecting File and then Save Bean from the menu bar after compilation is completed. If your program is an applet, the built-in applet viewer starts and loads the applet. If you are developing an application, the `main()` method is run. This process enables you to see the results of your work much quicker than waiting until you have finished the program's development. Iterating also enables you to catch problems before you lose track of what caused them.

A lot of errors are caught directly in the IDE. Every time you save a class or method, the code is compiled and any errors are reported immediately. This may seem annoying at first, especially if you are used to compiling an entire class or program at a time. VisualAge uses an incremental compiler; it compiles only what is necessary. For example, when you change a method, that method is the only thing that gets recompiled. This actually saves a lot of time, enabling you to concentrate on the particular method you are coding. Sometimes, especially when you are at the early stages of developing a class, this forced-compile-before-saving process can get in the way, reporting problems about unresolved names just because you haven't written that particular part of the class yet. In most cases though, you can save a method even though it has errors. As you continue developing the class, the errors are resolved. Always make sure that there are no unresolved errors in a class before running and testing your programs. VisualAge for Java gives you a visual cue for classes and methods that contain errors. Either a red or a gray X will mark these unresolved errors. Of course, you can also turn to the Unresolved Problems view in the Workbench to see all outstanding errors.

Creating Projects and Packages

By now, you have customized the Workbench, and you are ready to start building your first VisualAge for Java applet. Applet is a Java class in the java.applet package. In VisualAge for Java, all classes must be part of a package, and all packages must be part of a project. Before you start designing your applet, you will need to set up a project and a package. You could use one of the existing projects, but it is not a good idea to mix your Java classes with the projects shipped with VisualAge.

Projects

VisualAge for Java uses projects to organize the packages and Java classes in the Workbench. Each project has a unique name. A standard for naming projects is emerging: Projects names usually start in upper case and can have multiple words separated by spaces.

Before applets or applications can be built using the IDE, a project, which will contain the package with the beans for the particular applet or application, must be created.

With each new project created in the IDE, a subdirectory with the same name as the package is created using the IBMVJava\Ide\project_resources directory as the root. Any packages in the project also cause the creation of an additional subdirectory descending from the subdirectory with the name of the project. This subdirectory is where the IDE looks for resource files, like the .gif files needed to display graphics on some types of GUI beans. It also stores any resources it creates in that same directory. We will cover using the project_resources directory in a later chapter. This subdirectory is only created when a project is created first. It is not created when you import a project from another user or system. In that case, you must create the directory and manually place any resources.

Now let's create a new project for your first application with the following steps:

 In the Workbench, click the right mouse button on the upper pane. Select **Add Project**. You can also create a new project from the menu bar by selecting Selected and then Add Project or by pressing the New Project icon.

A SmartGuide to aid you in creating a new project appears, as shown in Figure 2.5. Enter **My Project** in the **Create a new project named** entry field. Press the Finish button to create the new project.

A new project called My Project was created in the IDE. Next, create a package within this project, which will contain all classes of the HelloWorld applet.

Packages

 With **My Project** selected, click the right mouse button on the top pane, and from the pop-up menu, select **Add Package**. You can also press the New Package icon from the tool bar.

A SmartGuide to aid you in creating a new package appears, as shown in Figure 2.6. Enter **helloWorld** in the **Create a new package named** entry field. Press the Finish button to create the package.

Packages are Java language elements and represent a logical group of classes that provide related services. Package names make up the directory structure of the classes they contained. Naming conversions are still evolving. The current trend is that package names start in lower case. Usually, when developing commercial packages, the company's Universal Resource Locator (URL) is used to make up the

Figure 2.5 Creating a new project.

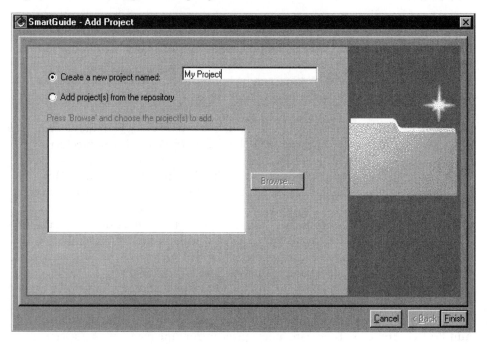

Figure 2.6 Creating a new package.

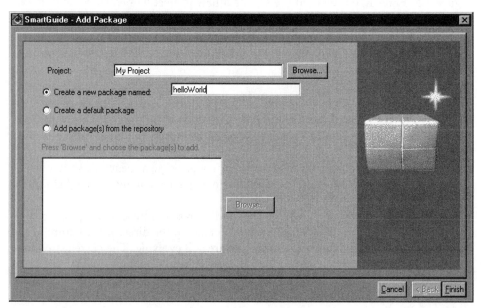

package name. The URL is used backwards; for example, IBM's URL is xxx.ibm.com, and any packages names originating from IBM start with com.ibm.xxx. Almost always there is an exception to the rule; that goes for naming conventions as well. If you look at the IBM packages in VisualAge, you will see that they start with COM.ibm.xxx, with COM in upper case. This is supposed to be changed for new packages, but changing it now would cause too many problems because package names are case-sensitive. Every other package shipped with VisualAge is named with the proposed convention as explained above.

When it comes time to deploy your program, packages can be exported out of the VisualAge environment in a single step. More on importing and exporting appears in a later section.

After you create the package, your Workbench should look like Figure 2.7.

Figure 2.7 My Project and HelloWorld.

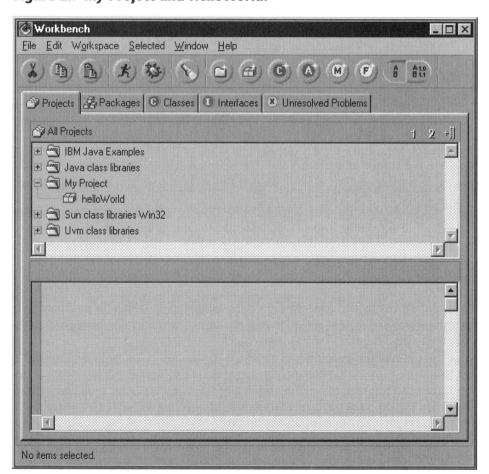

Making a New GUI Bean

You might have skipped some of the introductory information at the beginning of this book because you already had the product installed. It is a good idea to follow these first few chapters very closely to begin understanding how the VisualAge for Java development environment works. These initial steps are somewhat detailed to help the novice user become familiar with the graphical user interface and the tightly integrated IDE of VisualAge for Java. As you progress through the book, the steps will become briefer.

Now, you will construct a simple applet that is just a window that contains the words *Hello World* and the current date. It is probably the simplest program you can build, and it is a good way to familiarize yourself with the IDE. You will use the same steps when building more complex applications. In fact, you use these same steps throughout this book to build all the visual components of the exercises.

Because you have already defined the project and the package in the IDE, you can start defining the parts that will make up the applet. The project and package provide the structure for the IDE to contain and catalog your classes/beans in the repository. First, you will build and test the HelloWorld visual (or GUI) bean. Later, you will make a few changes to the user interface and add some function using connections, save your changes, and re-test the applet. Start building the Hello World applet by following these steps:

With the helloWorld package selected, click the right mouse button on the top pane and from the pop-up menu, select **New Class/Interface**. You could instead select the New Class icon on the Workbench tool bar.

In the Create Class or Interface SmartGuide, seen in Figure 2.8, enter **HelloWorld** in the Class Name entry field.

Naming conventions for Java classes are well defined. Class names start in uppercase, and the beginning of each new word is also in uppercase. No spaces are allowed. The SmartGuide warns you if you don't follow this convention. If you made a mistake entering the class name, the SmartGuide corrects it for you.

Initially, Hello World will be developed as an applet, which means it can only run inside a web browser or an applet viewer. To make an applet, the superclass for the HelloWorld class must be Applet.

You indicate the superclass by either typing the fully qualified name of the parent class in the Superclass entry field, in this case, java.applet.Applet. If you are not sure of the complete name, you can press the **Browse** push button opposite the Superclass entry field, which displays the Class Qualification window.

As you start typing the word **Applet** in the Pattern entry field, the choices in the Class/Interface Names list are narrowed down. See Figure 2.9.

Figure 2.8 Create Class/Interface SmartGuide.

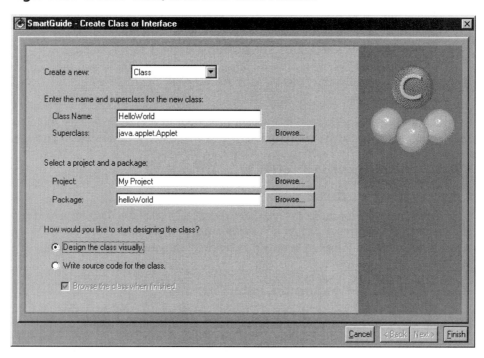

Figure 2.9 Class Qualification window.

After you have finished entering **applet**, the Applet class from the java.applet package should be selected. Once Applet is selected, press the OK button.

On the Create a Class or Interface window, make sure that the **Design the class visually** radio button at the bottom of the screen is selected, as shown in Figure 2.8. This option automatically opens the class in the visual builder. Press the Finish button to complete creating the HelloWorld class.

The Visual Composition Editor opens as shown in Figure 2.10. This window enables you to place the visual components that make up the HelloWorld applet.

Getting Acquainted with the Visual Composition Editor

The Visual Composition Editor is also referred to as *Visual Builder*, because it is used to visually build your beans. It is the default view when you open a GUI bean, and it provides a lot of support for creating and modifying beans. You

Figure 2.10 Visual Composition Editor.

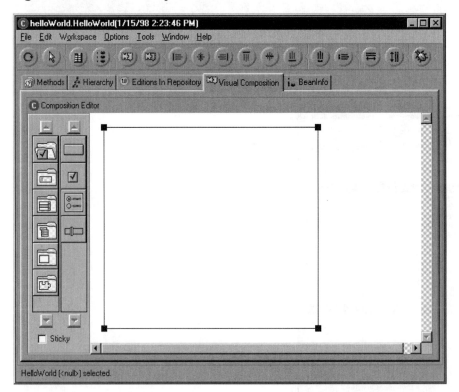

design the entire graphical user interface (GUI) for an application in the Visual Composition Editor.

The Visual Composition Editor is where you combine beans using visual connections to make composite beans and applications. The areas of the Visual Composition Editor are shown in Figure 2.11.

Categories and Beans

There are two columns of icons on the left side of the Visual Composition Editor. The left column is a scrollable list of folders called *categories*. These categories hold beans grouped by common types. The right column holds the beans contained in the currently selected category. Pressing the arrows at the top and bottom of each column enables you to scroll through the lists.

You see hover help appear when you place the mouse pointer over a category or bean and hold it there for a short time. Hover help makes it a lot easier to find the bean you need. A complete list of the default categories and beans is shown in Figure 2.12. It would be a good idea for you to copy it and keep it handy as a reference until you become familiar with the available categories and beans.

Figure 2.11 Visual Composition Editor areas.

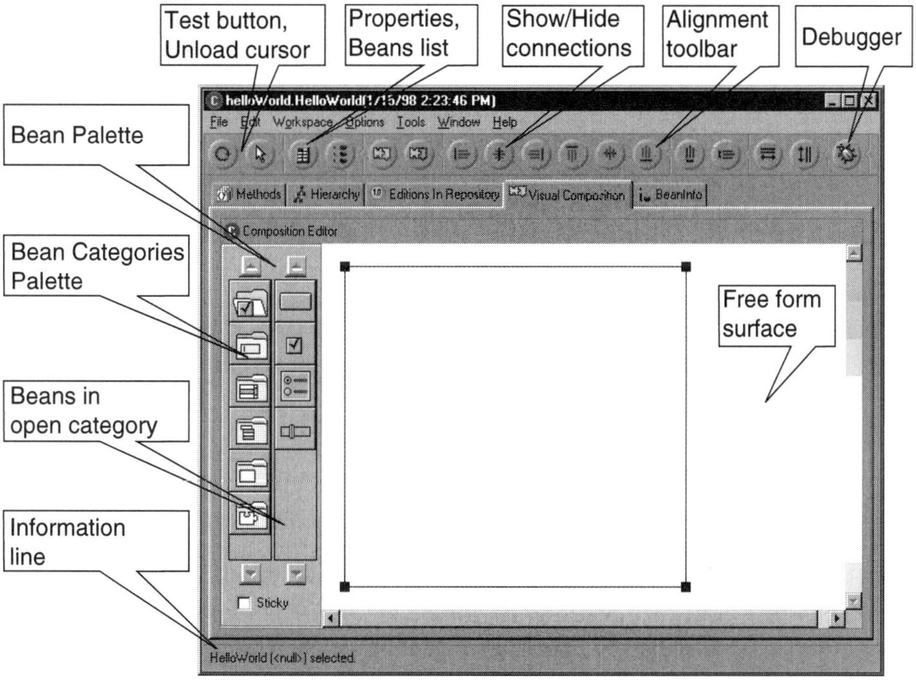

Figure 2.12 VisualAge beans.

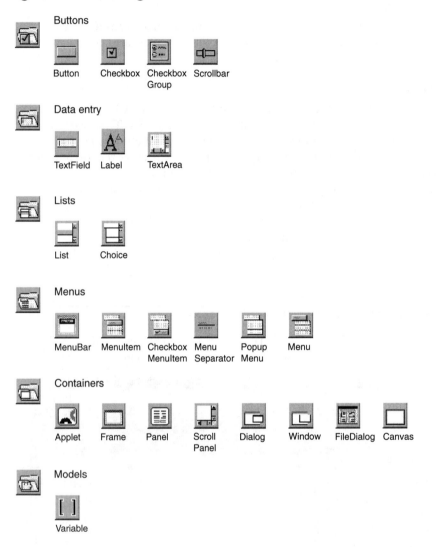

The Free-form Surface

The large blank area in the center of the panel is called the *free-form surface*, (see Figure 2.11). This is where you construct the user interface for the application and where you add nonvisual beans, those that represent business logic for your applet. The free-form surface grows as you add more beans. You may have to scroll the free-form surface to reach beans that are not in the current work area.

The free-form surface shows GUI beans exactly as they appear at run time. If your main bean is a Frame, its startup position is the same as the position of the window in the free-form surface, unless you write code to change its position.

Using Tool Bars

Like many of the applications available today, the Visual Composition Editor has tool bars to make it easier for you to select functions. These are first-generation tool bars with very basic functions like showing a group of icons and enabling you to cause actions by pressing the icons. You cannot choose to hide the tool bars, nor can you add your own buttons and functions to the tool bar. Many applications have second-generation tool bars that support drag and drop, have multiple views, and can be modified by the user at run time, however, you can edit and change the categories and folders in the bean palette.

Visual Composition Menu Bar

The menu bar has equivalent items for all the icons on the tool bar, except the Test button that is located on the left end. If more screen real estate is needed in the Visual Composition Editor you can hide the tool bar. You can do this by selecting the Options menu and then deselecting the Show Palette menu item. This setting is saved with the bean. The next time you open the bean, the Visual Composition Editor does not display the tool bar. Unfortunately, there is no means to make this the default setting for all Visual Composition Editors. In the sample illustrations in this book, we show the tool bar.

Making an Applet

Because you are creating a new GUI bean and you have selected Applet as the parent class (or *superclass*), the Workbench opened with an Applet object in the free-form surface, as shown in Figure 2.10.

    Applet provides very rich default behavior. The Applet class is a subclass of Panel, as shown in Figure 2.13. It has all the display functions of a panel along with the ability to be loaded into a browser. Because the applet will run in a web browser, it can't be resized and repositioned at run time.

    Look at the Hierarchy view by selecting the Hierarchy tab on the HelloWorld window. An Applet acts like a canvas or panel; it is a container. You can place other components like Buttons, Labels, TextFields, and many other types of GUI elements directly on an applet. Let's go back to the Visual Composition Editor and start adding components to the HelloWorld applet.

    Select the Visual Composition tab on the HelloWorld applet.

    Place the mouse pointer in the middle of the Applet and press the left mouse button to select the applet. The name of the selected Applet appears in the information area at the bottom of the Visual Composition Editor.

Figure 2.13 HelloWorld Hierarchy view.

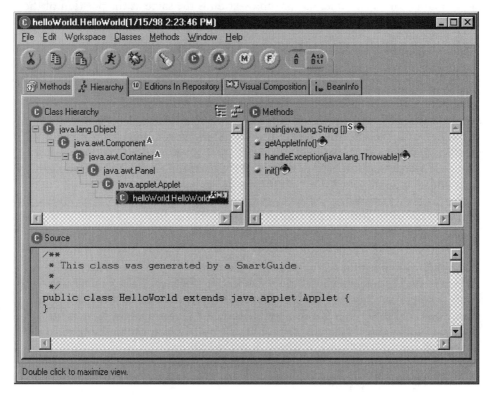

User interface beans are usually placed and positioned on canvases. AWT provides several layouts that are used with panels to control the spacing and alignment of GUI elements contained in the panel. Because the HelloWorld applet is your first project, we will keep it very simple and use a *null* layout manager, which is technically the same as not using a layout manager. With a null layout manager, you are free to place and size other components on the applet anywhere you wish. The use of a null layout manager is highly discouraged and considered poor design. Later in this book, we cover all standard layout managers by using them in other sample applications.

HelloWorld is basically an applet with text saying *Hello World*. Because the Applet class inherits from the Container class, it is capable of containing other GUI elements that can display text. The proper class to use for this purpose is the **Label** class. Add a label to the applet with the following steps:

Select the Data Entry category, which holds Label.

Click on the Label icon using the left mouse button.

[43]

BUILDING THE HELLO WORLD APPLET

You have now loaded the mouse pointer with a Label bean to drop on the applet. You can see that it is loaded because the mouse pointer appears as a cross hair as it is moved over the free-form surface. If you picked the wrong bean, just go to the correct icon on the palette and select that icon. You can unload the pointer by selecting the arrow icon (also called the *Selection tool*) on the tool bar.

Move the mouse to the applet and press the left mouse button to place the Label bean.

You now have a Label on the Applet; your Visual Composition Editor should look like Figure 2.14.

Naming Beans

You can select the various beans on the Visual Composition Editor by clicking the mouse pointer over them. Select the Label bean you have just added. Looking at

Figure 2.14 Adding a Label bean.

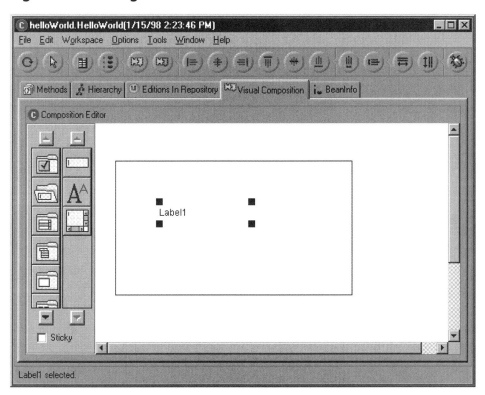

the bottom of the screen, in the information area, you see the name of the bean currently selected, in this case, Label1. Beans are given default names as they are dropped on the Applet. You should always identify your beans using names that describe their function. This becomes very important as the components you build become more complex. The name you give a bean is used by the code generator; using appropriate names will help you in debugging and understanding the generated code. To change the name of a bean, you have two options:

- Select the bean and click it with the right mouse button. Select **Change Bean Name** from the pop-up menu. Enter a meaningful name in the window provided.

- Double-click on the bean. This brings up the bean's property sheet. In this window, you can change many of the bean's properties, one of which is *beanName*.

Using either of these methods, change the name of the Label1 bean to **helloLabel**. The convention for bean names is that they start with lowercase and the first letter of all other words in the name is in uppercase. Bean names should reflect the type of the bean, that is why you called this bean helloLabel.

Editing Text

The default text for the helloLabel bean is **Label1**. For this applet, the text should be **Hello World**. The text for the label can be changed in two different ways:

- Enter the desired text by directly editing the bean's text. Place the tip of the mouse pointer on the label, and press and hold the Alt key and the left mouse button. A small editing window opens over the existing text. Type **Hello World** and click anywhere outside the editing window to close it. This method can be used to edit any beans that have a *text* property.

- Double-click on the bean. This brings up the bean's property sheet. In this window, you can change many of the bean's properties, one of which is *text*. See Figure 2.15.

Changing Fonts

Now, that looks a little bit better, but it is still pretty plain. Let's change the font size and foreground color to make it look even better with the following:

Select helloLabel by clicking once on the words **Hello World**.

Open the property sheet for helloLabel by either pressing the right mouse button and selecting **Properties**, or by double-clicking the left mouse button.

Find the *font* property in the table. Click the right side of the entry field for *font*. A small button appears; click it. This displays the Fonts window, as seen in Figure 2.16.

Figure 2.15 Label text changed.

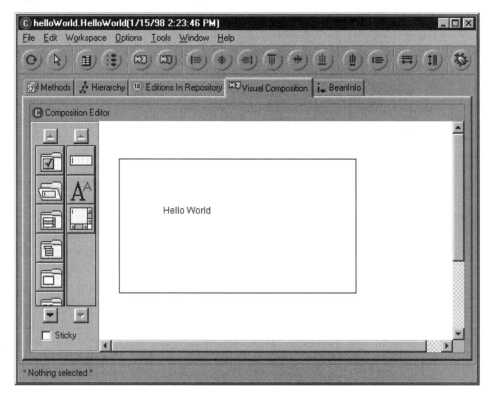

Select a font type, size, and style that looks good to you. For example, you could use a Helvetica font with a Bold Italic style and a size of 24 points.

Select **OK** on the Fonts window to close it; then close the property sheet to save your changes.

Your text should look like Figure 2.17. If the words **Hello World** appear clipped when the new font is applied, you have two choices:

- Select the Label bean and manually size it until all of the text is displayed.

- Select the text bean, bring up its pop-up menu and edit the width in the **constraints** properties to make it big enough to accommodate the text.

Generating Java Code

The next step is to save the applet and test it. As mentioned before, saving the bean also generates the Java code for all components in the Visual Composition Editor.

Figure 2.16 Changing the font attribute.

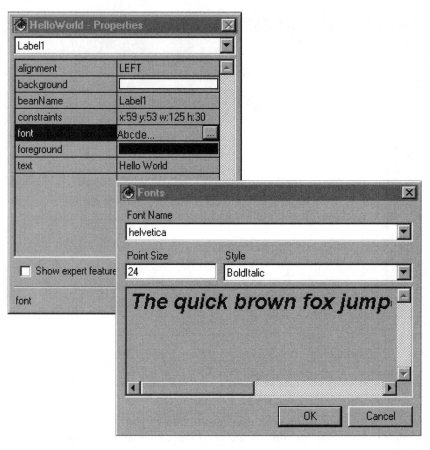

Select File and then Save Bean from the menu bar to save the applet. A new edition is created for the bean and stored in the repository; it also becomes the current edition in the workspace. The Java code for the HelloWorld class is generated and compiled.

To run the Applet, press the Test icon on the tool bar.

Pressing Test before saving causes the bean to be saved and recompiled. It is equivalent to performing the two steps with just one button. As soon as the code is compiled, the Settings window appears, and you are given a chance to enter any required parameters for the applet. Press the Run button to start the applet viewer and run HelloWorld as seen in Figure 2.18.

The HelloWorld applet runs in the applet viewer as seen in Figure 2.19. There is really nothing spectacular in Hello World, other than the fact that you just created your very first Java applet with VisualAge for Java. It compiled and ran without errors and you didn't have to write a single line of code! Real

Figure 2.17 HelloWorld with changed font.

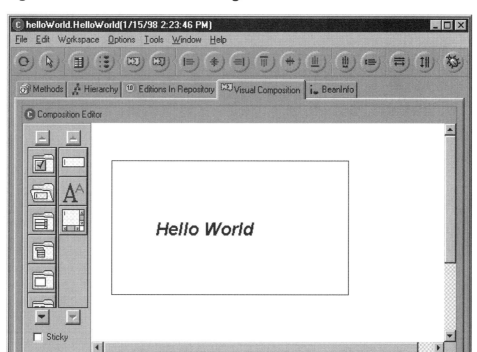

VisualAge for Java programs require that you write code, and you will have a chance to do this soon. You can rely on VisualAge for Java to generate most or all the code for the user interface.

You are probably interested in seeing the generated code. It can be seen in either the Methods or the Hierarchy view for the HelloWorld class.

Select the Methods view for the HelloWorld window as shown in Figure 2.20.

You will see a number of methods, as shown in Figure 2.20. These methods are:

- `main()`
- `getAppletinfo()`
- `gethelloLabel()`
- `handleException()`
- `init()`

Previously, we noted that one of the differences between Java applets and applications is that applets run within the confines of a web browser and are governed by the security model for applets. Applications have their own frame, run stand-alone, and are not subject to the same security model as applets.

Figure 2.18 Settings for HelloWorld.

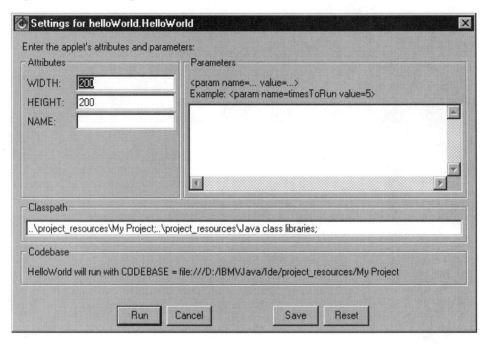

Applets start running when the Virtual Machine (VM) in the web browser constructs the Applet instance and calls the `init()` and `start()` methods.

Figure 2.19 Hello World running.

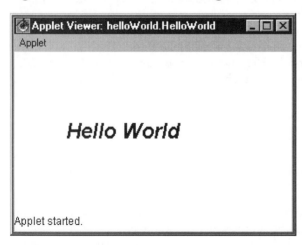

Figure 2.20 Generated methods.

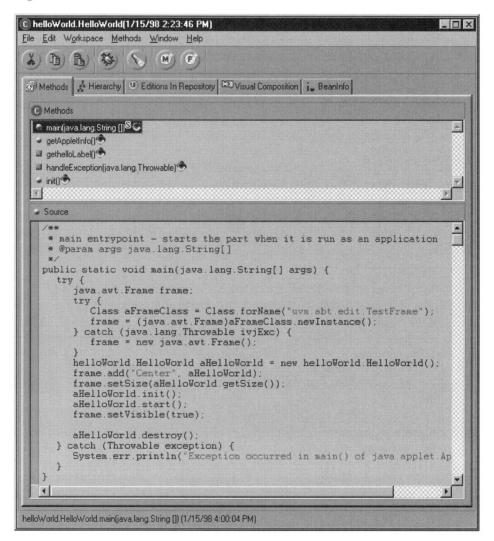

Applications start running when a stand-alone VM is started with the name of the class that contains the `main()` method. After instantiating the object, the `main()` method is called and execution starts.

You might be wondering why there is a `main()` method in the generated code of an applet. VisualAge generates this method for all visual components. It exists so that components can be tested in a stand-alone environment. Many times, you will develop components, such as panels, that cannot be run on their own. In order to test them, you would have to wrap them in an Applet or a Frame. To save you that trouble, VisualAge generates a `main()` method for them.

```
/**
 * main entrypoint - starts the part when it is
 * run as an application
 * @param args java.lang.String[]
 */
public static void main(java.lang.String[] args) {
  try
  {
    java.awt.Frame frame;
    try
    {
      Class aFrameClass =
        ClassforName("uvm.abt.edit.TestFrame");
      frame =
      (java.awt.Frame)aFrameClass.newInstance();
    }
    catch (java.lang.Throwable ivjExc)
    {
      frame = new java.awt.Frame();
    }
    helloWorld.HelloWorld aHelloWorld = new
     helloWorld.HelloWorld();
    frame.add("Center", aHelloWorld);
    frame.setSize(aHelloWorld.getSize());
    aHelloWorld.init();
    aHelloWorld.start();
    frame.setVisible(true);

    aHelloWorld.destroy();
  }
  catch (Throwable exception)
  {
    System.err.println("Exception occurred in
     main() of java.applet.Applet");
  }
}
```

Let's examine the generated `main()` method for the HelloWorld a applet in more detail:

- The `main()` function starts the application.
- A specialized kind of Frame, a TestFrame, is instantiated to hold the Applet. This frame knows how to close itself.

- A new HelloWorld bean is allocated in memory by the **new** operator; the HelloWorld bean's constructor runs and returns.

- The new aHelloWorld instance is added to the center of the frame object.

- The size of the frame is set to the size of the applet.

- The `main()` method simulates the web browser by sending the `init()` and the `start()` messages to the aHelloWorld instance.

- The frame is set to be visible and, by doing so, given focus.

- When the frame is closed, the aHelloWorld instance is destroyed.

All of this is coded within the proper, and necessary, try and catch blocks to handle any exceptions that might occur. There will be more on exception handling in a later chapter.

The HelloWorld window can be repositioned on the screen by pointing to the title bar, holding down the left mouse button and moving the window. You can also change the size of the Hello window by selecting one of the window edges with the left mouse button and moving the mouse. As the window resizes the **Hello World** text stays in the same relative position in the window because the applet has no layout manager associated. In a later chapters you will learn how to use layout managers to improve this behavior.

When you are done with the HelloWorld window, select the system icon in the upper left corner of the applet viewer and select **Close** to end this applet.

Adding More Function to Hello World

Now that you have built a very simple applet, you can add more function and iterate on the Hello World program. Return to the HelloWorld Visual Composition Editor.

You will add function to show the current date in the applet. You will add another Label and a Date class and make a visual connection to complete this function. This is accomplished, without writing any code, using the following steps:

- Select the Data Entry category, which holds Label.

- Click on the Label icon using the left mouse button.

- Move the mouse pointer to the applet below the Hello World text, and press the left mouse button to drop the Label bean onto the applet.

- Name this Bean **dateLabel**. (See Naming Beans earlier in this chapter.)

Next, you will add a Button bean that will set the Label to display the current date.

- Select the **Buttons** category.

- Click on the **Button** icon using the left mouse button.

- Move the mouse pointer to the applet below the Hello World text, and press the left mouse button to drop the Button bean on to the applet.

Now the applet has a Button. To change the default text of Button1, directly edit the text on the bean:

- Press and hold the Alt key; click the bean using the left mouse button.
- Type **Set Date**, move the mouse off the button bean, and press the left mouse button. Note that accelerator keys are not supported in Java.
- Name this Bean **pbSetDate**.

The HelloWorld bean should now look like Figure 2.21.

Selecting Beans

As you have seen, the left mouse button is used to select the beans. To select multiple beans, select the first bean; then press and hold the Ctrl key and click the left

Figure 2.21 New beans added.

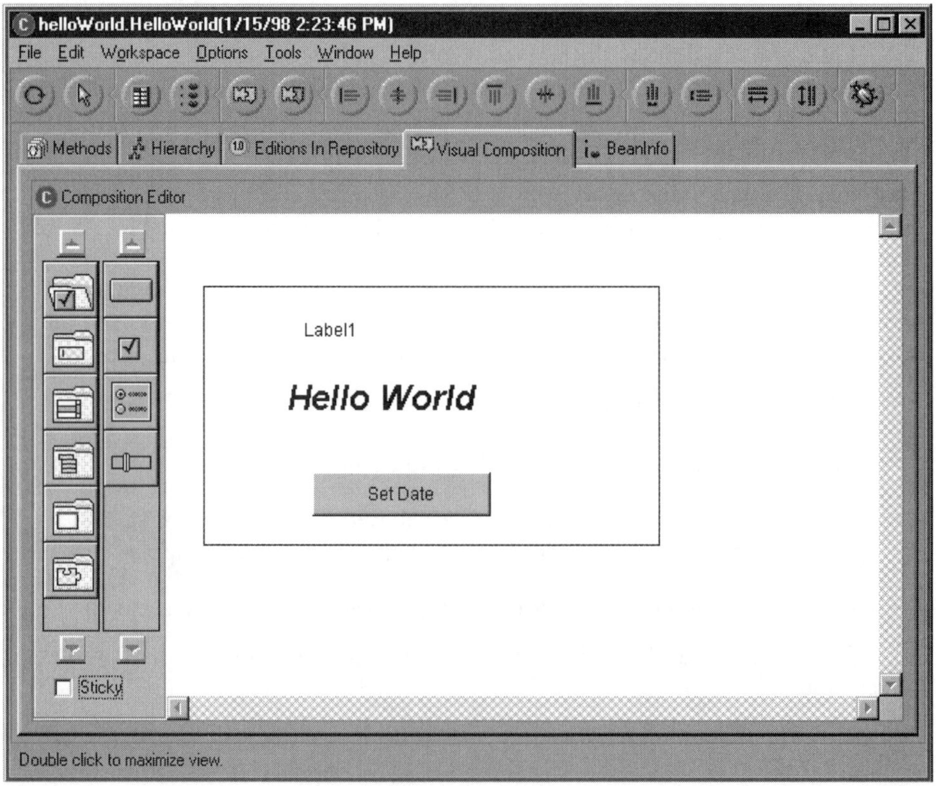

mouse button over any other beans you wish to select. The last bean selected is the one used as a reference when aligning all selected beans.

The beans on the applet need to be aligned so that they are centered. The default layout in the Visual Builder is **null,** which means that no alignment or sizing is done within the applet at run time. This can create some serious problems when you run your applet at a different resolution. As mentioned previously, we will cover layouts in a later chapter.

 Select the **Hello World** text and the **Set Date** button and press the Distribute Horizontally icon.

Using the Ctrl key, select the **dateLabel,** the **Hello World** Label, and the **pbSetDate** Button. All of the selected beans have boxes around them, and the last bean selected has black boxes or handles to indicate it will be used as a reference.

Press the Distribute Vertically icon to position the GUI beans in the applet.

There are also buttons to align to the left, right, top, bottom, and center. You can try these functions to see what they do, but they only work on a null layout and thus are not very useful.

Making Connections

When the applet runs and the user presses the pbSetDate button, it should set the text of dateLabel to the current date. To achieve this without VisualAge for Java, you would need to write some Java code. VisualAge for Java introduces the construction from parts paradigm, which enables you to build event-driven logic by connecting predesigned components. First, add a Date bean to the applet with the following steps:

From the menu bar, select Options and then Add Bean, or press Ctrl-B. The Add Bean window appears.

In the Class Name field, enter **Date,** then select the Browse button.

You must fully qualify any Java classes you add to an applet. The **java.util** package is the only currently loaded package with a Date class, so it is highlighted.

Select the OK button to close this window. Enter **aDate** in the Name entry field to properly name this bean.

Select the OK button to close the Add Bean window. See Figure 2.22.

Now the cursor is loaded with the Date bean. Move the mouse to the free-form surface and press the left mouse button to place the Date bean. Notice that because aDate is not a GUI bean, you are not allowed to drop it on top of the Applet.

Figure 2.22 Adding a Date bean.

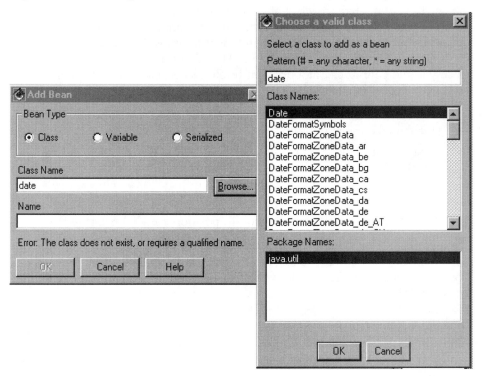

Make a connection from the **pbSetDate** bean to the dateLabel bean to set it with the current date when the button is pressed, as follows:

Place the mouse over the **pbSetDate** button, and press the right mouse button to get the context menu.

Select **Connect** from this menu.

This displays the preferred features list for a Button bean, seen in Figure 2.23. This is a short list of the most commonly selected connection items. Some items on the preferred list can be disabled or gray. The Visual Composition Editor prevents you from making some types of improper connections by graying out improper or invalid options.

Select the **actionPerformed(java.awt.event.actionEvent)** by clicking the left mouse button. This is source of the connection.

The mouse pointer changes its shape and looks like a spider attached by its web to the source of the connection. Now select a target for it. The spider needs a place to land.

Figure 2.23 Selecting the source connection.

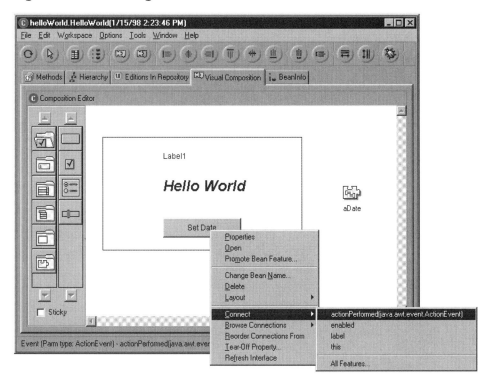

Move the spider to dateLabel in the HelloWorld applet and press the left mouse button to select the target for the connection. Notice that as the spider pointer moves over the objects on the Composition Editor, they receive focus clearly indicating the object you are about select.

This displays the preferred features list for the Label object shown in Figure 2.24.

Select the *text* item on the menu. Now you see a dashed line connecting the pbSetDate and the dateLabel objects. A dashed line indicates that the connection is incomplete. For now, this is correct, because we haven't yet told the connection what to set as the text when the button is pressed. A parameter is missing.

To complete the connection, pass a parameter into the connection with the following steps:

Move the mouse pointer so its tip is on the line representing the connection; press the left mouse button to select the connection. This displays a

Figure 2.24 Selecting the target connection.

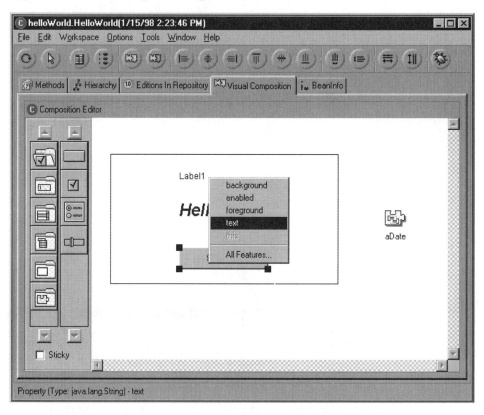

description of the connection listed in the information area at the bottom of the Visual Composition Editor. This is one way to find out what a connection does. Now make the following connection to pass the current date to the Label:

Select the connection from **pbSetDate** to **dateLabel**.

Making sure that the tip of the mouse is not over one of the handles or black squares on the connection, press the right mouse button to display the pop-up menu.

Select **Connect**, then select *value*.

Move the mouse to the aDate object on the free-form surface; then press the left mouse button.

Select **All Features**; a window appears. From the Methods column, select the **toString()** method to complete the connection and close the connection window. The HelloWorld applet should look like Figure 2.25.

Figure 2.25 Connection completed.

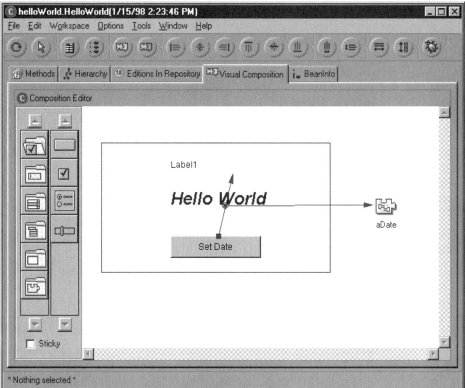

Saving and Testing the Improved Hello World Applet

Now you are ready to save and test your changes. It is really easy in the IDE: Select the Test button on the tool bar. The Visual Composition Editor saves the changes and compiles them into the workspace image. When you run the HelloWorld applet, it looks like Figure 2.26.

When the applet starts, the date does not appear in the dateLabel object; you see the default text of Label1. When you press the Set Date button, the date and time replaces the default text.

As you can see, it is very easy to create a graphical application with some basic function without writing any code! VisualAge for Java can generate most or all of the user interface code for your applications. Visual connections enable you to call methods in Java classes using event-driven programming.

Figure 2.26 Running applet.

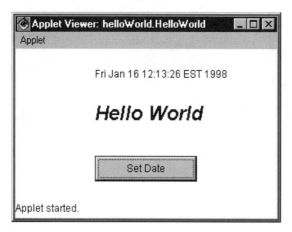

Viewing the Generated Code

For this simple sample, you can review the code generated by VisualAge for Java by switching to the Methods or Hierarchy view of the browser. Probably the most interesting piece of code in this applet is the code generated by the connection. Note that the connections in the Visual Composition Editor are development artifacts. They are translated into 100% pure Java code when the code is generated.

To see the generated code for any connection, the first step is to discover the connection number. You do this by selecting the connection (clicking it with the mouse) and looking in the information area of the Visual Composition Editor. In this case, we are interested in conn0; a corresponding conn0 method can be found in the Methods view. Notice that not all connections are translated into code: In this example, there is no method called conn1 for the parameter connection. See following code segment for the conn0 generated code:

```
/**
*conn0:(Button1.action.actionPerformed(java.awt.
*event.ActionEvent) --> dateLabel.text)
* @param arg1 java.awt.event.ActionEvent
*/
/* WARNING: THIS METHOD WILL BE REGENERATED. */
private void conn0(java.awt.event.ActionEvent arg1)
{
  try
  {
    // user code begin {1}
    // user code end
    getdateLabel().
```

```
        setText(getaDate().toString());
    // user code begin {2}
    // user code end
  }
  catch (java.lang.Throwable ivjExc)
  {
    // user code begin {3}
    // user code end
    handleException(ivjExc);
  }
}
```

There are a number of interesting points to observe in the code segment for the conn0 method above.

- Comments are inserted at the beginning of the class. They are in Javadoc format and can be printed to an HTML file using VisualAge for Java.

- Possible exceptions are handled by generating the appropriate try and catch blocks.

- The code for this method is regenerated whenever anything is changed and saved for the HelloWorld applet. Any modifications to this method will be lost the next time code is generated. To preserve your modifications, make them inside one of the user code areas.

```
    // user code begin {1}
    // Your code here
    // user code end
```

- You cannot make your own user code areas, but you will find that they are automatically generated in the appropriate places.

- This line of code does all the significant work in the method getdateLabel().

```
getdateLabel().
setText(getaDate().toString());
```

In Java, like in C++ and Smalltalk, messages to an object can be chained as long as the return type of the message is compatible with the next message. In this case, getdateLabel() gets a reference to the dateLabel object. If you look in this method, you will see that if it doesn't exist, the dateLabel object is created. The setText() method, just as its name implies, sets the text of dateLabel.

The next instruction is really the code generated by conn1, the parameter for the connection. The code getaDate().toString(), gets a reference to the aDate object, creates the object if it doesn't exist, and then asks it for its string representation, which in the case of a Date object is a formatted String with the date and time the object was created.

Now you can see why naming your beans is important. Reviewing the generated code would be a lot more difficult with the default bean names.

Summary

Well, you are off to a good start. You built a very simple Java application using VisualAge for Java. In this chapter, you:

- Became familiar with making projects and packages.
- Customized the Workbench with options.
- Learned the basic workings of the Visual Composition Editor using simple beans to design an applet.
- Edited beans to change their default attributes.
- Saved a JavaBean definition and generated Java code.
- Ran the compiled applet and saw the many default features of the application by using the AWT.

MAKING AN ADDING MACHINE

3

What's in Chapter 3

You have completed the Hello World applet and probably think this is very easy. This is one of the simplest Java applications you can develop other than the infamous "to do list" sample. Each chapter increases in difficulty and complexity, and this chapter covers visual programming in more detail. You will build an invisible bean and combine it with GUI beans to make an adding machine. You will write some simple Java code for the invisible bean to perform the calculation function. This chapter covers the following topics:

- JavaBeans Basics:
    - GUI beans
    - Invisible beans
    - Composite beans
- Overview of Layout Managers
- Building an Adding Machine:
    - Using a GridLayout
    - Using TextFields
    - Setting the tab order of GUI beans
    - Adding the contents of two TextFields

As you go through this book, we cover some object-oriented and visual development concepts. Many books exhaustively cover a particular object-oriented methodology or specific design technique. Because this book focuses on implementation, it covers only those object-oriented design concepts necessary to understand the applications you are building. The Adding Machine applet uses the Model-View-Controller design pattern that is common in object-oriented programming. First, you will build the View; later, you will build the Model part. This is okay, but in real life you will usually develop the Model parts first; then develop the View parts. This is because View (or GUI) parts are not supposed to influence the implementation of Model parts. It is unrealistic to say that View parts have no influence on Model parts, but this influence should be minimal.

Now that you have completed a simple applet (HelloWorld), it's time to look back at the steps and understand how you built it. Before you go on to more

[61]

complex programs, you need to understand the different types of VisualAge beans. This will help you design and implement your own Java applications. The JavaBeans definition is a fundamental concept of JDK Version 1.1, and you need to understand JavaBeans to fully utilize VisualAge for Java.

JavaBeans Basics

The notion of JavaBeans was introduced in JDK V1.1; VisualAge for Java uses JavaBeans and generates JavaBeans. End users of a program using JavaBeans neither know, nor have to care, that JavaBeans were used. JavaBeans were introduced primarily to assist Java developers; there are many changes to the JDK from V1.0 to support JavaBeans. In this section, you will learn the basics behind JavaBeans. You will learn more detailed information about JavaBeans classes and methods in later chapters.

Different types of beans or classes are used in the Visual Composition Editor. There are *GUI* beans, *invisible* beans, and *composite* beans. In this section, you learn about each type of bean. These JavaBeans terms are universal among the different tools that support Java, and they are different from the traditional VisualAge terms that have been used for years. If you are a veteran VisualAge developer, you will recognize that GUI beans are the same as Visual Parts, and invisible beans are the same as Invisible Parts.

GUI beans and invisible beans are Java classes. That's it, beans are classes, but there is a bit more to it than that. A comprehensive JavaBeans specification covers all requirements for a JavaBeans component available from the Sun web site. A few of the books cover the bean specification in great depth, and there are many articles that give a superficial overview of JavaBeans. If you are a Java tool developer, you need at least one in-depth book on the bean specification. Fortunately, VisualAge for Java generates JavaBeans, so it shelters you from some of the gory details relating to JavaBeans. However, it is important for you to understand how JavaBeans work.

The entire AWT class library was updated to support JavaBeans, including the new V1.1 event model. You can see how the event model works by examining the code generated by VisualAge for Java. Because AWT implements new methods supporting the new event model, all AWT-based classes inherit these special functions, which support the notification or messaging framework in the AWT class library. Implementation of a notification framework enables beans to notify or send messages to other beans. This critical function is what enables you to build program elements by making connections. As stated previously, this changes the way you develop your Java applications (it is better object orientation), but the end user will not notice any difference.

Deprecated Methods

Java V1.0 classes will work with Java V1.1 run-time support, but the V1.0 classes do not use the methods implementing the new event model. Although Java V1.0

classes are beans, they are stale beans that need some refining to be fully compat-ible with other JavaBeans. A number of methods in the AWT class library were replaced by new methods. These obsolete methods are referred to as *deprecated methods*. An example of a deprecated method is the Button **enable**() method, which is replaced with the setEnable(true) method. These old methods work in the compiler and at run time in the virtual machine, but eventually, they will not be supported. It is a good idea to use the new AWT methods.

Types of Beans

The most atomic or granular bean is called a *primitive* bean. GUI and invisible beans can be primitive beans. Examples of primitive beans from the AWT class library are Button, which is a GUI bean, and Color, which is an invisible bean. You can change the settings and default properties of primitive beans in the Visual Composition Editor.

Beans can be combined to create *composite* beans. When you combine two or more invisible beans, you have a composite invisible bean. For example, if you were building the invisible component of a Clock bean, you would combine the Timer and Date invisible beans in a composite invisible bean named **Clock.** The Clock bean would supply the services you would expect from such a bean, like setting and getting the time and date.

You create a composite GUI bean when you combine a GUI bean with one or more other beans. For example, you can combine the previously discussed invisible Clock bean with a user interface bean that displays the time and date and has buttons to perform the various clock functions. You could call this bean a **ClockView** (Figure 3.1). In fact, the clock could have multiple views like digital, analog, or a combination, which shows the date in digital format and the time, as a traditional clock with hands ticking.

GUI Beans

GUI beans are user interface controls in the AWT class library, such as Button, TextField, and Frame. The Visual Composition Editor generates Java code for all GUI beans in AWT. GUI beans supplied with the Visual Composition Editor are sometimes called *controls* or *widgets*. The terms *controls* and *widgets* come about

Figure 3.1 ClockView composite GUI part.

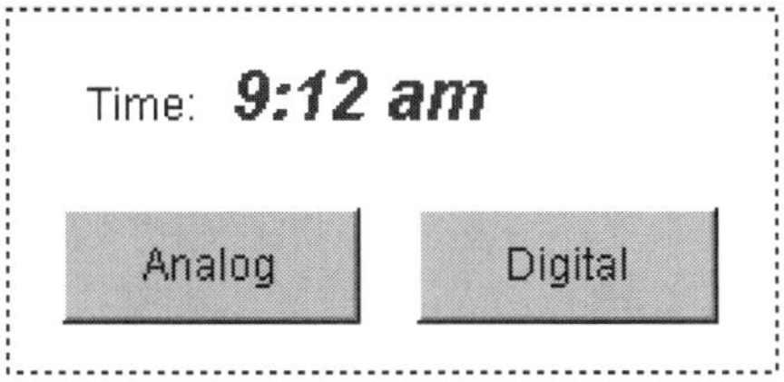

because the higher level definitions in Java AWT essentially map to the underlying graphical API for each windowing system running Java. When talking about GUI beans in this book, we will refer to them as beans or controls interchangeably.

All GUI beans are subclasses of **Component,** which is an abstract base class in the AWT class library. The **Component** class sets the base behavior for all user interface controls and for **Container,** as well. You can see this inheritance relationship in Figure 3.2.

Finding Beans

You may want to search for other JavaBeans in the Workspace when you are developing Java programs. Let's try searching for *Applet* with the following steps:

 Select the **Search** button on the Workbench toolbar.

The Search dialog appears, seen in Figure 3.3, allowing you to enter the following:

Enter **Applet** in theSearch for Name field.

Select **Workspace** in the Look in: dropdown list.

Press the **Start** button to begin the search.

Once the results window opens, open a browser for the Applet. You can select the **Open** menu item on the Applet popup menu.

When the Class browser opens, select the Hierarchy tab on the view as shown in Figure 3.4.

Now that you have found the Applet class, you can browse its definition and learn more about the class and its superclasses. If you ever need information about a bean, the search feature in the IDE is a quick way to retrieve that information. It will also verify whether the class is loaded in the Workspace and available to use.

Invisible Beans

Invisible beans contain business logic, such as mathematical computation, data access functions, and application logic. The AWT class library comes with a number of invisible beans that are very helpful in building applications. Most of these

Figure 3.2 Button inheritance hierarchy.

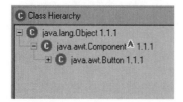

Figure 3.3 Search dialog.

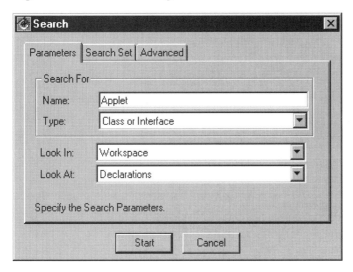

beans are designed for general-purpose use, and in many cases, they need to be subclassed to add application-specific function. In Figure 3.5, you see the composition of the ClockView application, combining both GUI and invisible beans.

Building an Adding Machine

In this chapter, you will build an Adding Machine application that combines GUI and invisible beans. First, you construct the GUI bean CalculatorView. Then you develop an invisible bean, Calc, which you use in combination with the GUI bean to perform the calculations.

The Adding Machine enables you to enter two numbers, press a button to add the contents of the two TextFields, and display the result in the output field. The application window has:

Three TextFields, two for accepting the numbers to be added and one to display the result

Three Labels for the TextFields

A Button for the Add function

An invisible bean, which performs the addition, signals that the operation has been performed, and that the result property in the Calc bean has changed

Let's begin by making a new applet in the Visual Composition Editor to build the view of the Adding Machine. You will build and test the CalculatorView GUI bean before building the Calc invisible bean. This is a new application, so you should make a new package before starting the new class. By

Figure 3.4 Applet hierarchy.

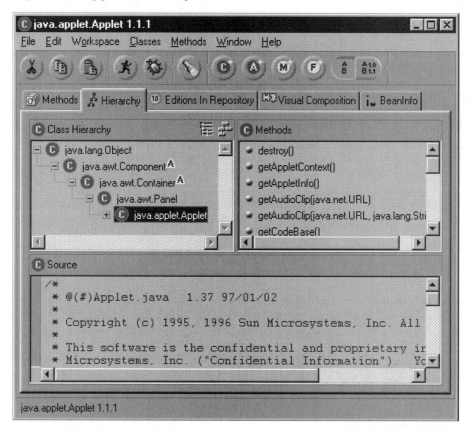

creating the new package, you keep the classes, methods, and, ultimately, the files for the different applications separate. If the VisualAge for Java Workbench is not started, restart it now (Figure 3.6).

Figure 3.5 ClockView composite with invisible beans.

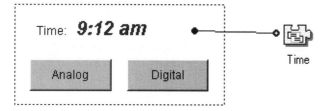

Figure 3.6 IDE Workbench.

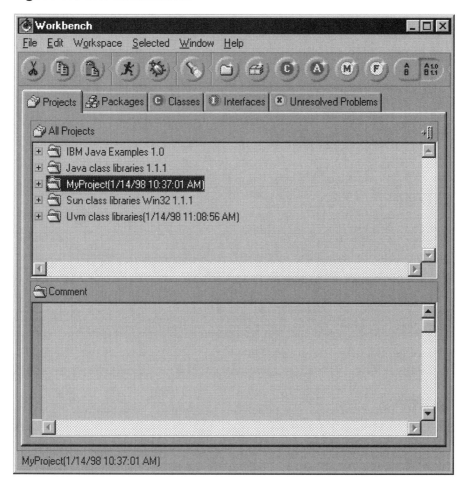

Creating a New Package

First, create the new package in the project we started for the Hello World applet.

In the Workbench, right-click on the upper pane (Figure 3.7).

Select the **My Project** project.

If you skipped Chapter 2, you need to create a new project in the Workbench. From the menu bar, select **Selected** and then **Add Project**, or select the **Project** icon on the tool bar. This displays the project SmartGuide, where you can enter the project name. Once you have a project to add new classes, you can proceed.

Figure 3.7 Add Project SmartGuide.

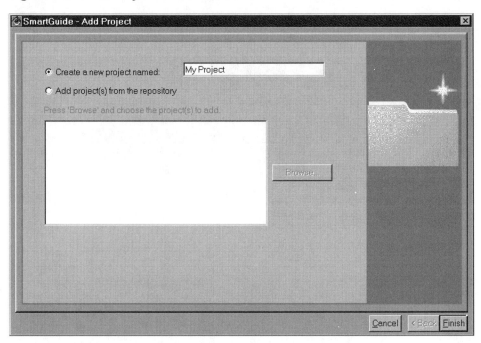

A new project called My Project was created. The next thing to do is to create the **package,** which will contain all the components of the Simple Calculator applet.

With My Project selected, right-click on the top pane. Select **Add Package** from the pop-up menu.

Enter **calculator** in the **Create a new package named** entry field. Press the **Finish** button to create the package (see Figure 3.8).

After the calculator package is created, your Workbench should look like Figure 3.9.

Creating a New Class

Now that you have defined the project and the package in the IDE, you can start defining the beans that will make up the Simple Calculator. The project and package provide the structure for the IDE to contain and catalog your beans in the **Workspace.** Packages are also used when exporting your Java classes.

First you will build and test the **CalculatorView** GUI bean, then you will go on to build the **CalculatorLogic** JavaBean. Initially, the **Simple Calculator** will be developed as an applet, which means it can only run inside a web browser or an applet viewer. To make an applet, the superclass for the **CalculatorView** must be **Applet.**

Figure 3.8 Add Package SmartGuide.

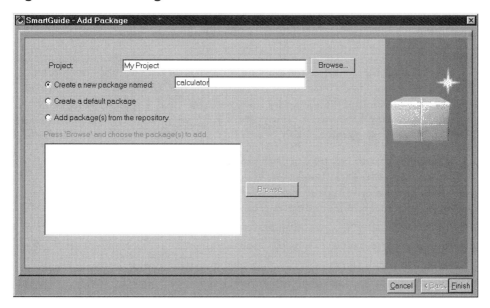

Figure 3.9 Workbench with My Project and calculator package.

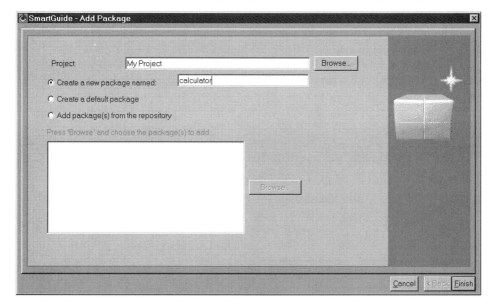

With the calculator package selected, click the right mouse button on the top pane, and select **New Class/Interface** from the pop-up menu.

In the Create Class or Interface SmartGuide shown in Figure 3.10, enter **CalculatorView** in the **Class Name** entry field.

Make sure you capitalize the class name. It is a Java convention to capitalize class or bean names and this is for a very good reason. The bean will have a constructor that is essentially a method with no return value. By capitalizing bean names, it is easy to differentiate constructors because they are capitalized methods with the same name as the bean.

Press the **Browse** button opposite the **Superclass** entry field and type the word **Applet** to select the Applet class from the java.applet package. Notice that as you type in the Class Qualifications Dialog, the choice of class and interface names are narrowed down, as seen in Figure 3.11.

Once the Applet bean is selected, press the **OK** button to save this selection and close the Class Qualifications Dialog.

Make sure that the **Design the class visually** radio button is selected on the Smart Guide, as shown in Figure 3.10.

Press the **Finish** button to complete the specifications for the applet so VisualAge for Java can generate the code to create the **CalculatorView** class.

Figure 3.10 Create Class/Interface SmartGuide.

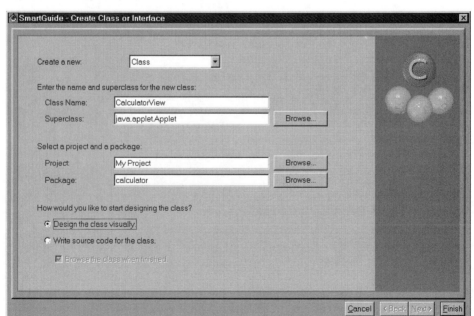

Figure 3.11 Class Qualification Dialog.

The Visual Composition Editor now opens to enable you to place the visual components that will make up the view of the Simple Calculator, as shown in Figure 3.12.

Layout Managers

The HelloWorld applet was built using no Layout Manager; actually, it had a Layout Manager set to *null*. Using a null layout is not a good design because it uses pixel coordinates to position the controls. This creates a new variation for Java applications: write once and run anywhere, but it will look rather ugly. Layout Managers are properties of Java AWT **Containers**, so the Layout Manager can be set easily in the property sheet.

Containers can use different Layout Managers; you can also make your own Layout Managers. This means that Frames, Applets, and Panels can all have their

Figure 3.12 Visual Composition Editor.

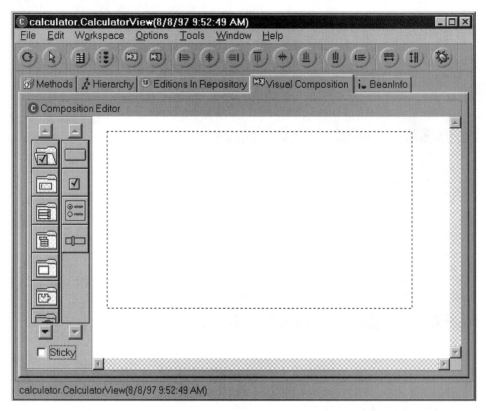

own Layout Managers. In this chapter, you will use GridBagLayout. Later, when you build the Advanced Calculator, you will use multiple panels with Layout Managers. When you combine Containers with different Layout Managers, you must be careful, because the different Layout Managers can produce conflicting behavior that will not provide the result you expect. This program is an Applet, and because an Applet is a Container, it will have its own Layout Manager.

Layout Managers are used to align, space, and size controls placed on an Applet, Panel or other Container. There are several types of Layout Managers, and only experience will make you comfortable using them. There are five basic Layout Managers in the V1.1 AWT:

- BorderLayout
- CardLayout
- FlowLayout
- GridBagLayout
- GridLayout

Each Layout Manager provides its own behavior and can be customized within the Visual Composition Editor. Each standard Layout Manager subclasses Object and implements either the LayoutManager or LayoutManager2 interface. Many Containers have a default Layout Manager if no Layout Manager is specified. It is best to specify the Layout Manager to insure your Container will perform as you expect. There is also a layout called *null,* which forces the positions of GUI beans to be fixed in the Container. In later chapters, you will use other Layout Managers like the Border, Flow, and GridBag layouts.

Custom Layouts

The Visual Composition Editor lists only the default Layout Managers in a Container's property sheet. If you create your own Layout Manager and you want to use it in a container, it will not display in the properties editor in the VisualBuilder. You need to break down and write a line of code in order to use the custom layout manager in a Container. The code would use the setLayout() method.

The Visual Composition Editor always generates a setLayout() method in the init() method of an Applet. You can see the code for the init() method shown in the next section. You would enter the code for the setLayout() method in a user code area provided in the generated code. All of the other code is regenerated, so you should put code here at your own risk. You can see the warning in the code that this method will be regenerated, and you will lose changes to the sources code.

Adding User Code The Visual Composition Editor provides places for you to enter **user code** with commented areas in the generated code. These locations are marked by commented lines:

```
// user code begin {1}
// user code end
```

You can put another setLayout() method between these comment lines like:

```
setLayout(MyCustomLayout);
```

Many people have asked, and a number of people have tried, to add additional **user code** areas in the generated code. This shows a lot of ingenuity and creativity, but, unfortunately, it does not work. The next time the Visual Composition Editor generates code for the Applet, these added **user code** areas will be gone.

Even the comment heading for the method is regenerated, so comments also need to be added to the **user code** areas. Hopefully, this will be fixed in the next release.

```
/**
 * Handle the Applet init method.
 */
/* WARNING: THIS METHOD WILL BE REGENERATED. */
public void init() {
```

```
super.init();
  try {
    setName("CalculatorView");
    setLayout(getCalculatorViewGridLayout());
    setSize(167, 289);
    add(getLabel1(), getLabel1().getName());
    add(getnum1(), getnum1().getName());
    add(getLabel2(), getLabel2().getName());
    add(getnum2(), getnum2().getName());
    add(getLabel3(), getLabel3().getName());
    add(getresult(), getresult().getName());
    add(getpbAdd(), getpbAdd().getName());
    // user code begin {1}
    // user code end
  } catch (java.lang.Throwable ivjExc) {
    // user code begin {2}
    // user code end
    handleException(ivjExc);
  }
}
```

Using a GridLayout

For the Adder applet, you will use GridLayout, which is used when you want to align a number of same-sized beans. This layout is frequently used for entry forms, because it can keep TextFields and Labels aligned.

Place the mouse over the applet and open its property sheet.

Select the **layout** field, which then displays a button.

Select this button to display the **Prompter** window.

Select the Layout Manager drop-down list, and select GridLayout from the list, as shown in Figure 3.13.

Now that you have changed the layout to GridLayout, the properties have changed in the Prompter window. Use the following steps to set properties for GridLayout:

Set the **columns** to **1**.

Set the **rows** to **7**.

Close the Prompter window and close the property sheet to save these changes. The Applet will not look any different because the Layout Manager will only affect the GUI beans that are placed on it and, currently, the Applet has no GUI beans.

Figure 3.13 Layout properties.

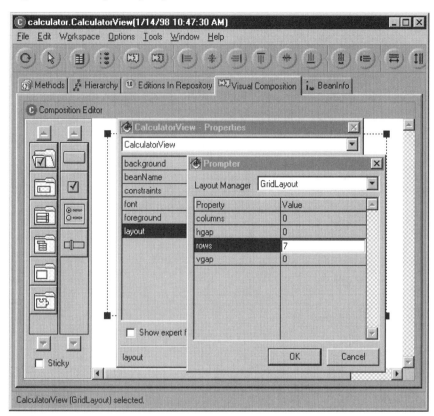

Adding GUI Beans to a GridLayout

The Simple Calculator needs the GUI beans for the user interface. Add the needed GUI beans to the GridLayout with the following steps:

Make the Applet smaller by resizing it. Select the Applet with the left mouse button, then select one of the handles (the black squares in the corners), and drag the handle to resize the Applet.

Place three **Label** beans on the applet. They are in the **Data Entry** category. See Figure 3.14 for suggested placing of controls.

Place three **TextField** controls on the GridLayout.

You may want to try the **Sticky** check box to make it easier to drop multiple controls of the same type. It is located at the bottom of the of the bean palette. To disable or stop the Sticky selection, either deselect the check box or select the mouse pointer button on the tool bar.

Figure 3.14 Applet with TextFields.

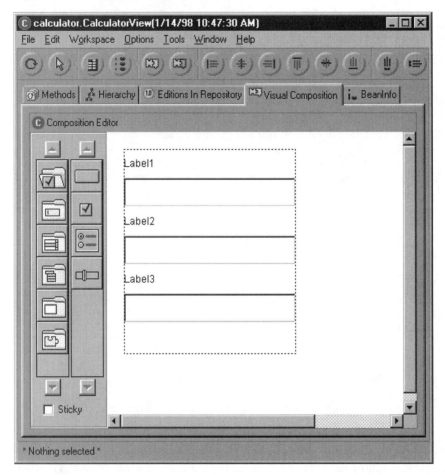

The Sticky function behavior is called *modal behavior* because you are in a specific mode. In general, modal behavior is not good for applications; it forces the user to figure out how to get into and out of a mode. However, in some very special cases, modal functions add some good function or actually improve application usability after you learn how the function works.

From the **Buttons** category in the bean palette, select a **Button**, move the mouse pointer to a position near the bottom of the dashed box on the composition editor, and press the left mouse button to drop the Button.

The dashed box represents the visual portion of the actual Applet instance, as seen in Figure 3.15. You may need to drag and drop the GUI beans a few times to get them in the proper order.

Figure 3.15 Applet with GUI beans.

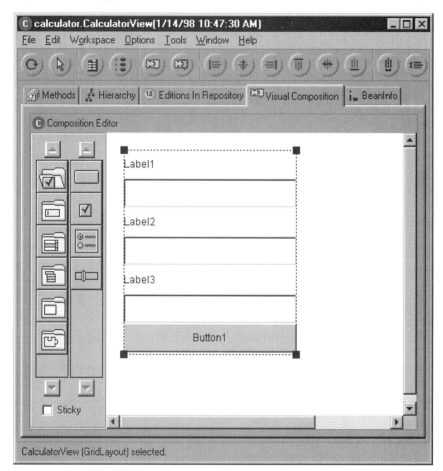

Editing Buttons

By placing the mouse pointer on the Button and pressing Alt and the left mouse button, you can directly edit the text of the Button. This also works for other controls. Change the text of the Button to **Add** with the following:

> Directly edit the Label controls to describe the TextFields below them.
> Use **First number, Second number, Result** for the respective Labels.
> When you finish the CalculatorView, it should look like Figure 3.16.
> You can also edit the Label **text** in the property sheet. Direct editing is usually faster.

Figure 3.16 Beans placement.

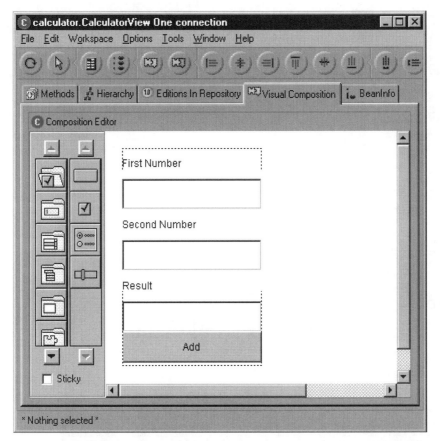

Naming Beans

Each bean you drop has a default name. The first TextField control you dropped is called TextField1. In addition, the first TextField dropped on the next composite you build will also be named TextField1. You can see that the proliferation of beans named TextField1could cause a debugging nightmare. Changing the name to something more meaningful will help you later to follow the generated code, and it provides some level of documentation for the code. So give the beans appropriate names. Change the bean names with these steps:

Point to a GUI bean, click the right mouse button, and select **Change Bean Name** from the pop-up menu.

Change the names of the TextFields to **efNum1, efNum2** and **efResult**.

Change the name of the Button to **pbAdd**.

Read-only TextFields

Because the result of the calculation will be supplied by an invisible bean (yet to be built), the result TextField should not allow keyboard input. One way to achieve this is to set the *editable* property to **False.**

Double-click on the efResult TextField to open its property sheet.

Select the **editable** field; from its pull-down menu, select **False.**

Close the property sheet to save the changes.

If you ever make any changes to a control in a property sheet and decide you do not like the changes, there is an easy way to go back to the old settings. After you close the property sheet, go to the **Edit** menu of the Visual Composition Editor and select **Undo.** You can step back through the changes until the bean has changed back to the way you want it. Remember that **Edit/Undo** is your friend. There is also a **Redo** function if you go too far in your undoing.

Testing an Applet

Now you are ready to try to run this applet for the first time. From the upper tool bar of the Visual Composition Editor, press the **Test** button. This generates run-time code for the applet.

Once compilation ends, a window appears to give you an opportunity to enter parameters, for example, to adjust the size of the applet. Press the **Run** button on this panel to continue. The applet viewer starts and runs the CalculatorView applet, as seen in Figure 3.17.

You can move between the first two fields, enter values, and press the **Add** button (of course, nothing happens yet). Nothing can be entered in the **Result** field because you made it noneditable. If you use the mouse to increase or decrease the window size, the GUI beans stay centered in the applet and the GUI beans expand, thanks to the GridLayout. It is usually good to have TextFields expand, but Buttons should not expand in the user interface. Close the applet viewer when you finish testing it.

Naming Conventions

Before you begin building the application is a good time to have a short discussion of naming conventions. When developing applications, it is prudent to adopt some consistent naming conventions. Java is a case-sensitive, type-specific language. This means that each class, method, and data field must have a unique name and a defined type. Use descriptive names to make your beans more usable. A good guideline is to have a set of prefixes and suffixes that can be used to ensure consistent naming. For example, the Hello World application used the *pb* prefix for Buttons.

Most people have their own naming conventions, as well as coding style conventions. In this book, the names of classes and beans start with an uppercase character.

Figure 3.17 CalculatorView applet running.

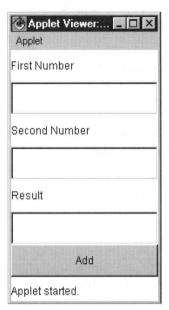

Each word in the name of a class or bean also starts with an uppercase character. For example, the adding machine view is called CalculatorView. Any properties of a class or bean start with a lowercase character. Each subsequent word in the name of the property starts with an uppercase character. For example, the property that holds the result of the calculation is called *result*. The convention for instances of a class is the same as that for properties. For example, the instance of the entry field that displays the calculation result is called *efResult*.

When you create an instance of a class, you should try to identify the type of class you are instantiating. For example, you can use *ef* as the beginning of the instance name for an entry field. Adhering to these simple suggestions makes it easier to follow and understand the generated code, as well as to understand the connection messages that are issued by the program at run time. It also improves debugging, in the rare event that you make a programming error.

What Are Tab Stops?

Tabbing is a useful feature in user interfaces that improves screen navigation. The term *Tab stop* describes the position or location where the cursor goes when the Tab key is pressed. Each control placed on a canvas can be designated as a Tab stop. This designation determines the position of the cursor after the user presses the arrow or Tab keys.

Pressing the Tab key moves the cursor from its current position to the next control that has been designated a Tab stop. The sequence is determined by the order in which the controls were placed on the container. This order can be viewed easily and changed visually.

Setting the Tab Order

This section describes how Tab stops and tabbing order can be defined. By default, AWT GUI beans have tabbing function automatically at run time. The tabbing order follows the sequence in which the GUI beans are added to the Container. Tabbing order can be determined from the Applet's pop-up menu. To see the Applet's current tabbing order, select the Applet. Make sure that the tip of the mouse pointer is not over one of the GUI beans; it should be at the bottom of the Applet where there is a small gap between the Button and the Applet.

Using the Beans List

As you can see, selecting some beans (like Containers) can be difficult. Sometimes the GUI beans are hidden or covered by other beans. In the case of Containers, controls can fill the Container bean so you can't access it. A special window enables you to select and work on beans. Let's use the Beans List window to view the Tab Stops with the following steps:

 From the menu bar, select **Tools** and then **Beans List.** The Beans List window appears. You could use the **Beans List** icon on the tool bar to open this window also.

Expand the CalculatorView by pressing the expansion (+) icon as shown in Figure 3.18.

This window is very helpful when accessing beans in a Container; it provides a graphical-tree view of all beans associated with this composite bean. This window lists all beans in this Applet, so you can select a bean easily and access all functions on its pop-up menu, like Properties, Delete, Open, and also Connections. You can drag and drop components in this window to put them in the desired order as well. The Visual Composition Editor will then generate the code with the components in the new order. If the TextFields and Buttons do not appear in the proper order, you can drag and drop them into the proper sequence by:

Selecting one or more controls

Using the mouse and drag the control to the proper position

Releasing the mouse button to drop the control and set its position

Now you are ready to see the Tab stops for the Applet by following these steps:

Select the second **CalculatorView** item and press the right mouse button to get the pop-up menu.

Select **Set tabbing** and then **Show Tab Tags** to see the tabbing order as shown in Figure 3.19.

Figure 3.18 Beans List for the Applet.

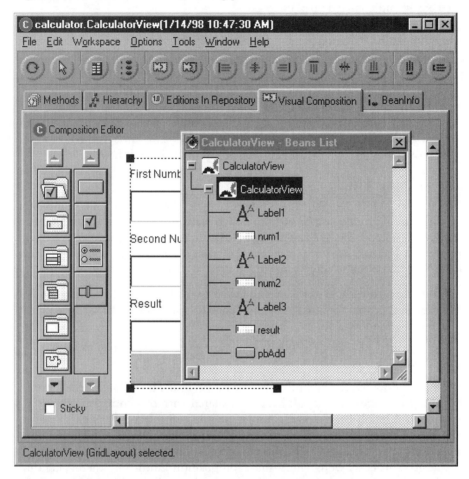

> **NOTE**
> After you have finished adjusting the Tab tags, you can hide them using
> the same process. When the Tab tags are showing, the popup menu item
> for the applet shows **Hide Tab Tags**.

The Visual Composition Editor now shows the Applet with little yellow
tab tags on each control in the Applet. The number in the tab tag indicates the
sequence that the cursor will follow when the Tab key is pressed. If the
TextFields and Buttons do not appear in the proper order, you can drag and
drop them into the proper sequence. Set the tabbing order so the tabbing

Figure 3.19 Setting Tab stops.

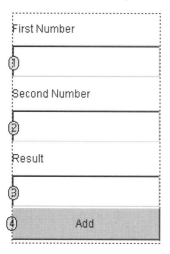

sequence starts with **efNum1** and then goes to **efNum2, efResult,** and **pbAdd,** as shown in Figure 3.17, with these steps:

Select one of these tags.

Use the mouse and drag the tag to the proper position.

Release the mouse button to drop the tag to set its position.

Continue to drag and drop the tab tags until they are in the proper order.

The new tabbing order will be saved when you save the Applet. The tab tags only show at development time, not at run time. You can hide the tags with these steps:

From the Beans List, select the pop-up menu for CalculatorView.

Select **Set Tabbing** and then **Hide Tab Tags**.

Close the Beans List window because it is no longer needed.

Running the Updated Adding Machine

You have completed the user interface for the CalculatorView applet. Now it is time to save and run the updated applet.

 Select the Test tool bar button to save, generate, compile, and run the applet.

When the applet starts, it should look like Figure 3.20. The user interface looks like it did the last time you ran the Adding Machine. You can enter numbers in the TextFields, and the tabbing works correctly. When you have finished

Figure 3.20 Running the Adding Machine.

reviewing the running applet, you can leave the applet running. In the next chapter you will add the logic to the applet, and you will be able to use that function by merely reloading the applet.

Summary

This was a little tougher than the Hello World application, but it was still fairly easy. You still need to make an invisible bean with the add function, which is covered in the next chapter. In this chapter you learned the following:

VisualAge JavaBeans Basics including:
- Composite beans
- GUI beans
- Invisible beans

How to build the Adding Machine application user interface including:
- Using a GridLayout
- Adding TextField, Label and Button beans
- Setting Tab order

These are the very basics of visual programming. In the following chapter, you will complete the CalculatorView and learn another important aspect to JavaBeans, namely bean features, including properties and methods.

MAKING INVISIBLE BEANS

4

What's in Chapter 4

You have completed the user interface for the Simple Calculator; now, you will learn how to make invisible beans. You will then combine it with GUI beans to complete the Simple Calculator. You will write some simple Java code for the invisible bean to perform the calculation. This chapter covers the following topics:

- Understanding JavaBean features
- Creating invisible beans
- Defining properties:
    Bound
    Constrained
    Indexed properties
- Deleting properties
- Defining methods
- Defining events
- Generating the BeanInfo class
- Types of connections
- Completing the Adding Machine:
    Property-to-property connections
    Event-to-method connections
    Adding code to methods
- Generating Javadoc

You have completed the user interface for the CalculatorView, and you have worked with a number of basic GUI beans. The next step is to develop an invisible bean to hold the logic for the applet. Before you develop the invisible bean, we will discuss another aspect of beans, namely JavaBeans features. We will cover the essential aspects of JavaBeans features in enough detail for you to feel confident in developing basic invisible beans. There are reference books available that discuss the JavaBeans specification and its features in far greater detail. The standardization of the Java class interface in the JavaBeans specification is a key reason that beans are open and extensible.

Understanding JavaBeans Features

In the previous chapter, we described JavaBeans and discussed the basic types of beans. Remember, beans are Java classes, and like classes, beans have a public interface. The public interface comprises JavaBeans features that other beans can call or address. There are three kinds of features: *properties*, *methods*, and *events*. Each feature has a Java type (for a method, it is a return type), so when you define one, you must specify a type. In this chapter, we describe these features and then show you how to define them in VisualAge for Java.

Java Types

When you first studied Java, you learned about the different types in the Java language and the AWT class library. In V1.1, there are both primitive types (like *int*, *float*, *boolean*) and beans that encapsulate them (like *Integer*, *Float*, and *Boolean*). When you specify the **type** for a property, remember the big difference between an *int* and an *Integer*. If you accidentally set a property to the wrong type, there is no SmartGuide to help you.

> **NOTE**
> Because Java has primitive types, it is not a purely object-oriented programming language. You could build a Java program and use only classes, but most beans, including those in the AWT class library, use primitive types.

What Are Properties?

In moving to a better object-oriented design, the V1.1 AWT class library adopted *properties*. The VisualAge products have had the notion of properties for quite a while, but they are referred to as *attributes*. Properties are, basically, public class variables, or *fields*, with a formalized interface. In good, object-oriented programming, you should not directly access variables, so properties are variables with a *get* and a *set* method as accessors. If you define a property named *foo* in VisualAge for Java, the SmartGuide generates a foo variable, a setFoo() method, and a getFoo() method. The convention is to use lowercase names for properties; also by convention, the Visual Composition Editor capitalizes the first character of the property name when it generates names for the get and set methods.

 Properties can be *bound* or *constrained*. Bound properties signal an event by calling a firePropertyChange() method whenever the property changes value or state. Constrained properties signal events, but the events are vetoable by the *listeners*. A later section on events describes listeners and how they work.

 Properties can also be *indexed*; that is, they have an array type. Examples of indexed properties are int[] and String[]. Indexed properties are not widely used, but they can be very helpful in special circumstances.

What Are Methods?

This may seem rhetorical, because as a Java developer, you are very familiar with methods. Methods must be covered as part of the definition of JavaBeans features. Method features are part of the public interface of the bean, so this implies that *method features* are public class methods.

Another term for public class methods is used in other VisualAge products: *actions*. With so many new terms associated with JavaBeans, it's nice that Java uses one term for methods. But this sometimes causes confusion in VisualAge for Java, because there are two places you can enter class methods. Just remember that method features are *public* methods.

What Are Events?

There are a number of improvements to the event model in JDK V1.1. These changes support a better object-oriented implementation through additional methods and classes.

There are many *events* in Java. Events can be caused by a user action like pressing a Button or closing a Frame. The AWT class library is full of events, and VisualAge for Java makes it easy to take advantage of this function. Events can also be caused by the system or by other invisible beans. For example, the data access beans in the Enterprise edition send a *connected* event whenever a Java program that uses them successfully connects to a database.

Events have a *source* and can have *listeners*. The source is the bean that signals the event. The listener is a bean that receives the event signal. Two methods control the registration of listeners: addListener and removeListener. For example, properties use addPropertyChangeListener() and removePropertyChangeListener(). All good beans should implement these methods so they can work with other beans.

The other VisualAge products also use events. Although the concept is the same, the implementation is completely different. Java events work with Java only.

Although events are messages, they are entirely different from Java *exceptions*, which are used for error detection. Exceptions are handled by using a Java *try/catch* block, when the code in the *catch* block is executed whenever the appropriate exception is caught. On the other hand, nothing happens when an event occurs unless the event has registered listeners. If your Java program isn't behaving the way you expect, check that events are actually being signaled and that the target classes are registered listeners.

The BeanInfo Class

As mentioned earlier, beans are designed to make Java tool development easier. So when you make a bean, additional information about the bean that is required at development time is stored in a BeanInfo class. This class is not needed at run time, so it is not deployed with the Java program. The Visual Composition Editor automatically generates the BeanInfo class whenever you add or change a bean feature. After you add features to a bean, you can review the generated BeanInfo class, but you should never edit the BeanInfo class. There is no reason to do this, because the Visual Composition Editor can always generate a BeanInfo class that matches the bean. If you edit the BeanInfo class, it may get out of sync with the bean that it represents.

> **NOTE**
>
> If you are coming to Java and VisualAge for Java with experience in another programming language or VisualAge product, one of the key hurdles is understanding the Java lingo. The AWT class library uses a number of terms for classes and methods that are different from the class libraries that you already know. Fortunately, once you know Java and AWT, you can speak a universal language with other Java developers.

Finishing the Adding Machine

VisualAge for Java generates pure JavaBeans, so all the background on JavaBeans is very helpful. This information is not specific to VisualAge for Java, but is part of Java V1.1 and used by many Java development tools available from many of the leading software development tool providers. Additionally, many smaller firms sell specialized beans for specific purposes. These beans can be used in any of the tools that support JavaBeans. This is a great example of a truly open development environment.

What Are Invisible Beans?

Invisible beans are usually subclasses of **Object,** which is an abstract base class in the AWT class library. You can see this inheritance relationship, shown in Figure 4.1, that shows the *Date* bean. Invisible beans can have many different functions, like managing the user interface, accessing a database, providing communications support, supplying print support, and running business logic. Invisible beans encapsulate Java function in a separate bean, which helps keep this function separate from the user interface or GUI beans.

VisualAge for Java comes with a number of invisible beans, and the Enterprise edition has additional code generators that create invisible beans. You can use VisualAge for Java to generate your own specialized invisible beans, with properties, events, and methods.

Creating Invisible Beans

Now let's use this knowledge of JavaBeans features to build the invisible bean for the CalculatorView. If the VisualAge for Java Workbench is not started, restart it now. First, you will build the **CalculatorLogic** JavaBean, then you will combine it with the **CalculatorView** GUI bean. You will use the same project and package for the invisible bean.

Figure 4.1 Date inheritance hierarchy.

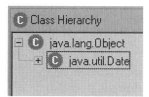

Select the package in the project we used for the CalculatorView Applet. The workbench should look like Figure 4.2.

Now that you have selected the project and the package in the IDE, you can start defining the invisible bean for the Simple Calculator. It is not necessary to

Figure 4.2 Workbench with My Project and calculator.

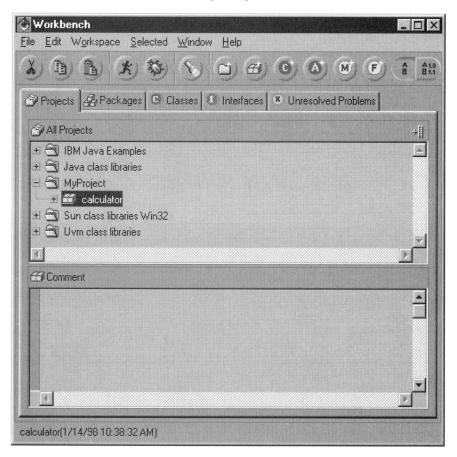

have the package selected, but it is very helpful. When you create a new bean, you must specify the project and project that contains the new bean. By selecting the package, it will be passed to the SmartGuide. You could put your math or calculation beans in another package, but for convenience, it is better to use the same package. So get started making a new bean with the following steps:

With the **calculator** package selected, click the right mouse button on the top pane and from the pop-up menu select **New Class/Interface**. This will cause the Create Class SmartGuide to display.

In the Create Class or Interface SmartGuide (see Figure 4.3), enter **CalculatorLogic** in the **Class Name** text field.

Leave the superclass as the default **java.lang.Object**, which is at the top of the Java class hierarchy.

You have entered all the information needed to generate the CalculatorLogic bean, but let's look at the other pages of the SmartGuide to see the additional information that could be used to generate a bean.

Press the **Next** button and see the second page of the SmartGuide, shown in Figure 4.4.

Figure 4.3 Create Class/Interface SmartGuide.

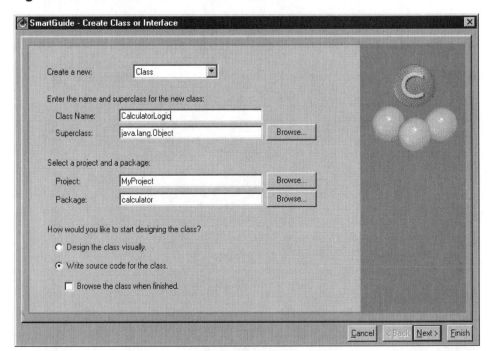

This page enables you to select a number of options for a bean. First, there is a list box to specify any **import** statements for the bean. You may feel it is easier to type these in the code, and you can always add import statements to the generated source code later. The SmartGuides are aides to help with the initial code generation. This dialog is very helpful, because it provides the handy browser to help you specify the class or package you want to import correctly.

You can specify additional modifiers for the class, including *abstract* and *final*. Abstract classes contain method declarations with no implementation. An abstract class cannot be instantiated at run time, primarily, because it is lacking method definitions. The implementation must reside in a subclass of the abstract class. By specifying the final modifier, you prevent a class from being subclassed. If you add either of these modifiers to a method, you see additional visual cues in the IDE. VisualAge for Java uses an F for final and A for abstract.

There are a number of common methods that many classes implement. Some of these methods are listed on the SmartGuide page as options for the method stubs to be generated, as shown in Figure 4.4. The Visual Composition Editor generates the method definition, and you must enter the specific implementation code for each method. The equals(), finalize(), hashCode(), and toString() methods all have a default implementation of calling the same method in the parent or superclass. The CalculatorLogic bean does not need any of these methods, so you do not need to select them.

Press the **Next** button and see the third page of the SmartGuide, as shown in Figure 4.5.

This page enables you to add interfaces to the classes. Remember that interfaces are a way that Java gets around multiple inheritance. When you add interfaces to the bean, VisualAge for Java generates the correct code in the class definition. You can always edit the source code and add *implements* to the bean definition. This is the last page of the SmartGuide; you have specified the bean.

There are additional modifiers that can be selected for a bean. These are the standard Java modifiers that you will recognize. By selecting any of these modifiers, VisualAge for Java adds them to the class definition. For this bean, you can use the default modifier *public*.

There are also a number of method stubs you can have VisualAge for Java generate for you. This is very helpful if you initially know that you will need a certain method like toString() in the bean. You still need to write the implementation code for the generated stub. Later in this chapter, you will learn how to add methods to a bean.

The SmartGuides are an easy way to specify information for the VisualAge for Java generator. This only happens when you are creating a new item. If you ever want to change the item, you will need to change the source code.

Press the **Finish** button to create the class.

Figure 4.4 Class Definition2.

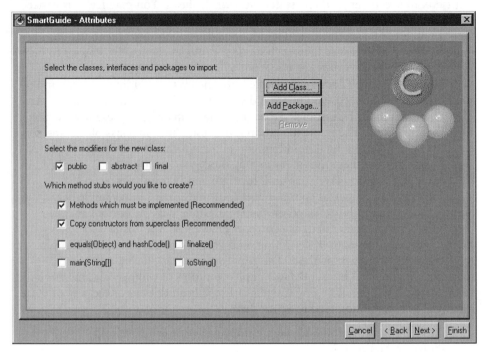

The SmartGuide closes, and VisualAge for Java saves the bean, generates the code, and compiles it. Focus goes back to the Workbench, and the new bean is highlighted. The Workbench should look like Figure 4.6.

You can see that the CalculatorLogic bean was added to the Workbench in the calculator package. You can add methods and variables (also known as *fields*) to the code for the bean in the Source pane. You can also edit or **open** the bean. This opens another view or window that enables you to work on the class. It is best to open a separate view for editing the class, because this frees the Workbench for browsing the other classes loaded in the workspace. You can still make changes to a class in the Workbench, but there are a lot more tools to help you work on a bean when you open the bean. Usually, you will find that you only make small changes to a bean in the Workbench.

Editing a Bean

If you have set the **Double Click in the Workbench** preference, double-click the mouse while it is over the bean. If you are using the default setting, click the right mouse button on the top pane and, from the pop-up menu, select **Open**.

The class/interface browser appears for you to continue developing this bean (see Figure 4.7). This browser looks like the Workbench, but it is very different. The browser can only work on this bean.

Figure 4.5 Class Definition3.

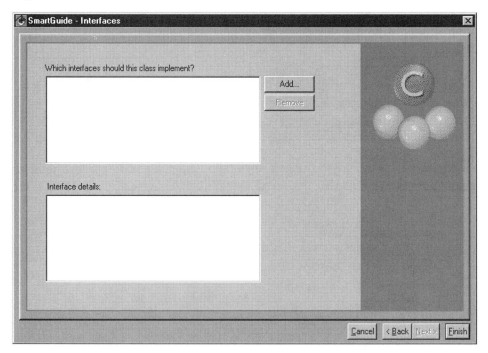

This browser has five pages, each of which has its own special functions. These pages are:

Methods. This page is used to work with private and protected methods for the bean. You can also enter or edit public methods, but public methods are bean features and need to be in the BeanInfo class so tools can work with them. It is also used to work with fields or variables for the bean. Just like methods, public fields should be properties and entered in the BeanInfo page.

Hierarchy. This page is a convenient way to see all superclasses of the bean.

Editions in Repository. This page shows all editions. You create new editions when you version the beans.

Visual Composition. All beans have a Visual Composition page in VisualAge for Java. You can use the Visual Composition Editor for both GUI beans and invisible beans.

BeanInfo. This is the page where you edit bean features, namely properties, methods, and events.

If the tabs on a browser are displayed as icons only (see Figure 4.8), there is a reason this happened and an easy way to fix it. You probably resized the browser

Figure 4.6 Added CalculatorLogic class.

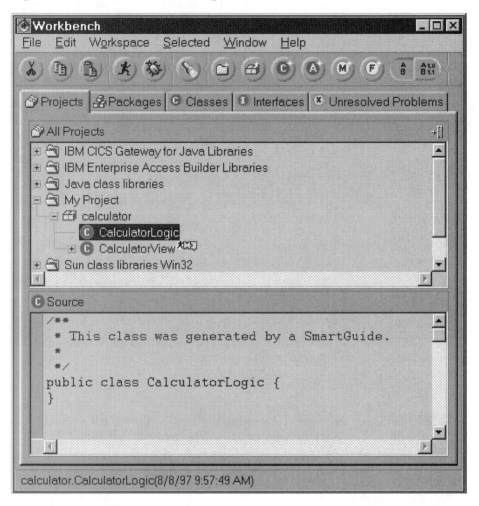

and made it smaller to conserve screen space. The text on the tabs of the notebook was automatically removed, leaving just the icons. You can increase the size of the browser window, and the text will magically reappear.

> **NOTE**
>
> You may wonder why the JavaBeans icon on the BeanInfo page is blue instead of brown like in the Sun samples. The reason is that these are for IBM blue beans.

Figure 4.7 Class browser.

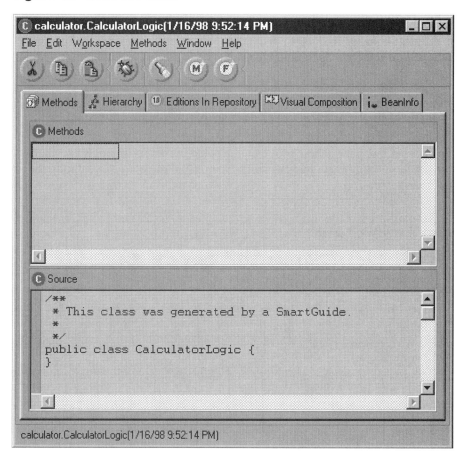

Defining Properties

This bean needs three integer properties to hold the two operands and the result of the calculation. Because we will be using this bean in the Visual Composition Editor, these properties must be enabled to send and receive notifications, so that

Figure 4.8 Icons on tabs.

the GUI and invisible representation of the values are synchronized. In other words, when the user enters a number in the user interface or changes the value of one of the numbers, the corresponding property in the invisible bean must be notified of this change. To do this, properties for the class should be defined in the **BeanInfo** page of the class/interface browser.

Select the **BeanInfo** page of the class/interface browser (see Figure 4.9).

Notice that the class browser's tool bar buttons change on every page. This page has the familiar cut, copy, and paste buttons, along with the Debugger and Search. There are three more tool bar icons (see Figure 4.10) that indicate the special function in this page. These tool bar buttons represent properties, events, and methods, and selecting these buttons starts a SmartGuide to aide in creating the desired bean feature.

Figure 4.9 BeanInfo page.

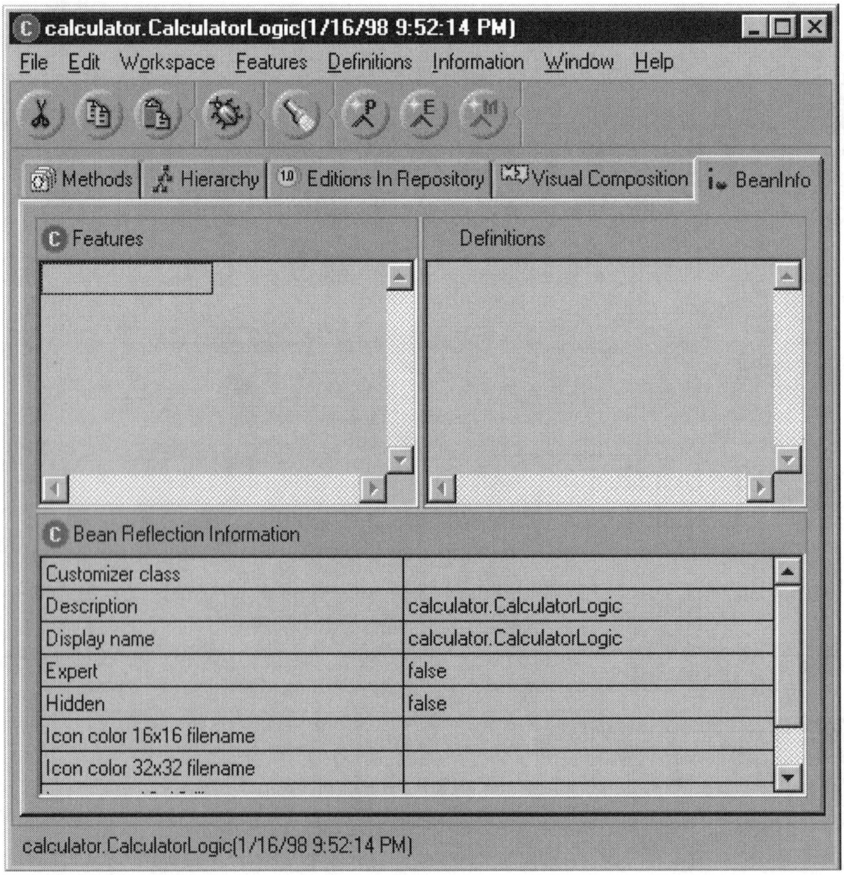

Figure 4.10 Property, event, and method icons.

Let's create a property and see how this works. Follow the next steps:
Right-click on the Features pane (top left) and select **New Property Feature** from the pop-up menu.

Enter **num1** in the **Property name** entry field.

Select **int** for the **Property type,** as shown in Figure 4.11.

> **NOTE**
> When you enter Java types, the VisualBuilder provides the Browse button on many of the SmartGuides. The browse function provides a search facility to find the fully-qualified name for a class including its packages. Since the browse function search for classes, you can not find the Java primitive types. If you need to enter a primitive type, you will need to select it from the initial dropdown list, or merely enter it in the field.

Figure 4.11 Adding a Property Feature.

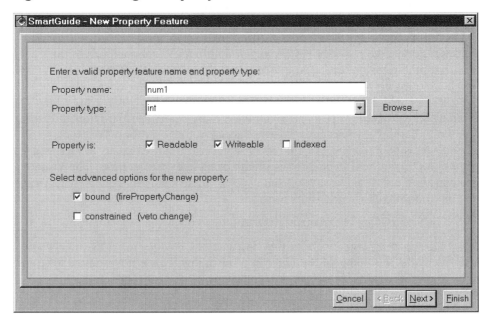

The **Readable** and **Writeable** check boxes are selected by default. VisualAge for Java automatically generates a *get* method and a *set* method for the property. If you want the property to be read-only, you can deselect the **Writeable** check box, and there will not be a set method. The properties in the CalculatorLogic bean need to have both get and set methods generated, so leave both check boxes selected.

It is very important to ensure that the **bound** check box is selected. This ensures that the property will emit a propertyChange event if you will be using this feature in a Visual Composition Editor connection.

You could press **Finish** at this time and accept the defaults for the remainder of the settings. You could also press **Next** to further define the interface of the property. Selecting defaults in the SmartGuide is generally okay, but in this case, select **Next** to see what else is available.

On the next page of the SmartGuide (see Figure 4.12), add a display name and a short description of the property.

When you enter a display name, it is used in the connections pop-up menu in the Visual Composition Editor, otherwise, the property name is used. This property is a primitive type, so it does not need a special property editor. These settings cause the Visual Composition Editor to generate code for a property descriptor method in the BeanInfo class. The property descriptor method in the BeanInfo class creates a *PropertyDescriptor* class for each property in the bean. The PropertyDescriptor class has a number of methods to get and set information about the bean. The specific methods for these descriptions are setDisplayName(String) and setShortDescription(String).

Expert and Hidden Features

You will notice two check boxes for *expert* and *hidden*. The methods in the PropertyDescriptor class for this information are setExpert(boolean) and setHidden. Expert features are those deemed by the bean developer to be advanced or seldom used features. AWT has a number of expert features; for example, the *enabled* property of a TextField is an expert feature. Hidden features are those that the bean developer deems should not be used by a Java tool.

There is no hard-and-fast rule about what features are expert, in fact, you may find that you will frequently use many of these expert features. The Visual Composition Editor shelters you from many of these bean API details by generating the BeanInfo class with all its methods.

The SmartGuide has enough information, so press the **Finish** button.

If the property you have added needs a specialized editor to set its value, you can specify the class name of the editor in this window. This is not required for common or primitive types such as **int**. It is frequently needed for user-defined types or

Figure 4.12 Property SmartGuide.

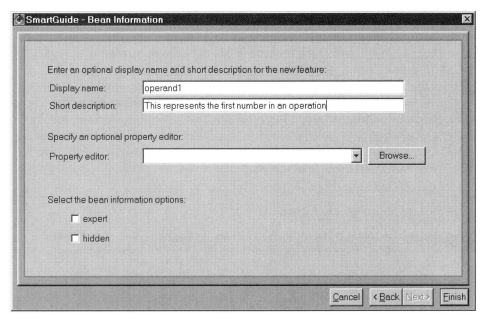

composite types, like Font and Color. The method in the PropertyDescriptor class for this information is setExpert(propertyEditorClass). This means that you need to construct a propertyEditorClass with all the needed settings and required data.

Finish defining the properties for this bean by creating two more **bound int** properties, using the steps that you used to make the **num1** property. Name these two properties **num2** and **result**.

Notice that as you add properties to the bean, the Visual Composition Editor adds the properties to the Features list in alphabetical order, not the order in which you define them. The Visual Composition Editor automatically generates the get and set methods to access the property.

Where Is the BeanInfo Class?

The *Features* pane in this window (see Figure 4.13) lists all bean features. Actually, it lists the bean features that are in the BeanInfo class. The properties have some trailing characters that were discussed in Chapter 1. These characters are a shorthand notation to help you identify the characteristics of the property. These characters came for the options in the SmartGuide when the property was generated, and they are:

R = Readable, has a get() method

W = Write, has a set() method

B = Bound, can fire a property change event

Any method created on the *Methods* page, or directly added in the source code, is not automatically added to the BeanInfo class. This pane has its own pop-up menu with the functions that apply to bean features.

The *Features* pane is actually a window into the BeanInfo class for this bean.

The lower pane on the BeanInfo page is used as two different editors. It is a BeanInfo editor when a bean *Feature* is selected and it is a source code editor when a bean *Definition* is selected. As mentioned earlier, you should not edit the generated BeanInfo class. The BeanInfo class can be generated by VisualAge for Java, which uses the *java.lang.reflect* functions to access information about the bean. This package contains the *Class* class, which is another addition to JDK V1.1. The Class class contains the information about the class, and it has a number of methods to access this information.

Figure 4.13 Bean information.

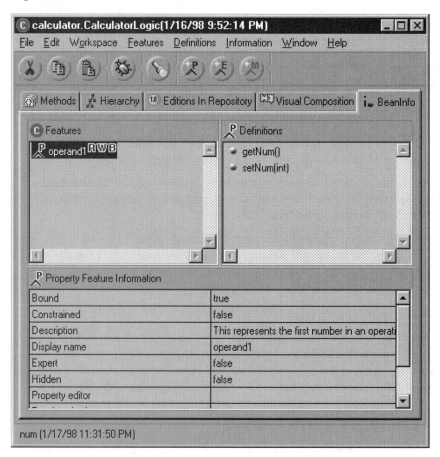

The *Definitions* pane of the BeanInfo page is used to display the methods and beans associated with each bean feature. Let's look at the generated methods for the **operand** property with the following steps:

Select a property feature in the Features pane; the corresponding get and set methods are displayed.

Select the **setNum1(int)** method; the lower pane is now the **Source** pane for the set method (Figure 4.14).

If you define the property as a **String** type, you see a String class (or String bean) in the Definitions pane. This is the default type in the SmartGuide, so you may have accidentally set one of the properties to String instead of **int**. This will not work correctly in the CalculatorLogic bean, because the add() method will

Figure 4.14 Source pane for setNum1.

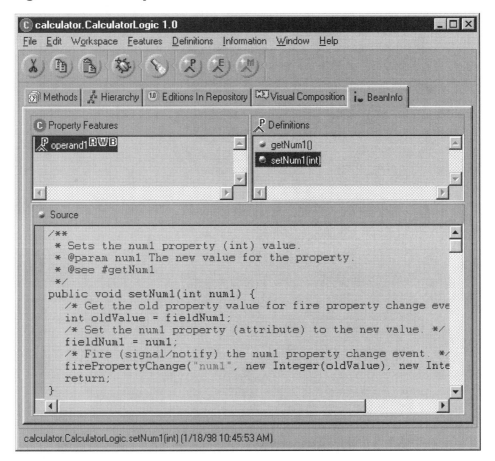

add the properties, and the result of adding Strings is different than adding ints. Check the property types with the following steps:

Select the **num2** property.

Select the **getNum2**() method in the Definitions pane.

The BeanInfo page Source pane should look like Figure 4.15. The definition for the num2 Property is:

```
public int getNum2() {
```

The num2 property is correct because it returns an **int**. Check the other properties and ensure that they return an **int**.

Figure 4.15 Property types.

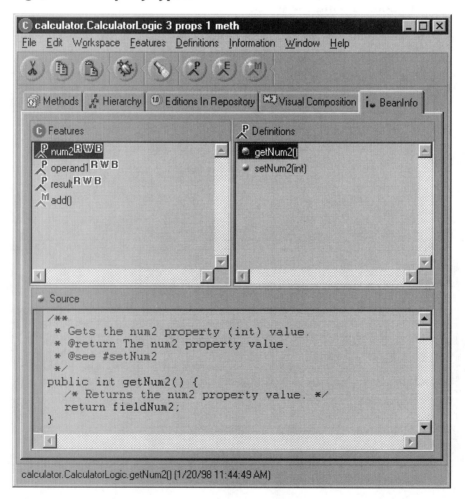

If any of the properties are of type **String**, you need to change the type to int. Because a property usually consists of a get and set method and a class variable, changing a property's type means editing a lot of code. You could do this, or you can follow the steps in the following section (Changing a Property's Type). Even if the properties have the correct type, you should review this section because you will probably need to do this some time.

Changing a Property's Type

If you ever want to change or delete a bean property, remember that a bean property usually consists of a get method, a set method, and a field (class variable). There is also code in the BeanInfo class for the property descriptors. Unless you have added code to either the set or the get method of the property, it is much easier to delete the property and create a new one if you want to change its type. If you have a **text1** property that is a String and you really want a **text1** property as an **int**, you need to:

Delete the property on the BeanInfo page.

The Delete features Dialog displays with the selected feature. The list shows the getter and setter methods that will be deleted, if they are selected. You must select the getter and setter methods for them to be deleted. If you forget to select them, they will still be in the bean and you will need to delete them individually.

Go to the source code for the class and delete the *fieldText1* field:

```
String fieldText1 = null;
```

Save the class.

Go back to the BeanInfo page, create the new property, and carefully select int as the property type as int.

You may wonder how the fieldText1 variable got in the class. When VisualAge for Java generates code for a property, it generates the appropriate accessor methods, and a variable to represent the property. The code generator creates a variable name by adding *field* before the property name. Let's see the properties in the generated class code for the CalculatorLogic class with these steps:

Select the Workbench page to view all the classes.

Select the Calculator View class and the code displays in the Source pane as shown in the following:

```
/**
 * This class was generated by a SmartGuide.
 *
 */
public class CalculatorLogic {
```

```
    protected transient java.beans.PropertyChangeSupport
propertyChange = new java.beans.PropertyChangeSupport(this);
  int fieldNum1 = 0;
  int fieldNum2 = 0;
  int fieldResult = 0;
}
```

This is another way to verify that the properties are the correct type. You can look at the class code and check the type of the fields corresponding to the properties. Of course, it helps to know what you are looking for. VisualAge for Java is a great tool for working with JavaBeans, but you need to understand JavaBeans and the generated code.

Defining Methods

Next, create a method to perform the addition operation.

While still on the **BeanInfo** page of the class browser's notebook, right-click on the upper left pane and select **New Method feature** from the pop-up menu.

Type **add** as the **Method name,** leave the method type as **void** and the **parameter count** as 0, as shown in Figure 4.16.

Press the **Finish** button. VisualAge for Java saves the new method, generates the code, and compiles it.

Figure 4.16 Creating the add method.

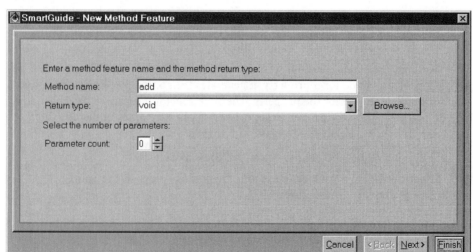

Using JavaBeans in the Visual Composition Editor

Now the only thing left is to bring the invisible bean into the Visual Composition Editor for the CalculatorView and make the connections.

Switch back to the browser showing the CalculatorView, and make sure the Visual Composition tab is selected.

From the menu bar of the Visual Composition Editor, select **Options** and then **Add Bean.** The Add Bean window appears.

Select the **Browse** button to show the list of available beans.

Type **CalculatorLogic** and press **OK** to choose this bean.

Enter a name for this bean (use **calculator**) and press **OK.**

Move the mouse pointer outside of the dashed box and over the free-form surface; click the mouse to drop the bean. You should now have a bean that looks like a jigsaw puzzle piece available for connections, as shown in Figure 4.17.

Types of Connections

You have already started to use visual connections in the HelloWorld applet. The Visual Composition Editor provides a number of connections to help you build Java programs:

Event-to-method

Event-to-property

Event-to-script

Property-to-property

All connections that start with an event are shown in green with an arrow pointing to the target. These different event connections are essentially the same. An event-to-property connection actually calls the set method for the property, and an event-to-script connection actually call a class method that has script, which is more commonly called Java code. Script connections are commonly used for calling other-than-public methods, although it's perfectly legal to call a public method using a script connection.

Property-to-property connections are bidirectional: A change in one property can cause a message, or an event, to be passed to the other property. These are very powerful connections, because they signal a **propertyChange** event. For example, in a TextField, a propertyChange event can occur every time you type a key. Because of this potential intensive messaging, beans with property-to-property connections create tightly coupled beans. There are many situations where tightly coupled beans are necessary, and there are other situations where they can be limiting. A tightly

Figure 4.17 Calculator invisible bean.

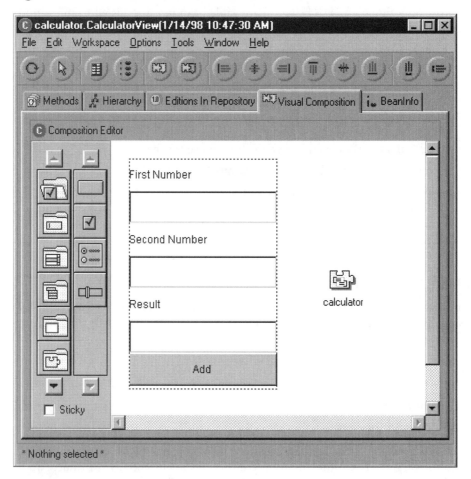

coupled bean cannot be easily moved to another system for distributed processing. This is common when using Remote Method Invocation (RMI).

You can also make connections to connections. This is used to pass parameters into connections like in the HelloWorld applet, where the **Date** is passed to the **setText**() method of the Label bean.

NOTE

It is better object-oriented design to pass objects as parameters than to pass primitive Java types as parameters. Many beans, including those in AWT, take primitive typed parameters, but this is usually only done for efficiency.

This is a lot of information about connections for those of you that are new to VisualAge. You will become familiar with these different connection as you complete the samples in this book.

> **NOTE**
>
> For those VisualAge for C++ users, you will see there is no event-to-custom logic connection.

Property-to-Property Connections

When CalculatorView runs, the values entered in the TextFields need to be copied to the invisible bean. This can be accomplished using property-to-property connections from the TextFields to the corresponding properties you defined in the CalculatorLogic bean.

The connection menu can be accessed by selecting the bean, pressing the right mouse button, and selecting **Connect** from the pop-up menu. The cascade menu contains the *preferred* properties, methods, and events available for connections. Preferred features have been used in the different VisualAge products and can be modified by the developer. However, the JavaBeans specification does not provide for preferred features, so there is no way to save them in the BeanInfo class. VisualAge for Java provides some default features in the preferred features list, and nonexpert, nonhidden properties of the bean are added to the preferred features list automatically.

The **All Features** selection at the bottom of each connection menu displays a window that contains all the possible features for this bean. You should use **All Features** to access the features that you need for connections, because the All Features window contains the properties, events, and methods in separate lists. These separate lists help ensure that you pick the desired feature for the connection.

Now perform the connections in the following steps:

Start the connection by opening the pop-up for the **num1** text field and select **Connect**, which displays the preferred features menu.

From the preferred features menu, select **text**. Now you see a line, which originates from the selected control and follows the mouse movements.

Take the end of the connection to the **calculator** bean and click the left mouse button. Another pop-up menu appears; it belongs to the **calculator** bean. To complete the connection, select operand1 or num1 (depending on whether you chose an optional display name).

This establishes a blue connection from num1(text) to calculator(num1), as shown in Figure 4.18.

Figure 4.18 Property-to-property connection.

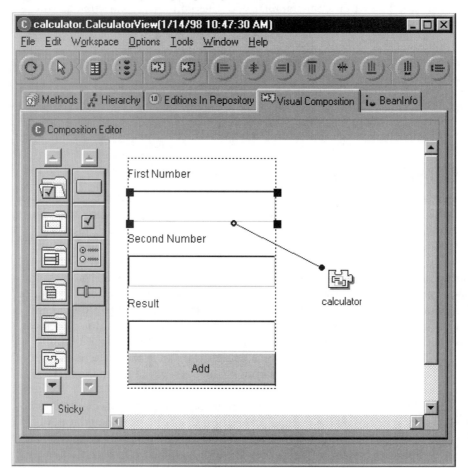

You get a warning that the source and target types are incompatible. This is because the *text* property of the text field is of type **String** and the *result* property is of type **int**. However, the Visual Composition Editor will generate the proper conversions to match the types at run time, so select **Yes** to continue.

Connect num2 (or operand2) (text) to calculator(num2) and set the source event.

Connect calculator(result) to result(text).

Connect pbAdd(actionPerformed(java.awt.event.ActionEvent)) to calculator(add). Remember to select **All features** from the pop-up menu, so that you can select the **add()** method to complete the connection.

You have made all the connections needed for the applet. It should look something like Figure 4.19.

Testing the Calculator

 There is quite a bit of function completed on the CalculatorView applet, so this is a good time to test it. Press the Test button to save and run the applet.

When the applet starts, it should look like Figure 4.20. You should notice that the Result TextField is magically set to 0. Actually, the magic comes from the connection to the Result TextField. This connection was drawn from the CalculatorLogic bean to the Result TextField. The **result** property in the CalculatorLogic bean is an int, so it is initialized to be 0. Therefore, the value of the *result* property in the CalculatorLogic bean gets passed to the Result TextField.

Enter a number in each text field and press the **Add** button. The Result field should show the value of adding the two numbers. Test this and enter **123** in the first field and **456** in the second field.

Figure 4.19 Completed connections.

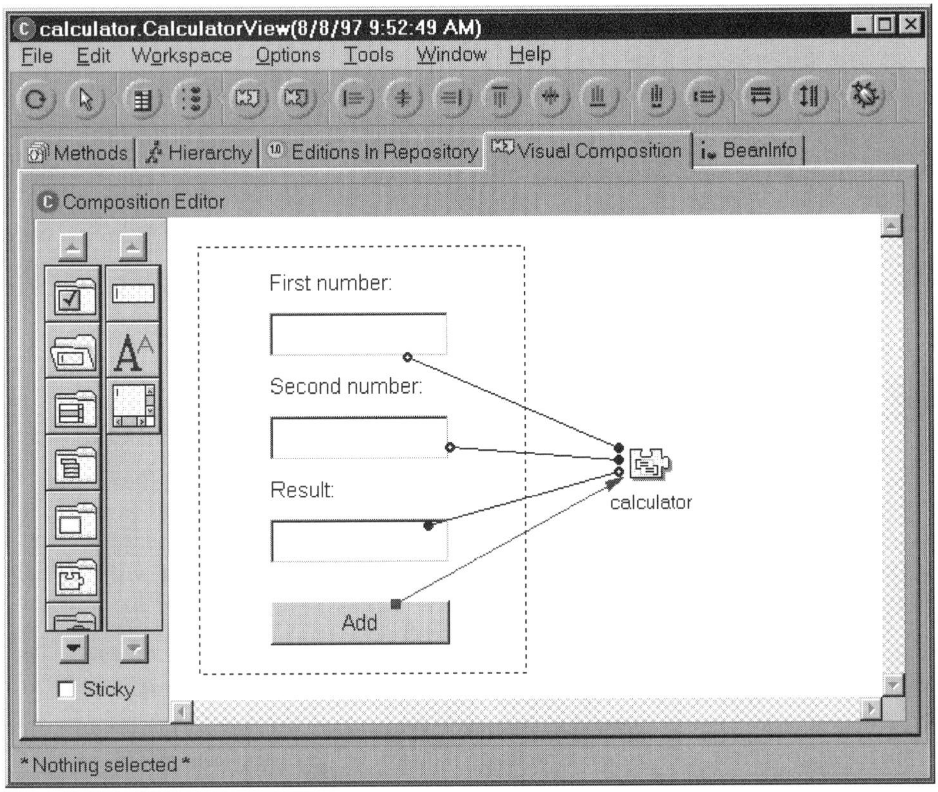

![Screenshot of calculator.CalculatorView(8/8/97 9:52:49 AM) showing the Composition Editor with First number, Second number, Result fields, and Add button connected to the calculator bean.]

Figure 4.20 Running CalculatorView.

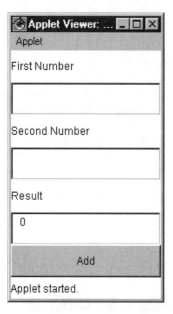

Press the **Add** button on the applet: nothing happens.

There is nothing wrong; the applet is not finished. There are two things that still need to be completed.

- As characters are typed in the TextFields, the events are not passing to the CalculatorLogic bean.

- The **add**() generated by the SmartGuide needs the logic to do the adding.

With these two changes, the CalculatorView applet is complete.

Property Events

As discussed previously, when a property changes, it passes an event. Some beans, like TextField, have a number of different events that can be passed at run time. The Visual Composition Editor does not know what event you might want to pass from a TextField, so this must be set during development. Set the event in the property sheet for the property-to-property connection with the following steps:

Open the property sheet for the connection. Either double-click on the blue connection line, or use its pop-up menu and select **properties**.

Set **Source Event** to **textValueChanged(java.awt.event.TextEvent)**. This tells the connection to fire whenever the text value of the source object (the num1 text field) changes (Figure 4.21).

Figure 4.21 Property-to-property connection.

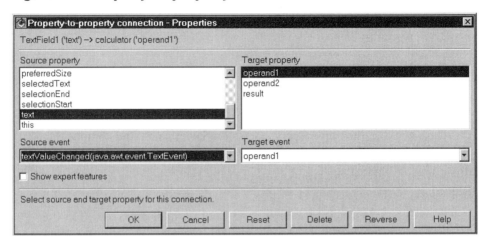

In a similar fashion, make the following property-to-property connections: Connect num2 (or operand2) (text) to calculator(num2) and set the source event.

Connect calculator(result) to result(text).

Adding Code to Methods

When the SmartGuide generates a method, it generates *stub* code. This stub code consists of the following:

A comment

The method definition

Another comment

The *return* for the method

The add() method for the CalculatorLogic bean looks as follows:

```
/**
 * Performs the add method.
 */
public void add() {
  /* Perform the add method. */
  return;
}
```

This stub code allows you to call the method and continue after it returns. This particular method has no return. You need to add the logic as Java code to the methods you generate.

Select the **add()** method in the Definitions pane (top right) to display the code for the method in the bottom pane.

Enter the following code to perform the calculation as shown in Figure 4.22:

```
setResult( getNum1( ) + getNum2( ) );
```

This code sets the *result* property on the **CalculatorLogic** bean with the sum of the values of **num1** and **num2**.

Right-click on the bottom pane and select **Save** to save and compile the code for the **add()** method.

Any errors are reported now. You can also use Ctrl-S to save and compile the bean.

If you select the **result** property on the Features pane and then select the **setResult(int)** method on the top pane, you will see how the notification

Figure 4.22 Code for add() method.

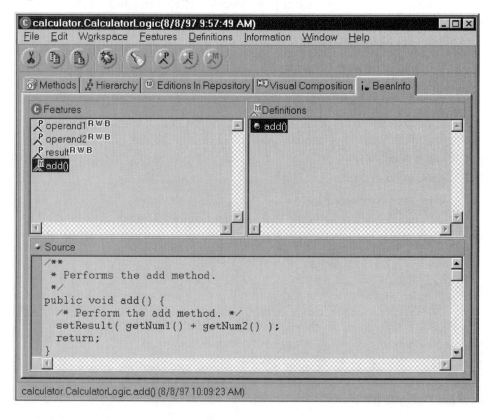

is sent to inform interested parties that the value of the *result* property changed.

You have created the invisible bean, which will perform the addition for you. You could easily improve this bean to perform subtraction, multiplication and division operations. You will do this later in the book.

Testing the Calculator Again

Now it is a good time to verify that everything is working in the CalculatorView applet. The TextFields can pass the event data to the invisible bean and the add() has code to perform the calculation. Test it with the following steps:

 Press the Test button on the Visual Composition Editor tool bar to save and run the applet.

Try again by entering a number in each of text fields and pressing the **Add** button. The Result field should show the value of adding the two numbers. Test this: enter **123** in the first field and **456** in the second field, as shown in Figure 4.23.

Select the **Add** Button, and the **Result** field should show **579**.

When you have finished testing the CalculatorView, close the applet.

Figure 4.23 Completed CalculatorView.

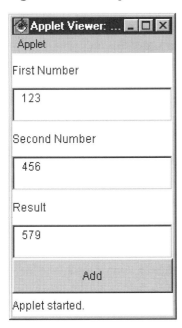

If you were coding this by hand, you might have just added an *add()* method to the CalculatorView class and put the necessary code in this method to do the adding. In addition, this applet does not have many refinements that are needed for a real applet that you could deploy. The next sample you build will be much more complete.

Generating Javadoc

As you have seen, VisualAge for Java has a number of code generators that help you to develop Java programs. The generated code includes comments to assist in documenting the purpose of classes, methods, and other information about a Java program. If you select the main() method in the CalculatorView applet, you see the following comment and the top of the method:

```
/**
 * main entrypoint - starts the part when it is run as an application
 * @param args java.lang.String[]
 */
```

What Is Javadoc?

Javadoc is a Java documentation technique for generating the documentation as an HTML (Hypertext Markup Language) file from the comments in the code. Javadoc uses //* to start a comment and */ to end a comment, as shown in the previous code sample. Because Javadoc generates HTML, you can insert HTML tags in the Java comments, and they will be passed to the generated HTML file. There are also a number of Javadoc tags that can be used to assist with documenting the code. The previous code sample shows the **@param** tag. The JDK includes a Javadoc generator, and there is one included in the VisualAge for Java IDE. Let's try generating the Javadoc for the CalculatorView Applet with the following steps:

Go to the Workbench.

Select the **CalculatorView** bean.

Display the pop-up menu and select **Generate javadoc**, which is at the bottom of the menu.

When the **Javadoc** window appears (Figure 4.24), you can accept the default values and press the **OK** button.

After the HTML files are generated, focus returns to the Workbench. You can run these HTML files from your browser. Figure 4.25 shows the Calculator HTML loaded into Netscape Navigator. In this HTML page, you can see the hierarchy map of the bean and all of its parents, and you can review all the fields, methods, and constructors for the bean. This is a very fast and easy way to make

Figure 4.24 Javadoc window.

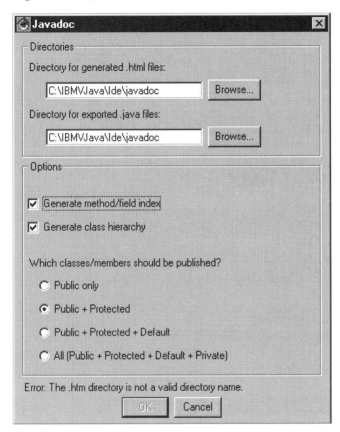

documentation for your Java programs. Because this function is integrated in VisualAge for Java, you can easily generate Javadoc while you are working on a Java program.

Summary

This was a little tougher than the Hello World applet, but it was still fairly easy. You learned about JavaBeans features and how to use a SmartGuide in the BeanInfo page to define your own invisible beans. In this chapter, you learned the following:

- How to create invisible beans
- Defining properties
- Defining methods

Figure 4.25 Viewing Javadoc in a browser.

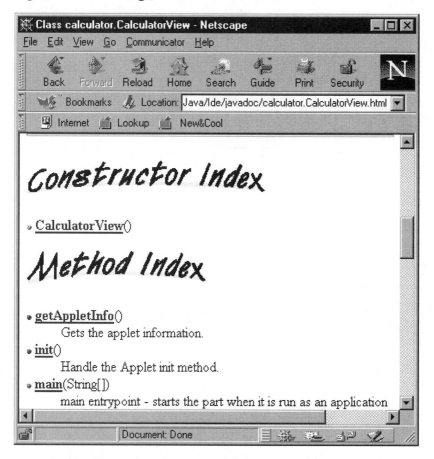

- Adding user code to invisible beans
- Connecting invisible beans in the Visual Composition Editor
- Generating Javadoc

These are very basic elements to visual programming. In the following chapters, you build on these basic elements and learn how to build more complex applications.

DEBUGGING BEANS

5

What's in Chapter 5

This chapter provides you with an introduction to using the debugging aids available in the VisualAge for Java development environment. You will be exposed to:

- Adding trace information to your programs
- The Scrapbook
- The methods in the uvm.tools.DebugSupport class
- The Java source-level debugger

These are very helpful tools for debugging applications. Because VisualAge generates a lot of the code for you, it may provide you with a false sense of security, as though the software knows what you want it to do.

This is the only chapter that covers debugging tools and techniques. You should use what you learn here in the other chapters if you have problems with your programs.

In the first few chapters of this book, you learned the basics about building simple programs with VisualAge for Java using beans. You built and tested the Hello World and Calculator applications. These applications are fairly simple and not prone to error. They introduced you to the basic user interface controls and the mechanics involved in composing, building, and running an application using the Building from Beans paradigm. You were also introduced to the world of connections and how they are used to make things happen in an event-driven program.

Introduction to Debugging

In this chapter, you will be exposed to several debugging tools and techniques that will aid you in finding logic, flow, and other problems in your Java programs. We will cover some debugging principles (that you probably already know from your experience with other programming languages and environments) by showing you how to apply them in VisualAge for Java. We will also cover the debugging tools and features that are exclusive to VisualAge.

Using System.out.println()

If you have a C or C++ background, you have probably used the printf() function to examine variables and print messages as a program is executed. Other languages have equivalent functions in some form of development environment. This technique is one of the simplest ways to obtain information from your program at run time. In Java, you can use the same approach using the System.out.println() method.

You can insert System.out.println() messages anywhere in your code to send messages to yourself and to examine variable and state information.

The println() method is defined in the **java.io.PrintStream** class. It is very versatile because of extensive overloading. Here are all the parameters it supports:

- println(boolean)
- println(char)
- println(char[])
- println(double)
- println(float)
- println(int)
- println(long)
- println(java.lang.String)
- println(java.lang.Object)

When passing a **java.lang.Object** to println(), the toString() method of that object is called and returns a string representation of that type of object.

All objects have the toString() method defined. In fact, this method is defined at the top of the Java hierarchy in the **Object** class. The default toString() method returns a string of the form *className@hashcode*. As you develop your own classes, it is good programming practice to override the default toString() method and supply your own string representation of your object.

Debugging Connections

By now, you are beginning to understand that programs generated with the VisualAge for Java Visual Composition Editor are event-driven and rely on the underlying event model provided by Java 1.1.

In traditional programming, when you receive unexpected results while executing your program, you resort to examining the code, analyzing the logic flow and operations, and often find yourself using the debugger to step through the program execution step-by-step.

Visual programming introduces a new level of complexity when debugging connections. This is partly because the connections are actually generated methods in the bean. There are at least three things that can go wrong with connections:

- The connection does not execute.
- The connection executes at the wrong time (out of sequence).
- The wrong connection executes.

When debugging connections, it is a good idea to trace that the connection is being executed. This helps you determine not only that it has executed, but also the sequence in which it executed in relation to other connections in the program. When you program visually, it is very easy to create connections that execute in the wrong order.

As mentioned before, in other programming languages, you probably used some type of tracing to send messages to yourself and to examine variables and state information at run time. When debugging complex connection problems, it may be necessary to use this technique again. You need to have the ability to "see" the connections executing in order to help you determine what the problem is. Tracing can easily be added to a program at strategic places in the code. Use the **System.out.println**() method to send messages to the Java console at the appropriate time.

Using the Console

In VisualAge for Java, the console provides a multiple-pane window where you can view messages sent to standard out (System.out) and standard error (System.err). You can also select from the threads waiting for input from standard in (System.in) and enter keystrokes for those threads. See Figure 5.1.

The console can be accessed at any time from the Window menu. The console also comes up automatically when a message is sent to it, and it remains visible until closed. These messages can be the result of a deliberate action, like executing System.out.println() or by the program or the VM executing exception code. In general, any message sent to System.out, System.err or System.in causes the console to appear.

When code is generated for connections, a description is included in the comments for the method that implements the connection. If you look at the code that implemented the connection between the pbSetDate Button and the dateLabel Label in the Hello World example, you will see the connection's description.

```
/**
 * conn0:(pbSetDate.action.actionPerformed
 *    ( java.awt.event.ActionEvent) --> dateLabel.text)
 * @param arg1 java.awt.event.ActionEvent
 */
/* WARNING: THIS METHOD WILL BE REGENERATED. */
private void conn0(java.awt.event.ActionEvent arg1)
{
  try {
    // user code begin {1}
```

Figure 5.1 Console window.

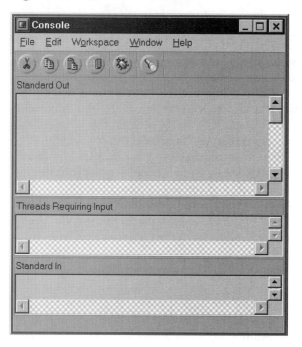

```
    // user code end
    getdateLabel().setText(getaDate().toString());
    // user code begin {2}
    // user code end
} catch (java.lang.Throwable ivjExc) {
    // user code begin {3}
    // user code end
    handleException(ivjExc);
  }
}
```

To add a trace point just before the code for the connection executes, insert the following line:

```
    ...
    // user code begin {1}
    System.out.println(
      "conn0:(pbSetDate.action.actionPerformed
         (java.awt.event.ActionEvent)-->dateLabel.text)");
    // user code end
    ...
```

The actual string passed to System.out.println() was copied and pasted from the comments of the method. Add your own code only between the lines designated as **//user code begin{1}** and **//user code end**. They are preserved when VisualAge regenerates code. Code that is added elsewhere in the method is lost the next time VisualAge generates code.

You can easily monitor the value of your program's variables because System.out.println() is so versatile. For example, to monitor the value of a variable int j as you execute a *for* loop, you could write the following code:

```
...
for (int j=0; I < 10; I++)
{
   // do something
   System.out.println("The value of j is " + j);
}
...
```

Notice how you can combine a String and an int into a single argument to System.out.println().

 As your program executes, messages appear in the Standard-out pane of the console. Contents of this pane can be cleared by selecting **Clear** from the pop-up menu, from the Edit menu, or by pressing the **Clear** button on the tool bar.

The handleException() Method

The Java compiler requires that every invocation of a method that has the **throws** keyword in its definition must be enclosed in a try/catch block. To be compiled successfully, code generated by VisualAge for Java must follow this rule.

In every catch block generated by VisualAge for Java, you will find a call to the handleException() method. See the following code segment from the Hello World applet:

```
/**
 * conn0:
 *(pbSetDate.action.actionPerformed
 *   (java.awt.event.ActionEvent) --> dateLabel.text)
 * @param arg1 java.awt.event.ActionEvent
 */
/* WARNING: THIS METHOD WILL BE REGENERATED. */
private void conn0(java.awt.event.ActionEvent arg1) {

   try {
      // user code begin {1}
      // user code end
      getdateLabel().setText(getaDate().toString());
```

```
    // user code begin {2}
    // user code end
  catch (java.lang.Throwable ivjExc) {
    // user code begin {3}
    // user code end
    handleException(ivjExc);
  }
}
```

In many cases, it is acceptable to do nothing in a catch block. In those cases, only the handleException() method will execute. The code in this method is all commented out and in most cases, this is fine. However, if you are getting strange results from your program or if it ends abruptly, you may want to remove the comments from handleException and see if an unrecoverable exception is being thrown. See the following code with comments removed:

```
/**
 * Called whenever the part throws an exception.
 * @param exception java.lang.Throwable
 */
private void handleException(Throwable exception) {

  /* Uncomment the following lines to print
     uncaught exceptions to stdout */
  System.out.println("--------- UNCAUGHT EXCEPTION
                     ---------");
  exception.printStackTrace(System.out);
}
```

Every class has a its own handleException() method, so depending on the complexity of your program, you might have to remove comments from code in one or more of the classes in the program path that is executing when the exception is thrown.

Introduction to the Scrapbook

The Scrapbook window can be accessed from the Window menu on the menu bar of the Workbench or on any of the browsers. See Figure 5.2.

The Scrapbook can be used to try out segments of code without having to write a method in a class. Fairly complex code segments can be entered in the Scrapbook's window and executed to prove a concept, verify the syntax of a method, or just observe the behavior of a few lines of code in isolation.

Code entered in the Scrapbook can be saved and loaded from the File menu on the window. These files are saved as text and can be manipulated outside the VisualAge environment by any text editor. By contrast, you can use the Scrapbook to edit text files, even those that are not necessarily Java source files.

Figure 5.2 Scrapbook window.

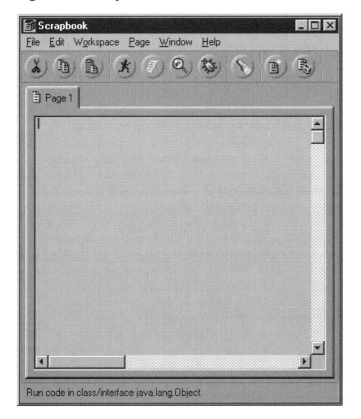

Most commonly, code debugged and tested in the Scrapbook ends up being copied and pasted back into a method in a class. The reverse is also true when code that is not giving the predicted result is copied from a method and pasted onto the Scrapbook for further testing and debugging.

Scrapbooks can have multiple independent pages. You add pages by selecting **New Page** from the Page menu or by pressing the **New Page** button on the toolbar. There is no interaction or interdependence between pages, and each page executes in its own context.

Execution Context

By default, code selected for compilation and execution runs in the context of the Object class. The context of a Scrapbook page can be changed to any class in the workspace. Code in the Scrapbook is treated as though it is a method in the class of the designated context. It has access to other methods and fields in that class and also classes in the same package. Classes in other packages must be fully qualified with their package names.

Each page in the Scrapbook can have a different execution context. Select **Run in** from the Page menu to change the context of the current page. From the Class/Interface Browser, pick the desired context.

Using the Scrapbook

Any valid Java expression can be run in the Scrapbook. If you attempt to compile an invalid expression, you get an error message indicating what the problem is. Error messages appear in-line with the line of code that produced the error. Error text is highlighted and can be removed by pressing the Backspace, Delete, or space-bar keys.

While the code in the scrapbook is running, and depending how long the process is, you see one of the following icons on the page tab as seen in Figure 5.3. If the contents of the Scrapbook were loaded from a file, or if you saved the contents to a file, the file name appears in the page tab.

Running code in the Scrapbook is as easy as selecting the code you want to run and pressing the Run button. You can also bring up the pop-up menu by right-clicking the mouse and selecting Run. You can select a portion of a line , a complete single line, or multiple contiguous lines. Depending on what ran, you may or may not see anything output on the screen. Typically, you will **Display** the value of an expression or **Inspect** the contents of a variable.

Open a Scrapbook window and enter the following lines of code:

```
int a;
a = 4 + 23;
```

Start by selecting 4 + 23, swipe the mouse pointer over the text while holding down the right mouse button, and press the Run button. The equation is compiled and run, but nothing is displayed.

To see the result of the calculation, highlight the same code, but this time press the Display button. You will see the answer (int) 27 highlighted right besides the equation. Press the Backspace key to remove the answer.

If you select the whole line and press the Display button, you get an error, because the code that defines the int a variable on the line above did not execute. To avoid the error, you need to select both lines of code and then press the Display button.

Figure 5.3 Scrapbook page icons.

Scrapbook page icons

	page is not associated with a file		page is busy running code
	file for the page is modified and not saved		page is busy running code
	file for the page is saved		page is busy running code

Inspector Windows

Sometimes you need to examine the value of a more complex object, for example, an array. Enter the following code in the Scrapbook:

```
int a[] = { 0, 4+23, 5, 12 };
return a;
```

 Select both lines of code and press the Display button; all you get this time is the internal representation of the array object, [I@b55. This number is the reference in memory and it will probably be different each time it is executed. To see the contents of array, you must press the Inspect button instead. Select the code again and press the Inspect button. An inspector window opens as shown in Figure 5.4.

In the case of the int array, you can see the value of each element. You can also change the value of any element in the array by selecting it on the Fields pane and over-typing a new value on the Value pane. Once you change the value of a field you have to save it. You can select **Save** from the Edit menu, or press the right mouse button over the right pane and select **Save** from the pop-up menu.

Inspector windows are very powerful; they let you get right in and inspect complex objects. Let's instantiate a **Frame** object and use an Inspector window to manipulate the object. In the Scrapbook, enter the following lines of code:

```
Frame f =
  new Frame("This is where the title goes");
return f;
```

Figure 5.4 Inspector window.

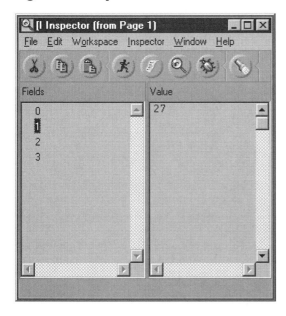

Set the context of this page to be the java.awt.Frame class. Select all lines and press the Inspect button. The code compiles and runs. When the line containing `return f;` is reached, an Inspector window is opened. The return statement is what triggers the Inspector to open; the object to be inspected is the object returned.

This Inspector lets you inspect and act on the `Frame f` object that is being displayed in the window as shown in Figure 5.5.

As you can see, an object of type **Frame** is fairly complex. In this Inspector, you can explore all of the Frame's properties. You can even open other Inspectors for the properties that represent objects, or open a browser for any of the typed properties in Frame. You do this by selecting the property you are interested in, bringing up the pop-up menu, and selecting either **Inspect** or **Open type.** You can also choose to see all fields or only the public fields of the object.

In the Value pane, you can inspect variables and also send messages to this particular object.

The first thing you will notice is that the Frame is nowhere to be seen on your screen. This is because Frames are created in a hidden state. To see the actual

Figure 5.5 Inspector for Frame f.

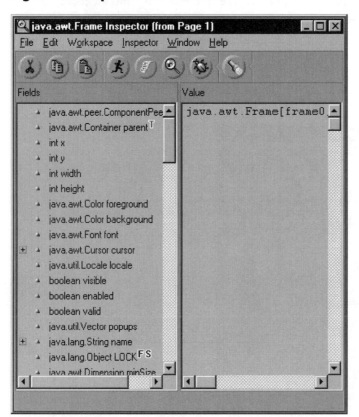

Frame, you need to call its show() method. Type **show**() in the Value pane, select the text, and press the Run button. Somewhere in your display, you should see a frame window with the title you entered on the code in the Scrapbook.

Try to send a few more messages to the Frame. Here are some ideas:

- setBackground(Color.green);
- setSize(200,200);
- width
- title

The last two, width and title, should be selected in the Fields pane. Their value is displayed and can be changed in the Value pane. They are properties of the Frame, so it does not make any sense to run them.

TIP

Be careful when you are entering commands in the Value pane; you should not select any items in the Fields pane. If you do, the command in the Value pane will fail when it is executed. Since you cannot deselect an item in the Field pane, you need to close and then re-open the inspector in order to continue entering commands in the Value pane.

There are more advanced topics to learn about Inspector windows; we will cover some of them in the Debugger section. You will also discover new features as you begin to use them while debugging your own programs.

The uvm.tools.debugger Package

A package in the Uvm Class Libraries project called **uvm.tools** is included with VisualAge for Java. In this package, you will find the **DebugSupport** class, which has methods very useful for debugging your programs. They are:

- bell()
- halt()
- inspect(java.lang.Object)

These are all static methods implemented in native code.

You can place **uvm.tools.DebugSupport.bell**() in your code where you want an audible indication that you have reached a certain spot in your program.

The **uvm.tools.DebugSupport.halt**() method is used to force the debugger window to display at a specific instruction in your program. Execution stops after the halt() instruction, giving you a chance to proceed testing your code in the debugger. This is the only way to bring up the debugger while you are executing code in the Scrapbook. You will rarely use halt() inside a method because you can always set up a debugger breakpoint in a method of a class.

The last method in this package allows you to inspect the value of a variable on the fly. As the Java Virtual Machine executes the uvm.tools.DebugSupport .inspect(java.lang.Object) method, an Inspector window opens with the current state of the object passed as the argument. Execution of the program does not stop, so the variable you are inspecting may be out of scope by the time you see it in its inspector, but you can still look at it as a snapshot of the way it was at the time the Inspector opened.

Introduction to the Debugger

Sometimes studying the output of trace information or exercising a portion of code in the Scrapbook does not provide enough insight to determine what is causing a program to go haywire. At other times the logic of a particular function or algorithm may be very complex and you want to better understand how it works. For these cases, you need to examine the code more closely, perhaps by setting a breakpoint at a particular instruction and monitoring state variables or single-stepping through the program. The source-level debugger that is part of the VisualAge for Java product is an excellent tool to use when the going gets tough.

Importing the Switcher Package

Before you can start using the debugger in this chapter, you need to import the switcher package into the repository from CD-ROM and move it into the workspace. In the CD accompanying this book, you will find the **switcher.dat** file. This file contains a buggy version of the Switcher program. You will use the classes in this package to learn how to use the source-level debugger in VisualAge for Java.

Importing the switcher.dat file into the workspace is a two-step process. First you import the package into the repository; next, you add the package from the repository into the workspace. Once the package is in the workspace, you can start working with it.

Importing into the Repository

Import the switcher.dat file into the repository by following these steps:

Select the My Project project.

From the File menu, select **Import**. The Import SmartGuide appears as shown in Figure 5.6.

Select **Interchange File**. Press the **Next** button. The Import from Interchange File SmartGuide appears as seen in Figure 5.7.

Interchange files are used to share projects and packages between programmers. They are the only type of export in VisualAge that not only saves all the programming elements in a project or package, but also preserves the information required to restore visual connections made in the Visual Composition Editor. Only versioned projects and packages can be exported as interchange files.

Figure 5.6 Import SmartGuide.

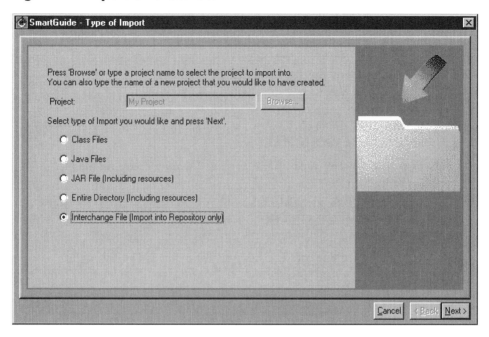

Figure 5.7 Import from Interchange file SmartGuide.

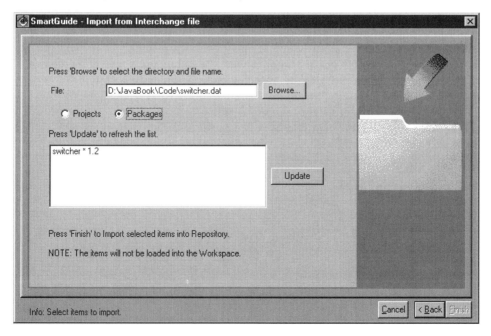

Enter the location of the file, or press the **Browse** button to locate it.

Because switcher.dat contains a package, select the **Packages** radio button.

Select the version of the package you wish to import and press **Finish**.

Adding a Package from the Repository

VisualAge for Java imports interchange files into the repository. The next step is to bring the switcher package from the repository into the workspace. For detailed steps on performing this action, see Chapter 1. For a shorter set of instructions, follow the steps below:

Select the My Project project, right-click, and from the pop-up menu, select **Add Package.**

In the New Package SmartGuide, select the **Add package(s) from repository** radio button and press the **Browse** button.

In the Add Packages SmartGuide, select the switcher package from the **Available package name** list. The **Editions** list is filled. The list might have more than one entry depending on the work you have already done on this package.

Select the edition you want to work with and move it to the **Editions to Add** list by pressing the Add button.

Press the **OK** button.

Press the **Finish** button on the SmartGuide to complete the operation.

Describing the Switcher Class

The switcher package contains several classes that implement a very simple program you will use to get acquainted with the debugger. Similar in construction to the Calculator project, the Switcher program is built following a view/model programming paradigm.

The view is built on a Panel using a GridBagLayout and is implemented in the **SwitcherPanel** class. The model is coded in the **SwitcherModel** class. The SwitcherPanel bean contains:

- Two Label beans
- Two TextField beans
- One Button bean

Each of the beans is placed on a Panel with a GridBagLayout. Each has its own GridBagConstraints to control its placement and other properties on the GridBag. You can use the property sheet for each bean to learn more about these settings.

The purpose of the Switcher program is to switch the values of the **First word** and **Second word** fields when the **Switch now** button is pressed. The logic to perform this operation is contained in the model bean, **SwitcherModel**.

Usually, model or domain beans have views associated with them. The views represent part of the model and, therefore, have some of the same properties. In this case, the Switcher model has two String properties representing **word1** and **word2**. The view has corresponding entry fields. The model has the logic to perform the switching of word1 and word2 in a public method called **switchNow()**. The view has the **Switch** button, which, when pressed, calls the switchNow() method to perform the operation.

The SwitcherPanel bean contains a SwitcherModel bean, which is named switcher. The proper connections have been made as seen in Figure 5.8. Feel free to open these beans in VisualAge browsers and observe the implementation details.

The SwitcherPanel bean can be run on its own within the VisualAge for Java development environment. This is because the code generator always creates a main() method for testing. However, before you can run it in a web browser, you need to place it inside an Applet. If you want to run it as an application, you need to place it inside a Frame. We have provided implementations for both options in the classes **SwitcherApplet** and **SwitcherApplication,** respectively.

Both classes are very straightforward; the SwitcherPanel is just placed in the center of a Applet or Frame with a BorderLayout.

Figure 5.8 SwitcherPanel bean.

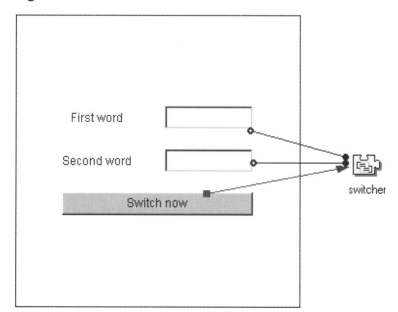

A connection gives focus to the **First word** field when the program completes its initialization. In the Applet, this is very easy; you just connect the init() event of the Applet to the requestFocus() method of the SwitcherPanel.

> **NOTE**
>
> The init() event is designated as an expert feature, so before you can see it in the list of available connections, you have to select the Show expert features check box in the connection window.

The features of the SwitcherPanel are encapsulated in the bean and are not accessible once it is placed on the Applet, which causes a problem. This problem is resolved by promoting the requestFocus method of the word1 TextField. You learn more about promoting bean features in a later chapter.

Because Frames don't generate init() events, you need to find another way to signal that the application has completed its initialization phase. A new *event interface* is defined to solve this problem. The new event is named **frameReady**. If you look at the code for the **windowOpened** method of the Frame, you will see how this event is fired at the appropriate moment.

```
public void windowOpened
   (java.awt.event.WindowEvent e)
{
   // user code begin {1}
   if (initialized == false)
   {
      fireFrameReady(new FrameReadyEvent(this));
      initialized = true;
   }
   // user code end

   if ((e.getSource() == this) )
   {
      conn1(e);
   }
}
```

Debugging the Switcher Program

Now back to the problem at hand. Select either the SwitcherApplet or the SwitcherApplication and run the program. Enter a distinct word on each of the text fields, for example, Justin and Jessica as seen in Figure 5.9.

Figure 5.9 Switcher application before switch.

Press the **Switch now** button and observe the change. The expected result is that Justin and Jessica will switch places: Jessica will be on top, and Justin will move to the bottom field. Actually, you end up with Jessica on both text fields as seen in Figure 5.10.

Even though the switch operation did not produce the expected result, you have ascertained several facts:

Figure 5.10 After switching.

- Pressing the button fired an actionEvent.
- A method was executed.
- Something in that method acted on the fields.

Setting Breakpoints

The next step should be to step through the code and see what is happening. If you look at the SwitcherPanel bean (see Figure 5.8) and click on the connection from the button to the model part, you will see in the information area that this is connection number 2, or **conn2**.

Select the Methods tab of the browser for SwitcherPanel and find the conn2 method. Click on it to display its source in the bottom pane of the browser as seen in Figure 5.11.

Figure 5.11 Setting a breakpoint at conn2.

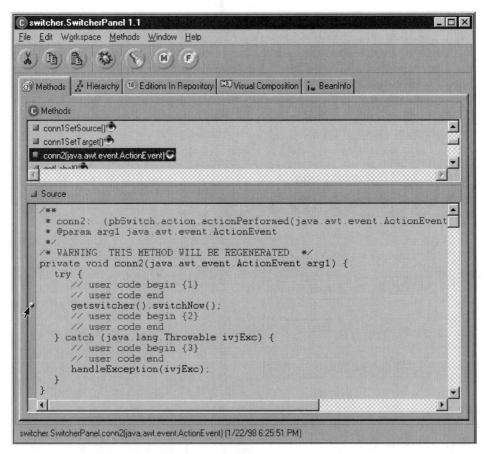

The gray column at the left of the source pane is used to manipulate debugger breakpoints. Place the mouse pointer on the column, aligned with the source line where the **switchNow**() method is invoked and double-click the right mouse button. Notice that a blue sphere appears next to the line indicating that a breakpoint exists. Breakpoints can be set at any valid executable line of code. Resetting the breakpoint is accomplished the same way by double-clicking on the blue sphere.

TIP

Avoid setting breakpoints in the constructor of beans created in the Visual Composition Editor. Their constructors are run in order to render the visual bean in the composition surface. A breakpoint in the constructor stops this process by bringing up the debugger.

Breakpoints can also be managed as a group from the Windows menu. Select **Breakpoint**. The Breakpoints window opens as seen in Figure 5.12; from here, you can temporarily enable, disable, or remove breakpoints in the workspace.

Figure 5.12 Breakpoints window.

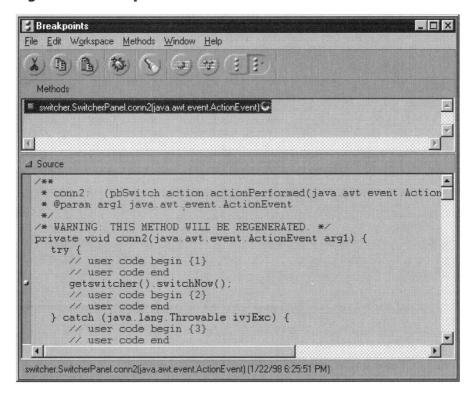

Source-level Debugger

To run the program again, switch to the Hierarchy or Visual Composition pages of the browser and press the Run or Test buttons. Enter some text in each field and press the **Switch Now** button. The program runs until it encounters the breakpoint; the debugger automatically comes up as seen in Figure 5.13.

The Debugger window is a complex window made up of many panes:

Pane	Displays/Function
Threads	Shows the threads available for debugging
Methods	Methods in the call stack
Visible Variables	List of variables which can be inspected
Value	Value of the currently selected variable
Source	Source code for the selected method

Panes can be sized by sliding the separator frames between the panes. You can maximize any pane by double-clicking its title. To restore it to its original size, double-click its title again.

The Threads pane lets you switch between threads that are stopped at their own breakpoints.

Figure 5.13 Debugger stopped at breakpoint.

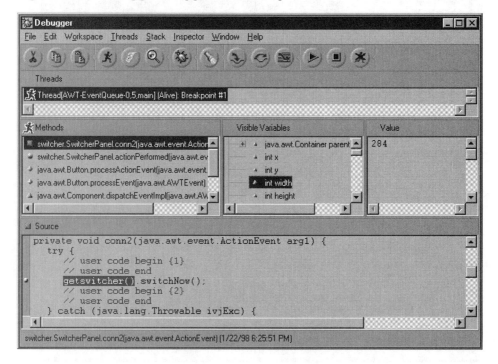

The Methods pane tells you how you came to this particular breakpoint by displaying the call stack. You can work your way back to examine the source code and variables at each point of execution.

The Visible Variables and Value panes are very similar to an Inspector window. You select the variable you are interested in and examine its value. You can change a variable's value by over-typing the current value and selecting **Save** from the pop-up menu. Notice that sometimes this option is grayed out, or unavailable. This happens if the variable is immutable (for example, a String) or if the variable you want to change is out of scope.

As long as you are stopped at a breakpoint, you can change the source code in the Source pane. You save your changes by selecting **Save** from the pop-up menu or by pressing Ctrl-S. Saving resets any breakpoints in the method that has been modified. Changes to the code take effect immediately after saving.

Debugger Tool Bar

The last six buttons of the debugger's tool bar are used to control the execution of the program while the debugger is in control seen in Table 5.1.

More Debugging

The debugger's window has now appeared, and the next statements to be executed are:

getswitcher()   press the **Step over** button
switchNow()   press the **Step into** button

Even though the statement at the breakpoint is a compound expression (getswitcher().switchNow();), each method call is executed and can be traced individually.

Table 5.1 Debugger Tool Bar Buttons

Button	Function	Description
	Step into	Steps into the highlighted method
	Step over	Executes method without debugging into method
	Run to return	Executes until the return statement of the method
	Resume	Resumes execution until next breakpoint or program end
	Suspend	Suspends the currently running thread at the next opportunity. It can then be resumed.
	Terminate	Terminates execution of the current thread

Now you have reached the switchNow() method and can analyze what is causing the two strings not to switch properly.

```
/**
 * Performs the switchNow method.
 */
public void switchNow() {
    /* Perform the switchNow method. */
    setWord1( getWord2());
    setWord2(getWord1());
    return;
}
```

At this point, you should verify that the String variables hold the same value as the fields in the view bean do. This would prove that the connections between them are firing properly.

Click on the plus sign next to the *this* variable in the middle pane.

It expands, and you see the two String variables, **fieldWord1** and **fieldWord2.** These names were made up by VisualAge as a result of the names of the String properties defined in this bean. If you click to select each of them, you can see their contents in the Value pane. They contain the same string as the field on the screen.

Upon examining the code, you realize that this is obviously a beginner's error. Every programmer knows that two variables cannot be switched without first storing one of the values in a temporary variable. You can change the code, right in the debugger's Source pane, so that the two strings will be switched properly.

```
public void switchNow() {
    /* Perform the switchNow method. */
    String temp;
    temp = getWord2();
    setWord2( getWord1() );
    setWord1( temp );
    return;
}
```

Press Ctrl-S to save and compile the method.

Press the Resume button to continue executing the program. The two fields switched properly: Justin moved to the bottom, and Jessica is in the top field.

It is very important to use the set method to set a new value into the bean's properties. Because these are instance variables, you could access them directly, for example:

```
fieldWord2 = fieldWord1;
```

This is a very bad idea, especially with bound properties. The code to fire propertyChange events is in the set method. If you assign values directly, the set method does not execute and therefore, property-changed events do not execute. The result is that no other components are notified that the property changed. See the following code segment:

```
public void setWord2(String word2) {
    /* Get the old property value for fire property
       change event. */
   String oldValue = fieldWord2;
  /* Set the word2 property (attribute) to the new
     value. */
   fieldWord2 = word2;
  /* Fire (signal/notify) the word2 property change
     event. */
  firePropertyChange("word2", oldValue, word2);
   return;
}
```

Killing Active Programs

It is possible to close the debugger while the program being debugged is stopped at a breakpoint. The program being debugged remains visible, but does not respond to keyboard and mouse events, and the program cannot be ended from the frame controls of the window.

In these cases, you can bring up the debugger and kill your program's thread. Another option is to resume execution from the breakpoint. If you find yourself in this situation, press the Debug button. A list of active threads will appear as shown in Figure 5.14. From this list, you can't really tell which thread is holding up your program.

Select all the threads in the list and press **OK**.

The debugger comes up with all threads selected on the top pane. You can attempt to determine which thread belongs to your program by selecting each one individually and pressing the Terminate button to end the thread, or you can terminate all threads at once.

Kill the running threads by selecting **Threads** and then **Terminate** from the Debugger menu bar.

Figure 5.14 Thread selection.

This concludes the introduction to debugging using VisualAge for Java. As you develop your own beans and combine them to form applets and applications, you will have lots of opportunities to hone the skills you started to develop in this chapter.

Summary

In this chapter, you were introduced to the trace and debugging facilities of VisualAge for Java. This chapter included the following activities:

- Adding trace information to a program by entering your own trace statements in the code

- Using the Java console to display trace information and to provide keyboard input

- Using the handleException() method to display uncaught exceptions

- Learning to test segments of code in the Scrapbook

- Learning about the uvm.tools.DebugSupport class

- Loading a program from an interchange file and bringing it into the workspace

- Debugging the Switcher application to fix a logic error

You should use the debugger to debug and inspect the Java programs that you develop. Debugging OO programs forces you to dive deep into the code, so don't be shy, you must do this to get your programs working properly.

BUILDING THE ADVANCED CALCULATOR GUI

6

What's in Chapter 6

This chapter builds on the topics already covered in this book. You will build on what you learned making the Adding Machine and improve it in a number of ways. The new application will have a much more sophisticated user interface, and you will add more math functions. In this chapter, you add user interface controls to support these new functions. This chapter covers the following topics:

- Copying beans in the IDE
- Using GridBagLayout
- Setting TextField and Label properties
- Setting GridBagConstraints properties
- Using the init() method

ased on your previous experience with the Simple Calculator, you will now construct a better calculator. This version will be able to perform operations to add, subtract, multiply and divide two floating-point numbers. It will also provide a Clear function and be able to detect an attempt by the user to divide by zero.

If you have closed VisualAge for Java, you need to restart it. The simplest way to start the VisualAge for Java is to double-click its icon.

Your Next Applet

Let's get started building the next applet with VisualAge for Java using the Visual Composition Editor. You will use the iterative development method, just as you did on the previous programs. You will develop the applet's user interface first, save your work, and test the Java code by running it in the IDE. You will iterate by adding more function and user interface elements, saving and testing again.

Packages

 With My Project selected, right-click on the top pane, and from the pop-up menu select **Add Package.** You can also press the New Package icon from the tool bar.

Enter AdvCalculator in the Create a new package named entry field.

Press Finish to create the package.

After creating the package, your Workbench should look like Figure 6.1.

Figure 6.1 AdvCalculator package.

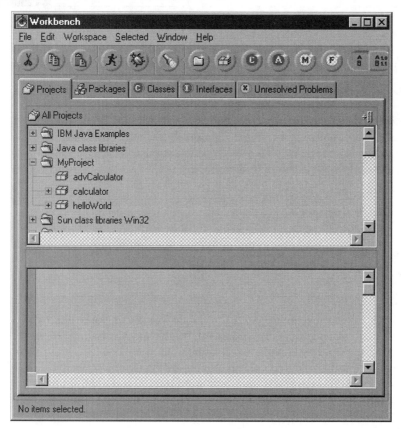

The Advanced Calculator builds on the Simple Calculator developed in previous chapters. It is much easier to start with the Simple Calculator than to build the Advanced Calculator from the beginning. This section covers copying beans, one of the most common forms of reuse.

Copying Beans

When copying a bean, you first select the bean that you want to copy in the Workbench. You then copy the bean using the pop-up menu. There is no other easier way to copy beans without exporting them.

In the Workbench, select the **CalculatorView**, then display the pop-up menu.

Select **Copy**; the Copying Selected Items SmartGuide appears.

Enter the package name for the Advanced Calculator, **advCalculator**, as the target package in the **Copy to** field as shown in Figure 6.2.

Figure 6.2 Copy SmartGuide.

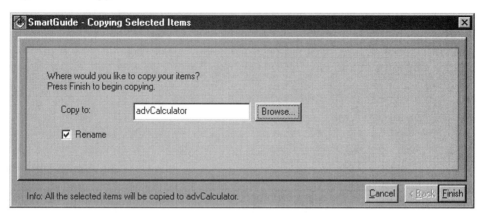

You can always use the **Browse** button to select the package name from those known in the workspace. The window prevents you from selecting an invalid package name by disabling the **Finish** button until a valid package name is selected. It is not necessary to rename this bean.

Deselect the **Rename** check box, and press the **Finish** button to start copying the bean.

TIP

If you copy a bean from one project to another, you get a warning, as shown in Figure 6.3. This message warns you that the classes being copied might not be able to find resource files (like bitmaps or icons) associated with GUI beans. The resource files are located in a subdirectory named like the project that contains the bean. When you copy beans, the resource files are not automatically moved to the target project. There is more information on working with resource files later in this book in the chapter that covers deploying Java programs.

CalculatorView is added to the AdvCalculator package in the Workbench, as shown in Figure 6.4. As the class is copied, a progress indicator is displayed. Note that the indicator lists that 12 problems were found. Notice the red X next to the CalculatorView bean in the Workbench. You only copied the bean, so why would it suddenly have errors? Did you copy it incorrectly? The error message in the info area at the bottom of the Workbench reads:

```
Type for field: private Calculator ivjcalculator, is missing
```

Figure 6.3 Copy warning.

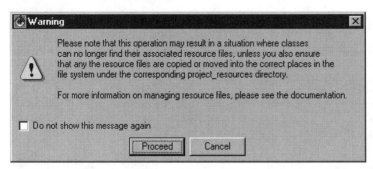

This is generated code, but let's look at it to see how to fix the problem. Look at the source code for the class where the variables are defined. If you select the CalculatorView in the Workbench, you can see the following:

```
private CalculatorLogic ivjcalculator = null;
```

By looking at the code, it is clear that the **ivjcalculator** has a type of **CalculatorLogic**. There is no qualification for the CalculatorLogic type. So the type for the field is not missing, but maybe it is out of scope in the workspace. Let's quickly review Java access conventions to see why this type may be out of scope.

Access Rules

Java has the same access modifiers for methods and fields as C++, as follows:

Private—access is limited to the class

Protected—access is limited to the class, all of its subclasses, and all the classes in the same package

Public—access is not limited

Java allows another type of access when an access modifier is not specified for the method or variable. This access is called *default* access and it is a very loose level of access control because it is implied. Default access allows any class in the package to have access to the method or variable.

When you refer to objects and methods, you refer to them by name. This name can be either unqualified or fully qualified, which includes the specific packages that contain the referenced item. Fully qualified names can be very long, so it is very common to use unqualified names. When you move a bean to another package, the unqualified names become out of scope.

Fixing Generated Code

As discussed earlier, there is no qualification for the CalculatorLogic type. The type relies on the fact that CalculatorLogic is in the same package. When you

Figure 6.4 Workbench with copied CalculatorView.

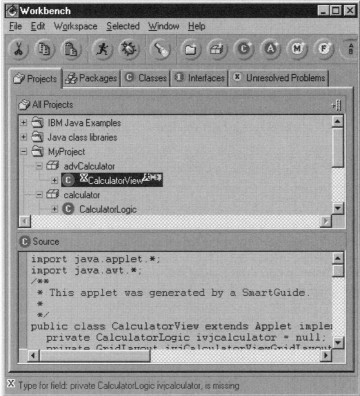

copied the class to another package, this assumption was shattered. There are a number of way to fix this error so that the variable type is correctly referenced. Three options are:

- Editing the generated code by fully qualifying the reference to CalculatorLogic

- Editing the generated code with an import statement to resolve the reference

- Having the Visual Composition Editor regenerate the code with the correct reference

The last option is a little easier, and if there any other invalid references, the Visual Composition Editor should fix those references, too. You can go to the Visual Composition Editor and force a regeneration. Fix the applet with these steps:

Go to the Visual Composition Editor for the AdvCalculatorView.

You must first make a trivial change to the applet. It can be to move the applet in the workspace or resize the applet.

This enables the save function, so select **Save Bean** from the File menu to save and generate the correct code.

When the Visual Composition Editor has finished saving the bean and generating the code, the red Xs should all go away. You can look at the regenerated code in the Workbench or on the Methods page of the browser. The Visual Composition Editor regenerates a fully qualified reference as shown in the following code:

```
private calculator.CalculatorLogic ivjcalculator
      = null;
```

The Generated main()

Another method in the advanced version of the CalculatorView is automatically generated by the Visual Composition Editor. When you define an applet in a SmartGuide, the Visual Composition Editor generates a main() method. Following is the code for the generated main():

```
/**
 * main entrypoint - starts the part when it is
   run as an application
 * @param args java.lang.String[]
 */
public static void main(java.lang.String[] args) {
  try {
    java.awt.Frame frame;
    try {
      Class aFrameClass =
        Class.forName("uvm.abt.edit.TestFrame");
      frame =
        (java.awt.Frame)aFrameClass.newInstance();
    } catch (java.lang.Throwable ivjExc) {
      frame = new java.awt.Frame();
    }
    calculator.CalculatorView aCalculatorView =
      new calculator.CalculatorView();
    frame.add("Center", aCalculatorView);
    frame.setSize(aCalculatorView.getSize());
    aCalculatorView.init();
    aCalculatorView.start();
    frame.setVisible(true);
```

```
    aCalculatorView.destroy();
  } catch (Throwable exception) {
    System.err.println("Exception occurred in
      main() of java.applet.Applet");
  }
}
```

The main() method is only generated once. If you intend to use the program as an applet only, there is no need for main(). If you ever want to run this as an application, you need to edit the main() method. When the bean was copied, the reference to the bean was not changed. Look at the code and you can see the following:

```
calculator.CalculatorView aCalculatorView =
new calculator.CalculatorView();
```

The main() method creates an instance of the CalculatorView in the old *calculator* package. After you have made a number of changes to the new CalculatorView, you will still see the old CalculatorView when you run it. You would probably find this problem by tracing the code, but it can be very confusing because it is the same class in different packages. The Advanced Calculator will only be used as an applet, so you do not need to edit the main() method.

TIP

The main() method is only generated one time by the Visual Composition Editor. If you copy or rename the class, you will need to edit the main() method so that it refers to the new class name. If you forget to edit main(), it will instantiate the old class when it runs.

Improving the CalculatorView

Now that the CalculatorView is cleaned up (or rather, it doesn't have any errors), you can start improving it with the following:

From the Workbench, open the **AdvCalculator** package; then open a browser to edit the **CalculatorView** class.

The Visual Composition Editor opens, enabling you to modify the applet and place the additional GUI beans.

The first thing to improve in the CalculatorView is the Layout Manager. For this applet, the GridBagLayout will help keep the GUI beans properly aligned at run time, and it is better suited for this applet. After you change the Layout Manager, you will add the additional Buttons for the new calculator functions.

GridBagLayout

The Simple Calculator was built using the applet in GridLayout to place other GUI beans. GridLayout kept the GUI beans in the correct place and the applet could be resized at run time. However, when you resized the applet, the TextFields and the Button got bigger. This is not a good design for a user interface; you would do better with GridBagLayout.

Building the Advanced Calculator involves using the applet with its own GridBagLayout Manager. The applet will have the same TextFields and Labels that were used in the Simple Calculator. The applet will also have a separate panel with a FlowLayout Manager that will contain the buttons for the calculator. This panel will be added to the applet as a component in the GridBagLayout.

GridBag Basics

As you learned earlier, Layout Managers are used to align, space, and size controls placed on a Container. GridBagLayout is a fairly complex Layout Manager, far more complicated than FlowLayout, the default Layout Manager for applets. GridBag is organized in rows and columns, with the numbering starting in the upper left corner. Rows and columns are addressed using integers, with the upper left corner cell having the address of row 0 and column 0, as shown in Figure 6.5. The GridBag properties for location are *gridX* for the column and *gridY* for the row.

Once a component is placed on a Container that has a GridBagLayout, the component has a new property. GridBagConstraint is a class in the java.awt package, and it holds properties for the behavior of the bean within the GridBag. The cells or coordinates in the GridBag are referred to as grids. The GridBag has the following properties:

- *anchor* determines the location in the GridBag cell in which the GUI bean anchors itself. Directional values for this property are center, north, northwest, northeast, south, southwest, southeast, east, and west.

- *fill* specifies which directions the GUI bean fills or grows as the GridBag is resized. Valid settings are NONE, BOTH, HORIZONTAL, and VERTICAL. The default value is NONE.

Figure 6.5 GridBagLayout addressing.

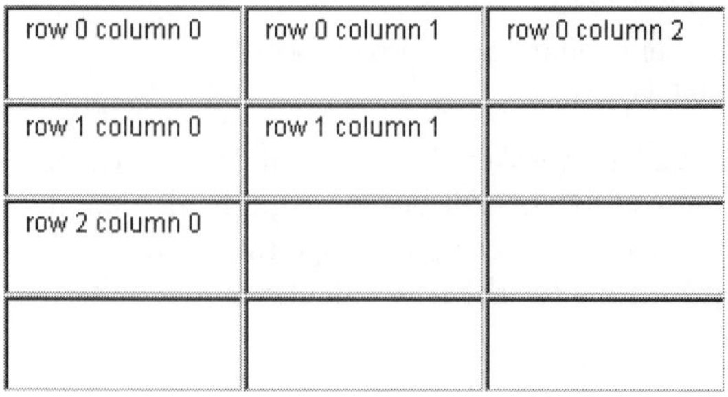

row 0 column 0	row 0 column 1	row 0 column 2
row 1 column 0	row 1 column 1	
row 2 column 0		

- *gridHeight* and *gridWidth* are the number of grids that the GUI bean spans or occupies. By default, the GUI bean is in one grid.

- *gridX* and *gridY* are the GridBag x and y coordinates for the bean.

- *insets* are the padding outside the GUI bean, specified in pixels. There are separate insets for top, bottom, right and left.

- *ipadx* and *ipady* are the padding inside the GUI bean. These are frequently used to increase the size of a GUI bean and they are specified in pixels.

- *weightX* and *weightY* specify how extra space will be used by the GUI bean.

As you can see, there are many different properties that can be set in GridBagConstraints. These properties can be set individually and in combination, thus adding to their complexity. The Visual Composition Editor generates default values for all of these properties, but you will need to modify the default settings to get the desired results.

Using GridBagLayout

The Visual Composition Editor makes it easy to work with more complex Layout Managers. Change the Layout Manager for the CalculatorView to GridBagLayout with the following steps:

Double-click on the dashed box, which represents the Applet instance, and bring up its property sheet (Figure 6.6).

Select the *layout* property from the list and select the ... button to open the prompter window where layouts can selected and customized.

Select **GridBagLayout** from the drop-down list, click OK to change the layout property, and close the property sheet.

After you change the Layout Manager, the Visual Composition Editor does not know where to place the GUI beans in the new Layout Manager. The Visual Composition Editor places all the GUI beans in one long row. You can move the GUI beans to a better arrangement with the following steps:

Drag and drop the GUI beans in the Applet so they are aligned in columns in the proper order (Figure 6.7).

As you drag the GUI beans over the GridBag, you can see some artificial lines that indicate the grids. You will probably need to drag and drop the GUI beans a number of times to get them in the proper order.

You can also see in Figure 6.7 that the TextFields are smaller than the TextFields in the previous programs. In addition, the Labels are no longer aligned with the TextFields. You will fix these after a quick test of the applet.

Figure 6.6 Setting the Applet Layout Manager.

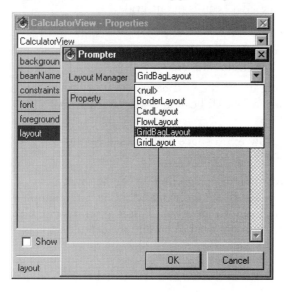

TIP

When you drop GUI beans in the GridBag, it is possible to place two GUI beans in the same grid. If you do this, the Visual Composition Editor generates the code successfully, and compiles and runs it. You will not get any errors that prevent you from doing this.

Figure 6.7 GUI beans arranged.

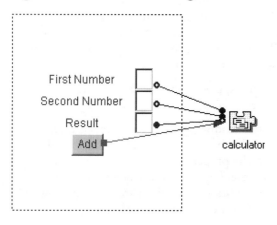

Test Iteration One

Let's test the applet with GridBag layout to see how it works:

Run the AdvCalculatorView by pressing the Test button; the applet should look like Figure 6.8.

Change the size of the applet. Notice how the controls are repositioned according to the behavior of the Layout Manager. The TextFields and the Button do not grow bigger as you resize the applet, instead, they stay in the center of the applet.

Try to enter numbers in the TextFields.

You can put the cursor in the TextFields, but you can't enter numbers in them. The TextFields can be fixed in the next iteration. Also notice that the Labels are not aligned any more. These too can be fixed in the next iteration. Even though you can't enter any numbers, the add function still works, although there is no way to verify it.

After you have finished testing the applet, close the applet so you can continue improving it.

Setting TextField Properties

The TextFields must be changed to enable the user to enter numbers in the applet. There should be a TextField property that controls its size. Many GUI beans are managed by their paint() method. TextFields have a *columns* property that specifies the number of characters the TextField can display. Increase the *columns* property with the following steps:

Figure 6.8 Running the GridBag layout.

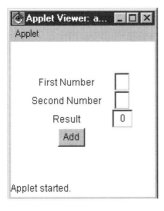

Open the property sheet for the efNum1 TextField.

You will see that the *columns* property is currently set to 0. This is why you can't enter any numbers in the TextFields. You can set the number of characters for the *columns* property so the TextField will work properly.

Enter **10** for the *columns* property as shown in Figure 6.9. Also change the *columns* property for efNum2 and efResult to 10.

TIP

You can keep the property sheet open when you need to change the properties of a number of beans. Select the next bean in the Visual Composition Editor; the property sheet refreshes itself with the properties for the new bean. This is a very handy feature that makes it a lot easier to edit bean properties.

Label Alignment

The Labels also need to be changed. The Labels are no longer aligned as they were in the Simple Calculator. You can affect the alignment of a Label though its GridBag Constraint or its own properties. In some cases, you need to use multiple

---

Figure 6.9 TextField columns properties.

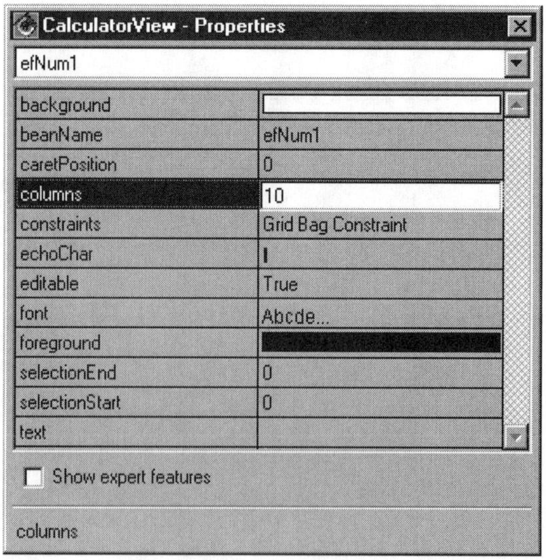

GridBag Constraint properties to get the desired result. Change the TextFields with the following steps:

Open the property sheet for the efNum1 Label. If you left the property sheet open, just select efNum1.

The default setting is CENTER. It would look better if the Labels are aligned RIGHT.

Select **RIGHT** in the drop-down list for the *alignment* property, as shown in Figure 6.10.

Change the alignment to RIGHT for the other two Labels.

When you complete these changes to the properties, the text will be right aligned, as shown in Figure 6.11. It is not right-aligned within the grid. This is not quite what you need, but there is another setting to make all the GUI beans right-aligned. The GridBag Constraints allow you to make property settings for each grid.

Setting GridBagConstraints Properties

If you look closely at Figure 6.11, you can see that the Labels are not right-aligned correctly. The Labels are readable, but it would look a lot more polished if the Labels were truly right-aligned and there were a little space between the

Figure 6.10 Property sheet for alignment.

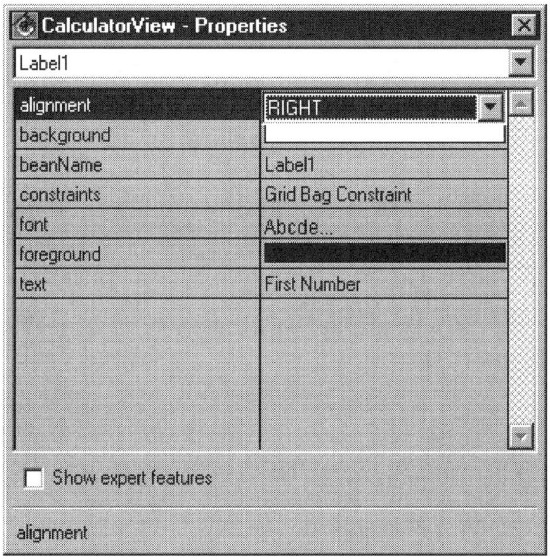

Figure 6.11 Right-aligned TextFields.

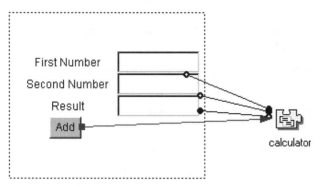

GUI beans. You learned about the many different GridBag constraints in a previous section. Now you will have a chance to use what you learned about the GridBag.

Using the Anchor Property

The *anchor* is the location or direction in the grid that the bean is oriented or attaches itself. The three Labels in the Advanced Calculator are different lengths, and the default anchor is *center*. If the user interface was centered this would be fine.

Select the *First Number* Label and bring up its property sheet.

Select *constraints* and open its property sheet.

Select *anchor* property and set it to **EAST** in the dropdown list as shown in Figure 6.12.

Repeat the previous steps for the Second Number and Result Labels.

When you are finished setting the properties, close the property sheets. the Labels should be nicely right-aligned as shown in Figure 6.13.

Using Insets

The insets properties of the Label. Make these changes with the following steps:

Select the efNum1 Label and bring up its property sheet.

Select *constraints* and open its property sheet.

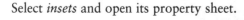

Select *insets* and open its property sheet.

Enter 10 for the right inset as shown in Figure 6.14.

Repeat the previous steps for the Second Number and Result Labels.

When you are finished setting the properties, close the property sheets. The composite bean now looks as shown in Figure 6.15.

Figure 6.12 TextField anchor properties.

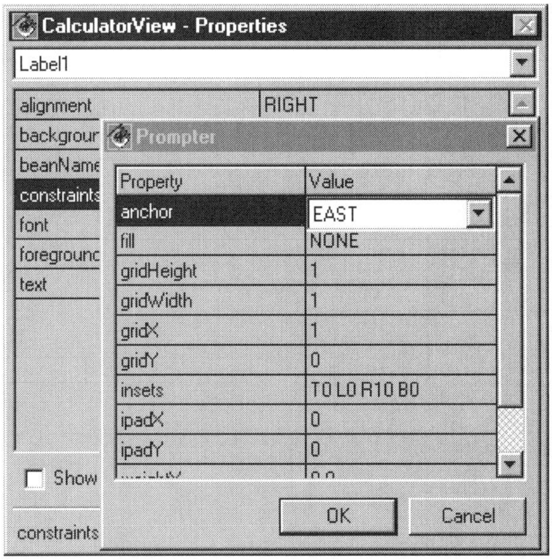

Property	Value
anchor	EAST
fill	NONE
gridHeight	1
gridWidth	1
gridX	1
gridY	0
insets	T 0 L 0 R 10 B 0
ipadX	0
ipadY	0

Building a Sub-Panel

You could add each additional button directly to the applet, but each button would need to be in a separate grid. The buttons should behave separately from the TextField GUI beans. They should stay together in a group and not increase in size or move around the user interface. Users like to rely on the location of buttons in the user interface.

It is better to combine multiple buttons on a Panel. An AWT Panel is a subclass of Container and it can have its own layout manager. You can add the panel to another Container like an applet. Build the buttons Panel with the following steps:

Figure 6.13 Right-aligned East-anchored TextFields.

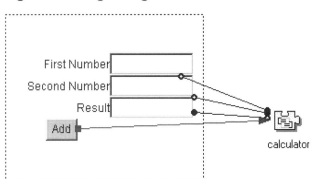

Figure 6.14 Setting an inset.

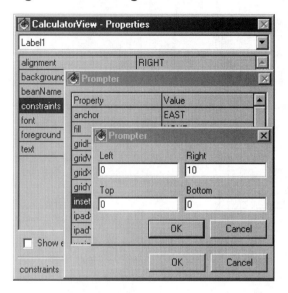

 In the AdvCalculatorView Visual Composition Editor, select the Container category on the beans palette.

 Select a **Panel** bean and temporarily drop it on the free-form surface outside the Applet instance, as shown in Figure 6.16.

 Select the **Sticky** check box, then select **Button** from the Buttons category. **Sticky** keeps the mouse pointer loaded with Button, enabling you to drop the same bean many times.

 Drop four Buttons on the Panel you have just added to the free-form surface; then turn off the **Sticky** option.

Select the pbAdd Button in the applet and drag it to the new Panel.

Figure 6.15 Applet with a right inset of 10.

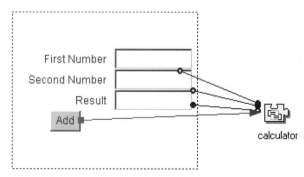

Figure 6.16 Sub-Panel on free-form surface.

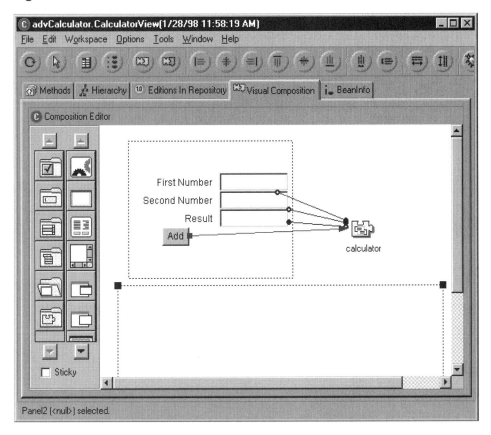

Notice how the buttons stay where you drop them on the Panel. That is because this Panel has a null Layout Manager. FlowLayout would keep the Buttons neatly displayed in different screen resolutions. Set the Layout Manager for the button Panel:

Double-click inside the dashed box that represents the Panel instance, and bring up its property sheet.

This time, set the layout to FlowLayout, and close the property sheet. Now the buttons are all aligned, flowing one after the other.

Directly edit the text on the new buttons to read **Subtract, Multiply, Divide** and **Clear**.

Adjust the size of the Panel until it is just large enough to hold all the buttons in one row, as shown in Figure 6.17.

Figure 6.17 Buttons Panel.

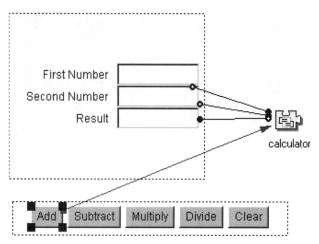

Adding a Panel to a Container

The sub-panel will be a component of the applet, but as a component it will initially be placed in one grid.

Drag and drop the buttons Panel onto the *lower* section of the Applet instance, just under the efResult Label.

Notice that as you moved the mouse pointer over the top of the Applet, distinct areas appeared as dashed boxes inside the Applet. These are *drop zones*, and they show the GridBag cells in the Applet. These lines are shown only at development time and appear when a GUI bean is moving over the GridBag. Your CalculatorView should now look like Figure 6.18.

Spanning Multiple Grids

The ability for GUI beans to span multiple grids is a unique feature of the GridBag layout. The Panel1 panel is a large GUI bean and it should span multiple grids, which are easily changed in the GridBag Constraints. Change Panel1 so that it spans three grids with the following steps:

Figure 6.18 AdvCalculatorView with buttons Panel.

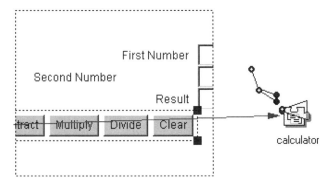

Select the Panel1 panel and bring up its property sheet.

Select *constraints* and open its property sheet.

Select *gridWidth* property and set it to 3 as shown in Figure 6.19.

When you are finished setting the properties, close the property sheet.

The updated Advanced Calculator applet should look like Figure 6.20. All the GUI beans are properly aligned and the button panel is visible spanning multiple grids.

Figure 6.19 Buttons Panel, spanning grids.

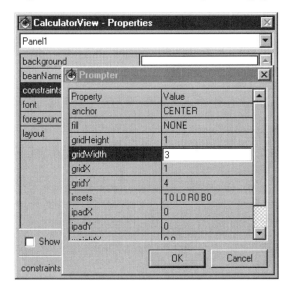

Figure 6.20 All GUI beans are aligned.

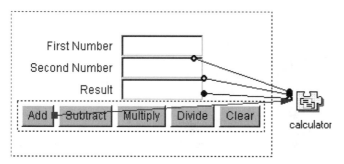

Test Iteration Two

Run the **AdvCalculatorView** by pressing the Test button. It should look like Figure 6.21.

Change the size of the applet and notice how all the GUI beans are repositioned according to the behavior of the Layout Managers.

The GridBag Code

You have completed the user interface for the advanced calculator. You used the GridBag Layout with a number of GUI beans, and you made a lot of property settings. Let's look at all the generated code for the applet using a GridBag. This code is added to the applet in the init() method as shown in the following code segment:

```
/**
 * Handle the Applet init method.
 */
```

Figure 6.21 Running iteration two.

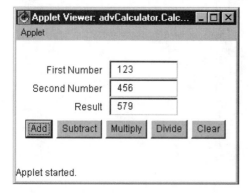

```
/* WARNING: THIS METHOD WILL BE REGENERATED. */
public void init() {
  super.init();
  try {
    java.awt.GridBagConstraints constraintsLabel1
      = new java.awt.GridBagConstraints();
    java.awt.GridBagConstraints constraintsefNum1
      = new java.awt.GridBagConstraints();
    java.awt.GridBagConstraints constraintsLabel2
      = new java.awt.GridBagConstraints();
    java.awt.GridBagConstraints constraintsefNum2
      = new java.awt.GridBagConstraints();
    java.awt.GridBagConstraints constraintsLabel3
      = new java.awt.GridBagConstraints();
    java.awt.GridBagConstraints
      constraintsefResult = new
      java.awt.GridBagConstraints();
    java.awt.GridBagConstraints constraintsPanel1
      = new java.awt.GridBagConstraints();
    setName("CalculatorView");
    setLayout(new java.awt.GridBagLayout());
    setSize(285, 153);

    constraintsLabel1.gridx = 1;
    constraintsLabel1.gridy = 0;
    constraintsLabel1.gridwidth = 1;
    constraintsLabel1.gridheight = 1;
    constraintsLabel1.anchor =
    java.awt.GridBagConstraints.EAST;
    constraintsLabel1.weightx = 0.0;
    constraintsLabel1.weighty = 0.0;
    constraintsLabel1.insets = new
      java.awt.Insets(0, 0, 0, 10);
    ((java.awt.GridBagLayout)
    this.getLayout()).setConstraints(getLabel1(),
      constraintsLabel1);
    this.add(getLabel1());

    constraintsefNum1.gridx = 2;
    constraintsefNum1.gridy = 0;
    constraintsefNum1.gridwidth = 1;
    constraintsefNum1.gridheight = 1;
    constraintsefNum1.anchor =
      java.awt.GridBagConstraints.CENTER;
    constraintsefNum1.weightx = 0.0;
    constraintsefNum1.weighty = 0.0;
```

```
((java.awt.GridBagLayout)
this.getLayout()).setConstraints(getefNum1(),
    constraintsefNum1);
this.add(getefNum1());

constraintsLabel2.gridx = 1;
constraintsLabel2.gridy = 2;
constraintsLabel2.gridwidth = 1;
constraintsLabel2.gridheight = 1;
constraintsLabel2.anchor =
    java.awt.GridBagConstraints.CENTER;
constraintsLabel2.weightx = 0.0;
constraintsLabel2.weighty = 0.0;
constraintsLabel2.insets = new
    java.awt.Insets(0, 0, 0, 10);
((java.awt.GridBagLayout)
this.getLayout()).setConstraints(getLabel2(),
    constraintsLabel2);
this.add(getLabel2());

constraintsefNum2.gridx = 2;
constraintsefNum2.gridy = 2;
constraintsefNum2.gridwidth = 1;
constraintsefNum2.gridheight = 1;
constraintsefNum2.anchor =
    java.awt.GridBagConstraints.CENTER;
constraintsefNum2.weightx = 0.0;
constraintsefNum2.weighty = 0.0;
((java.awt.GridBagLayout)
this.getLayout()).setConstraints(getefNum2(),
    constraintsefNum2);
this.add(getefNum2());

constraintsLabel3.gridx = 1;
constraintsLabel3.gridy = 3;
constraintsLabel3.gridwidth = 1;
constraintsLabel3.gridheight = 1;
constraintsLabel3.anchor =
    java.awt.GridBagConstraints.EAST;
constraintsLabel3.weightx = 0.0;
constraintsLabel3.weighty = 0.0;
constraintsLabel3.insets = new
    java.awt.Insets(0, 0, 0, 10);
((java.awt.GridBagLayout)
this.getLayout()).setConstraints(getLabel3(),
    constraintsLabel3);
```

```
        this.add(getLabel3());

        constraintsefResult.gridx = 2;
        constraintsefResult.gridy = 3;
        constraintsefResult.gridwidth = 1;
        constraintsefResult.gridheight = 1;
        constraintsefResult.anchor =
          java.awt.GridBagConstraints.CENTER;
        constraintsefResult.weightx = 0.0;
        constraintsefResult.weighty = 0.0;
        ((java.awt.GridBagLayout)
    this.getLayout()).setConstraints(getefResult(),
          constraintsefResult);
        this.add(getefResult());

        constraintsPanel1.gridx = 1;
        constraintsPanel1.gridy = 4;
        constraintsPanel1.gridwidth = 3;
        constraintsPanel1.gridheight = 1;
        constraintsPanel1.anchor =
          java.awt.GridBagConstraints.CENTER;
        constraintsPanel1.weightx = 0.0;
        constraintsPanel1.weighty = 0.0;
        ((java.awt.GridBagLayout)
        this.getLayout()).setConstraints(getPanel1(),
          constraintsPanel1);
        this.add(getPanel1());
        initConnections();
        // user code begin {1}
        // user code end
    } catch (java.lang.Throwable ivjExc) {
        // user code begin {2}
        // user code end
        handleException(ivjExc);
    }
}
```

As you can see, the Visual Composition Editor generated a lot of code, about 90 lines of pure Java. Each property that you set in the Visual Composition Editor causes the appropriate code to be generated for the GridBag. The Visual Builder is a great help in generating the code for the more complex GUI beans.

Naming the GUI Beans

Each control has a default name. The first TextField control you drop is called TextField1. Remember that changing the name to something more meaningful is a good idea. It aids you in following the generated code and provides some level of documentation to the code.

Change the names of embedded beans by clicking the right mouse button on the bean and selecting **Change Bean Name** from the pop-up menu. Change the name of the buttons to **pbSub, pbMult, pbDiv,** and **pbClear**, respectively.

You don't need to change the names of the TextFields because they retain the names efNum1, efNum2, and efResult. Just like the Simple Adder, the result of the calculation is supplied by the AdvCalculatorLogic bean (yet to be built), and the efResult TextField should not allow keyboard input. The efResult TextField was set to be uneditable in the Simple Calculator, so this does not need to be set again.

Using the init() Method

When an applet is loaded by a browser, the init() method is executed. After the init() method completes, the init event is sent. The init event is very good for triggering initial behavior in your beans. You might have noticed that when the applet runs, you must select a TextField with the mouse in order to enter data. By default, focus is not set in an applet. You can easily set the initial focus to a specific TextField with a simple visual connection.

Setting Focus

When you tested the Advanced Calculator, you had to place the mouse in the TextField in order to enter numbers. When a window or an applet displays, it is very helpful to set the focus. In this case, focus should be set to the efNum1 TextField. This can be accomplished by adding code in the init() method or by making a connection in the Visual Composition Editor. Usually, user interface settings should not be made with visual connections; this is a good example of using the init() method. You will make a connection from the applet's init() method. The applet's features can be accessed from the pop-up menu on the free-form surface. Make this connection with the following steps:

Move the mouse to the free-form surface and select the pop-up menu.

Select **Connect** and then **All Features**.

Select the *init* event as the source for the connection. If you can't find the *init* event, select the **Show expert features** check box at the bottom of the connection window as shown in Figure 6.22. Close the connection window.

Move the mouse to efNum1 and bring up the connection menu. Select **All Features**.

On the connections window for efNum1, select the requestFocus() method.

Figure 6.22 Selecting the expert init event.

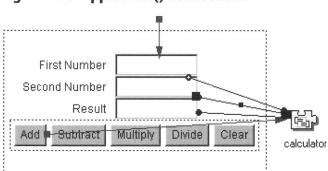

As indicated by the green line, this is an event-to-method connection, and it requires no parameters as seen in Figure 6.23. You could also have accomplished the same result by adding the following line of code directly to the init() method:

```
getefNum1().requestFocus();
```

It is far more efficient to write a line of code in the init() than to use the visual connection. However, the visual connection is much easier to see in the Visual Composition Editor and, therefore it is easier to change.

Figure 6.23 Applet init() connection.

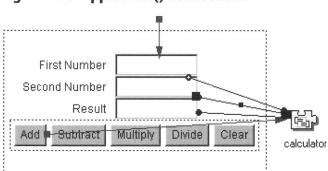

Test Iteration Three

The AdvCalculatorView is good enough to test. Run the applet by pressing the Test button.

The user interface for the Advanced Calculator is much cleaner than the user interface for the Simple Calculator. Resizing still works as in the previous tests. When the applet starts, the cursor is automatically placed in the first field.

When you are finished testing, close the applet viewer.

Summary

In this chapter, you completed a much more complicated user interface. You improved the Simple Calculator in many ways. There were a number of topics covered, including:

- Copying beans and dealing with invalid references
- Understanding GridBagLayout
- Setting TextField and Label properties
- Using GridBagConstraints
- Using the init() method to set initial focus

The applet is now the Advanced Calculator and the user interface is ready for you to add the additional function for the CalculatorLogic bean.

Building the Advanced Calculator Logic

7

What's in Chapter 7

In this chapter, you continue to improve the Advanced Calculator. The new application will have a much more sophisticated user interface and you will add more math functions. In this chapter, you will add user interface controls to support these new functions. This chapter contains the following topics:

- Extending invisible beans
- Exception handling
- Using a message box
- Modifying the bean palette
- Using a numeric-only TextField

You will apply all these concepts in completing the Advanced Calculator applet. After you have finished this chapter, you will have a better understanding of what it takes to develop more complex Java programs.

Based on your previous experience with the Simple Calculator, you will now construct a better Calculator. This version will be able to perform operations to add, subtract, multiply, and divide two floating-point numbers. It will also provide a Clear function and will detect an attempt by the user to divide by zero.

If you have closed VisualAge for Java, you need to restart it. The simplest way to start the VisualAge for Java is to double-click its icon.

Extending an Invisible Bean

Let's continue and construct the **AdvCalculatorLogic** invisible bean. Although you reused the CalculatorView, in this case you will make a new invisible bean. The CalculatorLogic used in the Simple Calculator had properties of type *int*. The AdvCalculatorLogic bean will also have three properties, but they will be of type *float*. Start building the bean with the following steps:

From the Workbench panel, select the **advCalculator** package, right-click, and **select New Class/Interface**.

Name the class **AdvCalculatorLogic** and keep the superclass for this class as the default java.lang.Object, which is the topmost class in the Java class hierarchy.

Select the **Browse the class when finished** check box. Press the **Finish** button to create the class as shown in Figure 7.1.

The Class/Interface Browser opens for you to continue developing this class.

This bean needs three properties of type **float** to hold the two operands and the result of the calculation. Because we will use this bean in the Visual Composition Editor, these properties must be enabled to send and receive notifications. This enables the visual and invisible representation of the values to remain synchronized. In other words, when the user enters a number in the user interface and changes the value of one of the numbers, the corresponding property in the invisible bean must be notified of this change. To do this, properties for the class need to be defined in the BeanInfo page of the Class/Interface Browser. Use the following steps to make the properties:

Select the BeanInfo page of the class browser.

Right-click on the Features pane and select **New Property Feature** from the pop-up menu.

Enter **num1** in the **Property name** entry field and select **float** from the **Property type** list. It is important to ensure that the **bound** check box is selected if you will be using this property in a connection in the Visual Composition Editor (see Figure 7.2). If you accidentally set the wrong type, delete the property and go to the source code for the class and delete the variable for the property.

Figure 7.1 Added AdvCalculatorLogic class.

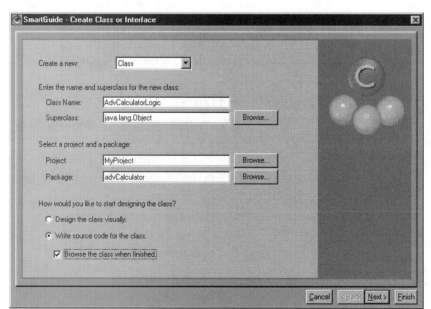

Figure 7.2 Adding properties.

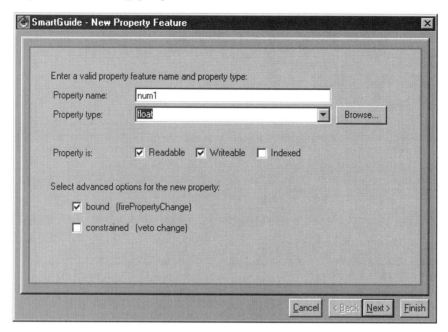

NOTE

Be very careful and make sure you are using little *float*, which is a primitive Java type, and not big *Float*, which is a Java class.

At this time, press **Finish** and accept defaults for the remainder settings or press **Next** to further define the interface to the *num1* property.

Repeat the previous steps to create the *num2* and *result* properties. Make them both of type float and with **bound** properties.

Next, you need to create the methods in the bean that will perform the calculator operations:

Right-click on the Features pane and select **New Method Feature** from the pop-up menu (see Figure 7.3).

Type the method name **add**. Press the **Finish** button.

Repeat these steps to add new method features for the **clear, subtract, multiply,** and **divide** operations.

The SmartGuide generates stubs for the user-defined methods you created in the BeanInfo page. You need to add the code to perform the added math functions

Figure 7.3 Creating the add method.

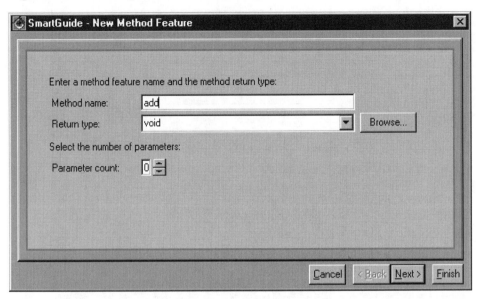

in the AdvCalculatorLogic bean, as you did with the CalculatorLogic bean. Enter the code to perform the calculation in the bottom pane, as shown in Figure 7.4. This code sets the *result* property on the **AdvCalculatorLogic** bean with the sum of the values of *num1* and *num2*.

Select the *add* property in the Features list, then select the **add**() method in the Definitions list.

Enter code for the add() method.

Right-click on the bottom pane and select **Save** to save and compile the code for the add method. Any errors are reported now. You can also use Ctrl-S to save and compile.

Enter the code for all operation methods in the AdvCalculatorLogic bean as shown in Table 7.1.

Adding the GUI Bean to the Visual Composition Editor

You have finished adding the math functions to the invisible bean that will perform operations for the calculator. Now, you can bring the invisible bean into the Visual Composition Editor for the **CalculatorView** and make the necessary connections with the following steps:

Switch back to the class browser that is showing the **CalculatorView** class, and make sure the Visual Composition tab is selected.

Select **Options** and then **Add Bean,** then select the **Browse** button to show the list of available classes.

Enter the name of our calculator bean, **AdvCalculatorLogic,** and select **OK.**

Enter a name for this bean (for example, **advCalc**) and select **OK.**

Move the mouse pointer outside of the dashed box and over the free-form surface; click the mouse to drop the bean. advCalc should be near the old calculator bean on the free-form surface.

You should now have a bean that looks like a jigsaw puzzle piece available for connections (see Figure 7.5). You are ready to connect the GUI beans to the model or logic bean.

Figure 7.4 Code for the add method.

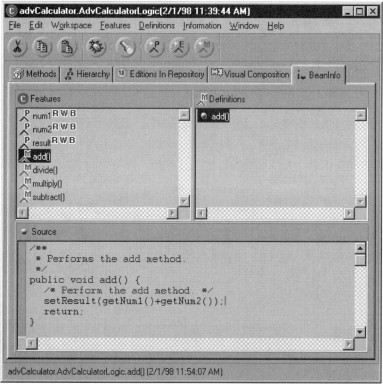

Figure 7.5 New invisible bean.

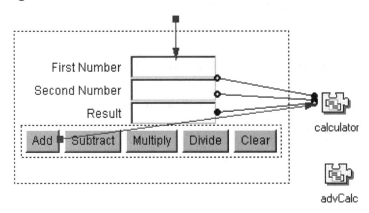

Figure 7.6 Conn0 moved to advCalc.

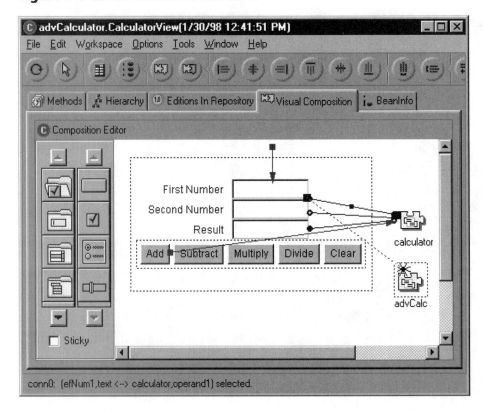

Table 7.1 Operation Methods

Method	Code
add()	setResult(getNum1() + getNum2());
subtract()	setResult(getNum1() – getNum2 ());
multiply()	setResult(getNum1() * getNum2 ());
divide()	setResult(getNum1() / getNum2 ());

Advanced Calculator Connections

One of the benefits of visual programming is the ability to see method calls between classes. You can modify any of these method calls quickly and easily by modifying the visual connections. Once the program has visual connections, you can change the source event or the target method of the connection. You can also move the source or target of the connection to a different bean in the Visual Composition Editor.

Moving Connections

The connections for Advanced Calculator are very much like the ones used in the Simple Calculator. In fact, the AdvCalculatorLogic bean is designed similarly to the CalculatorLogic bean so you can move the existing connections from the CalculatorLogic bean to corresponding properties in the AdvCalculatorLogic bean. Move the connections to AdvCalculatorLogic with the following steps:

Select the property-to-property connection from the **num1** TextField to the CalculatorLogic bean.

The selected connection has black handles for moving and positioning. Verify that you have the correct connection. The information area at the bottom of the window indicates the selected item. It should read:

conn0: (efNum1,text <->calculator1, operand1) selected.

Place the tip of the mouse on the end of the connection handle; press and hold down the left mouse button.

With the mouse button still down, move the end of the connection to the **advCalc** bean and release the left mouse button, as shown in Figure 7.6.

Because the CalculatorLogic bean and the AdvCalculatorLogic bean have the same *num1* property, the connection automatically completes. If the properties were not an exact match, then the Visual Composition Editor would prompt you with a list of properties to select.

The other two TextFields need their connections moved to the AdvCalc bean. In a similar fashion, move the following connections:

- **efNum2** (text) connection to AdvCalc's *num2* property
- **efResult** (text) connection to AdvCalc's *result* property

Automatic Conversion

When you move these connections, the Visual Composition Editor does not warn that the source and target types are incompatible. However, the *text* property of the TextField is of type String, and the *result* property is of type float. If you made a new connection, you would get the warning message. However, the Visual Composition Editor correctly generates the proper conversions to match the types at run time when the connection was initially made. Let's look at the generated code for this connection, conn0, to see how this is handled.

First, save these changes by selecting **Save Bean** from the File menu. The applet is saved, and the code is regenerated.

To view the class code, you can go to the Workbench or the Methods page of the class browser. Refer to the following code segment:

```
/**
 * conn0SetTarget:  (efNum1.text <--> advCalc.num1)
 */
/* WARNING: THIS METHOD WILL BE REGENERATED. */
private void conn0SetTarget() {
   /* Set the target from the source */
   try {
      if (ivjConn0Aligning == false) {
         // user code begin {1}
         // user code end
         ivjConn0Aligning = true;
         getadvCalc().setNum1(new
         Float(getefNum1().getText()).floatValue());
         // user code begin {2}
         // user code end
         ivjConn0Aligning = false;
      }
   } catch (java.lang.Throwable ivjExc) {
      ivjConn0Aligning = false;
      // user code begin {3}
      // user code end
      handleException(ivjExc);
   }
}
```

As you can see, when the setNum1() method is called, it is passed a parameter that uses the floatValue() method. This method converts the String to a float.

Property Events

Remember from the CalculatorView that TextFields have a number of events that can be passed on property-to-property connections. These events were set when you built the CalculatorView. You do not need to reset these events in the AdvCalculatorView. However, it is a good idea to verify that these events are set correctly:

Open the connection's property sheet for the previous connections (see Figure 7.7). Either double-click on the blue connection line or use its pop-up menu and select **properties**.

Look at the corresponding event drop-down list and verify that it is set to **textValueChanged(java.awt.event.TextEvent)**.

Close the connection's property sheet when you have verified the correct event settings.

Moving Method Connections

Now you need to move the add method call to the new invisible bean. It is the same process as moving the previous connections. It's easier now that you have already done it a few times. Move the connection as follows:

Select the green connection between the pbAdd Button and the calculator bean.

Move the end of the connection from the calculator bean to advCalc.

Figure 7.7 Verifying connection properties.

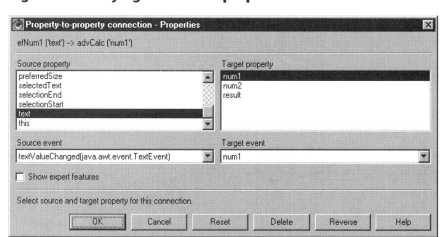

When you have moved all the connections, the applet design in the Visual Composition Editor should look like Figure 7.8.

Testing the Add Function

There are enough changes in the Advanced Calculator to test it. Execute the following steps:

Press the Test button on the upper tool bar of the Visual Composition Editor to generate and run the applet.

Enter values in the TextFields and try all the operations of the calculator.

The **Result** field should show the correct value of the addition operation on the two numbers, as shown in Figure 7.9. If it does not add correctly, use the debugger to trace the values in the AdvCalc bean and check the add() method execution.

When you are finished testing, close the applet viewer.

TIP

Notice how the **Result** field displays 0.0 when it starts. This is because the connection for this TextField starts at the AdvCalc bean as the source and points to the efResult TextField as the target. The source value sets the target value when the objects are instantiated at run time. The float property in the AdvCalc bean is initialized to be 0.0, so this value sets the value in the efResult TextField. efNum1 and efNum2 do not have 0.0 as an initial value, because both TextFields are sources for the connections. They are of type String and set the appropriate values in the AdvCalc bean.

Figure 7.8 All calculator connections moved to advCalc.

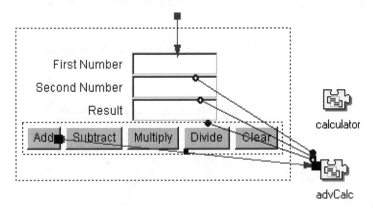

Figure 7.9 Running the Advanced Calculator.

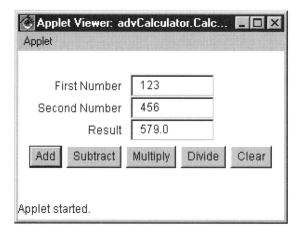

Deleting Beans

The Advanced Calculator ran fine when you tested it. There were two invisible beans that provide calculation functions, but only one of the invisible beans was called by the applet. The invisible beans placed on the free-form surface are instantiated or NEWed at run time. The Visual Composition Editor generates the call to the constructor of the bean using its default constructor. After you have moved all the connections to the AdvCalc bean, there is no need to keep the old calculator bean on the free-form surface. Delete this bean as follows:

Select the calculator invisible bean from the free-form surface of the AdvCalculatorView applet.

Either press the Delete key or point the mouse at the calculator invisible bean and select **Delete** from the pop-up menu.

More Connections

Now that you have made a number of connections in the Visual Composition Editor, the instructions in the book for making connections will be much briefer. These shorter instructions indicate the source bean and its feature followed by the target bean and its feature. Try to use **All Features** to ensure that you are selecting the proper feature for the connection. Verify that you have the correct connections by referring to the screen captures that follow a number of connection instructions.

Each math function in the AdvCalc bean needs to be called when the corresponding button is clicked (see Figure 7.10). Make the following connections from the math buttons on the applet to their corresponding method in the invisible bean as follows:

pbSubtract (actionPerformed(java.awt.event.ActionEvent)) to calculator (subtract)

pbMultiply (actionPerformed(java.awt.event.ActionEvent)) to calculator (multiply)

pbDivide (actionPerformed(java.awt.event.ActionEvent)) to calculator (divide)

Adding a Clear Function

Another function that is common to calculators is a Clear function. There are several ways to implement this function:

1. Set properties in the GUI beans, as shown in Figure 7.11.
2. Set properties in the AdvCalc bean.
3. Create a class method that sets the variables.
4. Create a method in the AdvCalc bean that sets the properties.

Options 1 and 2 require three connections. These are not good options because each connection generates a new method in the class, additional visual clutter, larger code, and slower execution. Most important, with option 1 and 2, each additional TextField in the user interface would need an additional connection for the **Clear** button.

Figure 7.10 All math buttons connected.

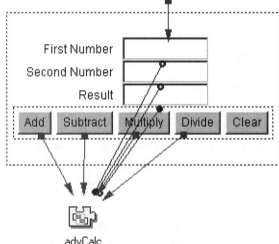

advCalc

Figure 7.11 Clearing fields.

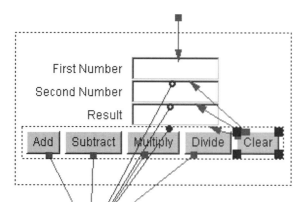

Option 3 is less costly, but it puts behavior for the bean at the applet level. It is usually better to place this function with the invisible bean. However, in some cases it is better to keep this type of function with the GUI bean.

Adding Another Method

For this applet, option 4 is a good option to implement. Add the clear() method to the AdvCalc bean with the following steps:

Go to the BeanInfo page of the AdvCalculatorLogic class browser.

Create a new method called **clear** with no return type (void) and no parameters.

Select the **Finish** button to save and generate the clear() method.

Now add the Java code to the clear() method to set the three properties to 0 with the following code segment:

```
setNum1(0);
setNum2(0);
setResult(0);
```

Save these changes to the code by selecting **Save** from the pop-up menu in the Source pane.

Although this is not the only way to clear the values for the Advanced Calculator, it is one of the best ways. It requires only two methods, one for the AdvCalc bean and one for the generated connection. It can be easily extended by adding additional code in the clear() method. This technique is even more efficient with user interfaces that have many properties to set. Each property change is merely another line of code.

Connecting the Clear Button

Now that there is a clear() method in the AdvCalc bean, you can call this method from the applet user interface. Make the following connection (see Figure 7.12):

pbClear (actionPerformed(java.awt.event.ActionEvent)) to AdvCalc (clear())

TIP

The previous example shows one of the better ways to minimize connections in the Visual Composition Editor. It may seem ironic, but connections need to be used sparingly to get the best performance results. By using connections only for higher-level function, the Visual Composition Editor view of the bean has fewer lines, is easier to understand, and easier to debug. This minimizes what is referred to as *visual spaghetti*.

Figure 7.12 All buttons connected.

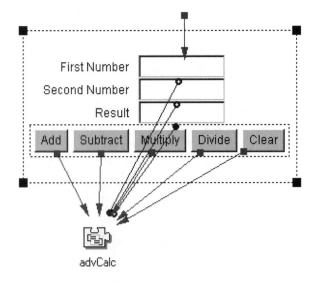

advCalc

Testing the Math Functions

Now that all the math functions and the clear function are complete, it is a good time to iterate and test the applet.

 Press the Test button on the upper tool bar of the Visual Composition Editor to generate and run the applet.

Enter numbers in the TextFields and try all the operations of the calculator. The **Result** field should show the correct value of the selected operation on the two numbers.

Try multiplying two really big numbers. The result will be *infinity*. This is a special Java term used for arithmetic results. (Hopefully, it will be needed to calculate our book royalties.)

Try multiplying a really big number and a really big negative number. The result will be *-infinity*, as shown in Figure 7.13. This is another special Java term used for arithmetic results. (This new term is possibly anticipating future calculation of the national debt.)

Try to divide a number by 0. What happens? The result is *NaN*, the Java term for *Not a Number*. The traditional math term for this is undefined, but at least Java translates a divide-by-zero error into something you can use.

Try the clear function: It should set all the fields to 0.0.

When you are finished close the applet viewer.

Figure 7.13 Multiply function.

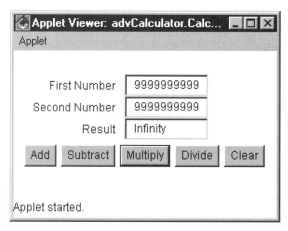

All the basic functions for the Advanced Calculator are complete. The Layout Manager works well, the focus is initially in the first TextField, all the math functions operate, and the clear function works.

Exception Handling

What happens if you enter 0 in the **Second Number** field and press the **Divide** button? The result of NaN is not very useful to most end-users. It would be much better to intercept this error and handle it programmatically. Exceptions are the standard way to handle errors in Java. Method calls that could throw an exception should be placed in a *try/catch* block. If the method throws an Exception, the code after the *catch* is executed.

The connections in the Visual Composition Editor generate methods that call the target in a *try/catch* block. The following code segment shows the code that calls the divide() method:

```
/**
 * conn7: (Button3.action.actionPerformed
   (java.awt.event.ActionEvent) -->
   advCalc.divide())
 * @param arg1 java.awt.event.ActionEvent
 */
/* WARNING: THIS METHOD WILL BE REGENERATED. */
private void conn7(java.awt.event.ActionEvent
     arg1) {
  try {
    // user code begin {1}
    // user code end
    getadvCalc().divide();
    // user code begin {2}
    // user code end
  } catch (java.lang.Throwable ivjExc) {
    // user code begin {3}
    // user code end
    handleException(ivjExc);
  }
}
```

That is because even though you are throwing the exception in the logic for the divide function, nobody is catching the exception. An appropriate action is to display a message to the user to let him or her know about the problem. This is easily incorporated into the CalculatorView by performing the following steps:

Using Exceptions

The declaration of the divide() method needs to be changed to indicate that it can throw an exception if division by zero is attempted.

```
public void divide() throws
   java.lang.ArithmeticException {
```

The code for the divide() method tests to see if the second operand, num2, is zero. If it is, an exception is created and thrown as shown in the following code segment. Make sure that your version of the method looks exactly as shown in the following code segment:

```
public void divide() throws
   java.lang.ArithmeticException {
if( getNum2() == 0 )
   throw( new java.lang.ArithmeticException("Divide by zero not
   allowed"));
else
   setResult( getNum1() / getNum2());
return;
}
```

If you select the **setResult(float)** method from either the BeanInfo tab or Methods tab of the class browser, you will see how the notification is sent to inform interested parties that the value of the *result* property has changed.

Importing a Bean

There are a few ways to notify the user of the exception message. You could have the computer beep, but that can be annoying. It is better to display an error in an information area or to display an error in a message box. Let's use a message box in the Advanced Calculator applet.

You could use the generic java.awt.Dialog bean, but it is not suited to easily display exceptions. An OKDialog bean is provided on the CD-ROM with this book that is designed to display exceptions. You can import OKDialog into the repository so you can add it to the Advanced Calculator. Follow these steps:

From the Workbench, select **Import** on the File menu.

From the Type of Import window shown in Figure 7.14, select **Project**.

After you have specified the Project and the type of import, press the **Next** button and Import Files dialog displays as shown in Figure 7.15.

From the Import Files window, select the OKDialog.class and the MultiLineLabel.class files. You may want to use the Browse button to select the files from a file dialog. Both of these classes are on the CD-ROM included with this book.

Press the **Finish** button to load OKDialog into VisualAge for Java.

Figure 7.14 Type of Import SmartGuide.

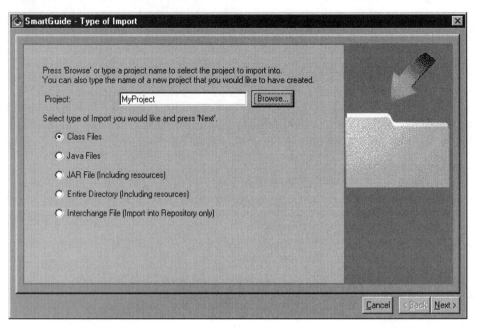

The OKDialog class uses the MultiLineLabel class to display the exception message. It must be imported with the OKDialog class for it to work properly.

Using a Message Box

Once the OKDialog bean is in the Workbench, you can use it with Java programs. Let's use it in the Advanced Calculator to display the exception to the user. Add the OKDialog bean as follows:

Go back to the class browser for the Advanced CalculatorView. Select **Add Beans** from the Options menu.

On the Add Beans window, select or enter **OKDialog** and press the **OK** button.

Place OKDialog on the free-form surface for Advanced Calculator. Call it errorDialog.

The OKDialog will be instantiated at run time, so all you need to do is call it when the exception is thrown by the AdvCalc bean. All of the connections in the Visual Composition Editor are generated as methods. The method calls inside connections are placed in a try/catch block. You will see examples of this convention later in this chapter when we review the code for connections. When an exception is thrown inside a try/catch block, the code after the catch is executed. This is the standard Java and C++ method for handling exceptions.

Figure 7.15 Import Files SmartGuide.

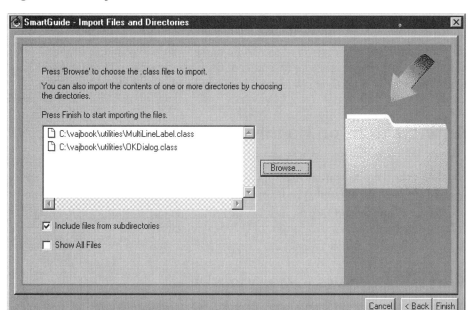

The connection from the pbDivide Button to the AdvCalc divide() method is executed in a try/catch block. The Visual Composition Editor enables you to make a connection that intercepts exceptions or return values from methods called in connections. You will make a connection from the pbDivide Button connection to the OKDialog bean. Connect the OKDialog bean with the following steps:

Click on the pbDivide (actionPerformed(java.awt.event.ActionEvent)) to calculator (divide) connection to select it.

Right-click on the selected connection; from the pop-up menu, select **Connect** and then **exceptionOccurred**, as shown in Figure 7.16.

Move the mouse to errorDialog and select the **showException(java.lang.Throwable)** method, which is found on the **All Features** list.

Notice that this a dashed or broken connection, which means it is a method call requiring one or more parameters. This connection merely displays the message box without any information. The exception object holds message text for the specific exception. You should pass this exception object as the parameter to the showException() method. This is easily accomplished in the Visual Composition Editor with the following steps:

Open properties for this new connection and select the **Pass event data** check box, as shown in Figure 7.17.

Select the **OK** button to save this change and close the property sheet.

This causes the Exception object to be passed as the parameter to the showException() method. Note that Exception is a subclass of Throwable, so it's a valid parameter type. The completed Advanced Calculator should look like Figure 7.18.

Testing Exception Handling

Let's see if this works. Save these changes and test it with the following:

- Press the Test button on the upper tool bar of the Visual Composition Editor to generate and run the applet.

- Run the applet and test the new connections by performing a calculation that divides by zero.

Figure 7.16 Connecting from an exception.

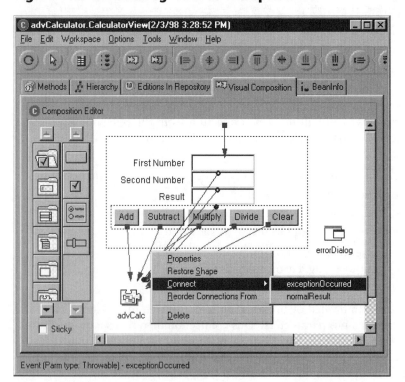

Figure 7.17 Exception connection properties.

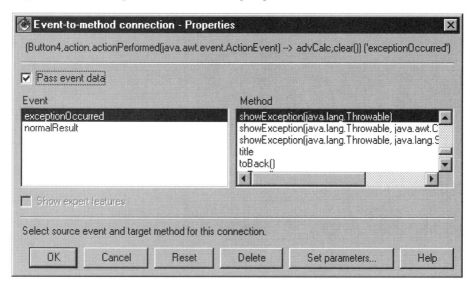

The exception is thrown and caught. The message box appears as shown in Figure 7.19, telling the user of the error.

Close the message box and close the applet when you are finished testing.

Figure 7.18 Completed connections.

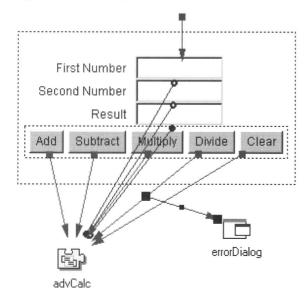

Figure 7.19 Message box display.

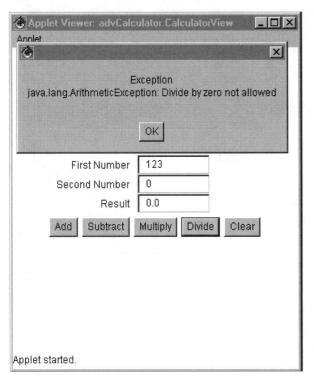

As you can see, it is easy to work with exceptions using VisualAge for Java. However, it can become tedious to add connections for all the exception handling. When you are developing larger applications, you will need to look at developing an exception handler bean. This bean would handle the exceptions caught for the application.

How Does the Exception Work?

This seems like magic: How do the connections handle the exception? Let's look at the code for the connections to see how it works. As discussed earlier, each connection is a method that is generated by the Visual Composition Editor. Each connection method is automatically named by the Visual Composition Editor as *connX()*, where X is the number of the connection. You can see all the connections on the Methods page of the Advanced Calculator.

Analyzing Connections

You need to find out the connection name for the **Divide** button connection. The information area in the Visual Composition Editor displays the connection name. Let's find out the name of the Divide connection by the following:

From the Visual Composition Editor for the Advanced Calculator, select the Divide connection.

Look in the information area at the bottom of the Visual Composition Editor as shown in Figure 7.20. The Divide connection is conn7, which means that the Visual Composition Editor generates a conn7() method in the CalculatorView bean.

> **NOTE**
>
> Your connection numbers may be different than those in this book. You may have made the connections in a different order, you may have changed connections, or you may have deleted a connection. All of these actions can affect how connections numbers are assigned, so your method may have a different connection number.

Figure 7.20 Divide connection.

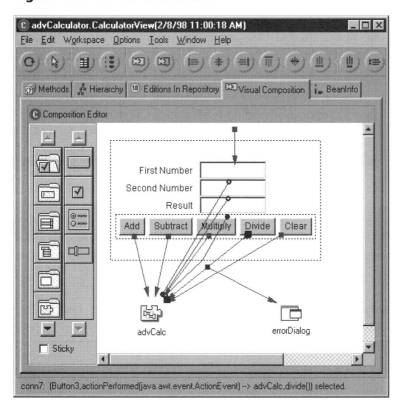

If you go to the Methods page, you can select and view the code for conn7(). The following code segment shows the method for the **Divide** button:

```
/**
 * conn7: (Button3.action.actionPerformed
   (java.awt.event.ActionEvent) -->
   advCalc.divide())
 * @param arg1 java.awt.event.ActionEvent
 */
/* WARNING: THIS METHOD WILL BE REGENERATED. */
private void conn7(java.awt.event.ActionEvent
    arg1) {
  try {
    // user code begin {1}
    // user code end
    getadvCalc().divide();
    // user code begin {2}
    // user code end
  } catch (java.lang.Throwable ivjExc) {
    // user code begin {3}
    // user code end
    conn9(ivjExc);
    handleException(ivjExc);
  }
}
```

As you read the code, it makes good sense. The connection method calls the AdvCalc divide() method inside a try/catch block. The exception is caught. The Visual Composition Editor generated a method call to another connection method, in this case conn9, which passes the exception as a parameter. Let's look at the code for conn9 in the following code segment:

```
/**
 * conn9:  (
(Button3,action.actionPerformed(java.awt.event.ActionEvent) -->
advCalc,divide()).exceptionOccurred -->
errorDialog.showException(java.lang.Throwable))
 * @param exception java.lang.Throwable
 */
/* WARNING: THIS METHOD WILL BE REGENERATED. */
private void conn9(Throwable exception) {
  try {
    // user code begin {1}
    // user code end
    geterrorDialog().showException(new java.lang.Throwable());
```

```
    // user code begin {2}
    // user code end
} catch (java.lang.Throwable ivjExc) {
    // user code begin {3}
    // user code end
    handleException(ivjExc);
  }
}
```

This connection method calls errorDialog's showException() method, passing the exception as a parameter. In this case, the Visual Composition Editor generates all the code to catch the error and display it to the user. You could circumvent this connection by adding a call to the errorDialog's showException() method after the catch statement in the Divide connection method.

Modifying the Bean Palette

As described earlier in the book, the bean palette on the left side of the Visual Composition Editor contains standard AWT beans that are supplied with VisualAge for Java. You may want to add other frequently used AWT beans or your own beans to the bean palette. The OKDialog is very helpful; you may want to use it in other programs for displaying exceptions. Try adding this bean to the palette as follows:

Select the Visual Composition page of the class browser for the Advanced Calculator.

From the Options menu, select **Modify Palette** and then **Add New Bean**.

The Add to Palette window appears as seen in Figure 7.21, where you can specify the information for the bean as follows:

This is a **Class** bean, so leave this radio button selected.

Use the **Browse** button to specify the fully qualified path for the OKDialog bean.

Select **Containers** from the **Category** list.

Press the **OK** button when you are finished.

If you go to the Containers category and scroll to the bottom of the list, you can see the OKDialog bean. The modified palette is saved with the Workbench when you exit. When you open class browsers for other beans, the OKDialog will be on the bean palette for you to use.

It is also possible to add new bean categories and even delete AWT beans that you rarely use. The beans are retained in the repository; the bean palette only refers to beans that are loaded in the workspace.

Figure 7.21 Add to Palette window.

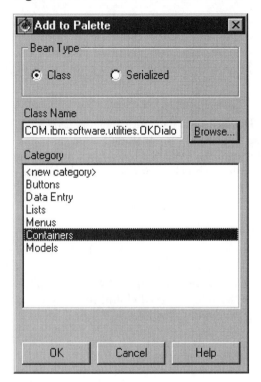

Making a Numeric-Only TextField

The Advanced Calculator uses the same AWT TextField GUI bean that you used in the Simple Calculator. When you tested the Advanced Calculator, you might have found that you could use alphabetic characters in the TextFields. It would be good if the TextFields prevented the user from entering characters other than numerals.

Importing More Java Files

A bean called **IntTextField**, provided on the CD-ROM with this book, can help solve this problem. IntTextField has a number of constructors and methods, so you will load this prebuilt bean instead of building it. Import the IntTextField into the repository and the workspace with the following steps:

In the Workbench, select the My Project project.

From the File menu, select Import. The Import SmartGuide appears as shown in Figure 7.22.

Figure 7.22 Import SmartGuide.

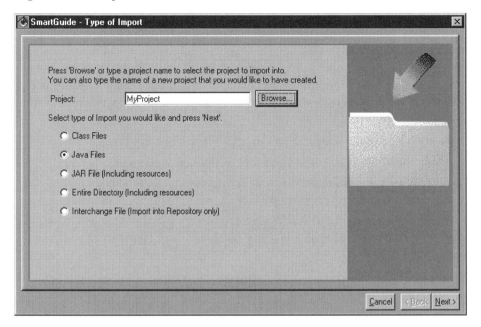

Now you can enter the information needed to load the .java files into the Workbench with the following steps:

Make sure that **My Project** is entered in the **Project** field.

Select the **Java files** radio button, then select the **Next** button. The Import Files SmartGuide appears.

Select the **Browse** button and choose the **FilteredTextField.java** and the **IntTextField.java** files. These files are added to the Import Files SmartGuide as shown in Figure 7.23.

Make sure the **Include files from subdirectories** check box is selected.

Select the **Finish** button to start loading the .java files. After the .java files are loaded, they can be viewed in the Workbench.

Using a Filtered TextField

Now that you have IntTextField loaded in the workspace, you can add it to the Advanced Calculator.

From the Options menu, select **Add Bean**.

Select **IntTextField** using the **Browse** button in the Add Bean window, as shown in Figure 7.24.

Then press the **OK** button to load the cursor with the IntTextField bean.

Move the mouse to the free-form surface and drop the IntTextField bean.

Switching GUI Beans

One of the neat things about working in the Visual Composition Editor is that it is easy to update your programs by switching beans. In this section, you replace the standard AWT TextFields with the recently imported IntTextField. Switch the beans with the following steps:

Select the efNum1 TextField and drag it to the free-form surface.

Move the IntTextField to the grid where efNum1 used to be.

After you have substituted the IntTextField for the TextField, set the IntTextField *columns* property to 10.

The substituted IntTextField in the Advanced Calculator should look like Figure 7.25. You might need to resize the applet to get the IntTextField to display showing 10 columns.

Repeat the previous steps and substitute an IntTextField for the efNum2 and efResult TextFields.

Figure 7.23 Import files SmartGuide.

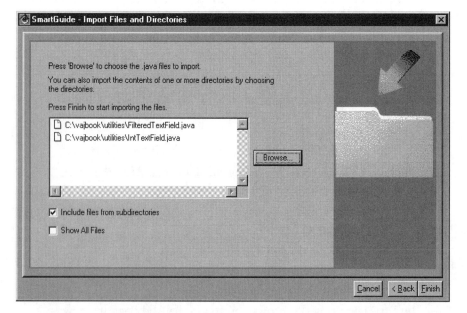

Figure 7.24 Add Bean window.

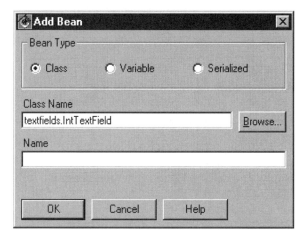

> **NOTE**
>
> The efResult TextField does not accept input, so it does not really need to be changed to be an IntTextField. If you do not change the efResult field, the Advanced Calculator will still run correctly. For consistency, it is probably a good idea to use the IntTextField.

Figure 7.25 Substituting an IntTextField.

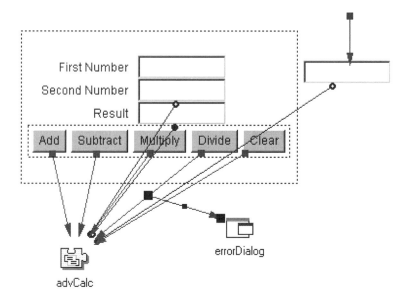

Changing Connections

You can move connections between beans just as you did when you replaced the CalculatorLogic bean with the AdvCalculatorLogic bean. You can drag either end of a connection to a new source or target.

Select the connection from efNum1 to the *num1* property.

Move the TextField end of the connection to the corresponding IntTextField in the Applet.

Repeat these steps for the efNum2 and efResult TextFields.

If you substituted the efResult TextField with an IntTextField, you get a warning, as shown in Figure 7.26. You can ignore this warning and press the **Yes** button. The Visual Composition Editor generates the correct code for the conversion.

TIP

Sometimes it is easier to redraw simple connections. If you have problems moving these simple connections you may want to just redraw them. However, you will find that connections with a number of parameters are much easier to move than to redraw.

Delete all the old TextFields that are on the free-form surface.

Rename all the new IntTextField beans to IntTextFieldNum1, IntTextFieldNum2, and IntTextFieldResult.

When all the TextFields are replaced with the IntTextFields, the Visual Composition Editor looks like Figure 7.27. The applet looks as it did before you added the IntTextFields.

Figure 7.26 Warning for incompatible types.

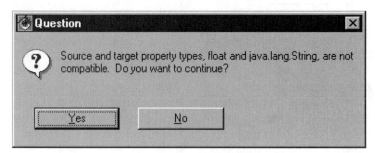

Figure 7.27 All TextFields replaced.

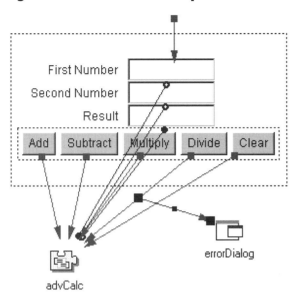

> **NOTE**
>
> If you have VisualAge for Java Version 1.0 installed and have not applied any of the patches, the IntTextField does not work properly in the IDE. When you test the IntTextField in the IDE, it allows you to enter any character. The Entry edition provided on the CD-ROM with this book has a patch applied, and the IntTextField works properly in the IDE.

Testing the IntTextFields

Let's see if this works. Save these changes and test the applet with the following:

Press the Test button on the upper tool bar of the Visual Composition Editor to generate and run the applet as seen in Figure 7.28.

Run the applet and try entering numbers in the TextFields. All the calculation functions should work.

Try entering alphabetic characters in the TextFields. You should not be able to enter characters in the IntTextFields.

When you are finished testing the applet, close it.

Figure 7.28 Running Advanced Calculator.

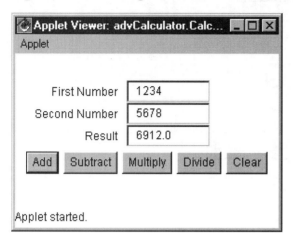

How Does the IntTextField Work?

Because you did not develop the IntTextField bean, you probably want to see how it works. This section will show you the classes used to make the IntTextField and how the code works.

IntTextField Hierarchy

If you open the IntTextField, you see its superclasses as shown in Figure 7.29. IntTextField is a subclass or FilteredTextField, which is a subclass of TextField. FilteredTextField is an abstract class that defines behavior for the IntTextField bean. We could have directly subclassed the TextField, but it is a more flexible design to subclass the FilteredTextField.

After you have reviewed the code for the IntTextField bean, you will be prepared to make other subclasses of the FilteredTextField class, like an AlphaTextField or an UpperCaseTextField. You should use the browser to review the constructors and methods for both the IntTextField and FilteredTextField beans.

IntTextField Source Code

The key method in the IntTextField bean is the filter() method. The code for the filter() method is shown in the following code segment:

```
/**
 * filter method comment.
 */
protected void filter(java.awt.event.KeyEvent e) {
  String allChars = "0123456789";
  String allSigns = "-+";
```

Figure 7.29 IntTextField hierarchy.

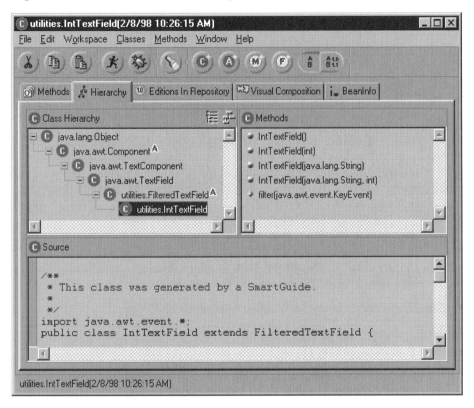

```java
char aChar = e.getKeyChar();
if(e.isActionKey() == true) {
  return;
}
if(((int)aChar == KeyEvent.VK_DELETE) || ((int)aChar ==
KeyEvent.VK_BACK_SPACE))
  return;
else
if( (allSigns.indexOf((int)aChar) != -1 ) &&
  (getCaretPosition() == 0) ){
  return;
}
else
if( (aChar == '.') && (getText().indexOf('.')
  == -1)){
  return;
}
```

```
  else
  if( allChars.indexOf((int)aChar) != -1) {
    return;
  }
  else {
    e.consume();
  }
}
```

Two Strings (allChars and allSigns) hold the allowed characters for the IntTextField. The *if* statement handles the different types of characters that may be pressed. As each valid character is parsed, the method *returns*. Finally, all invalid characters are consumed at the end of the *if* statement. This is the preferred design for filtering characters in TextFields, because the consume() method prevents the characters from displaying.

Summary

Well, this chapter covered a lot of topics. You built a Java program with a bit more function using VisualAge for Java. In this chapter, you:

- Extended invisible beans with additional methods.
- Added exception handling to an applet.
- Used a message box to display an exception.
- Modified the bean palette.
- Used a numeric-only TextField.
- Learned how to switch beans and connections in the Visual Composition Editor.

Each chapter is building on the information used in the previous chapters. This is about all you will do to the Calculator applet. In the next chapters, you create new programs using VisualAge for Java. You will learn additional tips and techniques that will aide you in building beans with VisualAge for Java.

DEPLOYING JAVA

What's in Chapter 8

Now that you have used VisualAge for Java to build several applications and applets, you are ready to distribute the programs to others. This chapter covers the considerations for deploying your applet to the World Wide Web or your application to the desktop. Additionally, you will learn how to share your code with other developers:

- Exporting code from the IDE
- Running applets outside of the IDE
- Running applications outside of the IDE on the Desktop
- Distributing beans

VisualAge for Java is a powerful tool for building both applets and applications in Java. However, to fully realize the fruit of your labors, you will want to make your work available to both end users and other developers. With VisualAge for Java, you have several options for deploying and sharing your code. The following sections cover specific information about how you can place your applets on a web server and your applications on a user desktop. Additionally, this chapter discusses and gives advice on how to effectively share code with other developers without compromising source code integrity.

Exporting from VisualAge

When you are working in the IDE, all source code is stored in a monolithic repository. Using this repository allows you to version, compare code across versions, and to apply complex configurations to your code for multiple customer situations. For more information on the repository, see Chapter 2. While there are many benefits to using the repository, you must export the code from the repository at some point if you want to enable others to use or share the code. VisualAge offers several means and file formats for accomplishing the goal of exporting. You can export your work from VisualAge to byte-code, source code, .jar file format and a VisualAge-specific format: the interchange file (.dat).

Exporting Java Byte-Code (.class Files)

When using VisualAge for Java, the compiled source code (byte-code) is stored in the workspace. In order to use the code outside of the IDE, you must export it to the file system. One option is to export the byte-code as .class files.

Why Export Java Byte-Code

To use the application, applet, or bean outside of the VisualAge IDE, you must export them to the file system. Exporting byte-code, or .class files, is an excellent choice for initial attempts at deployment. By exporting each Java class as a .class file, you are able to make modifications and only have to export those classes that changed. Once you have successfully deployed a set of .class files, you will probably want to examine the use of .jar files or the VisualAge Publish option.

A .class file can be reimported into your VisualAge for Java workspace. These .class files can also be given to other VisualAge for Java developers for importing. However, this makes the byte-code available only and essentially hides the source code.

When exporting byte-code as .class files from VisualAge for Java, you can export projects, packages, classes, and interfaces. You may not export classes or interfaces that contain unresolved problems, classes that were previously imported as .class files, or individual methods.

TIP

It is possible to have two different versions with the same name in the repository at the same time. It is much better to have a unique name for each version for easy identification. You should reversion the items with unique names to reduce confusion.

An Example of Exporting Java Byte-Code

An IBM-supplied sample, COM.ibm.ivj.examples.vc.todolist, can be used for demonstrating how to export byte-code (.class files) from VisualAge. This sample is found in the **IBM Java Examples** project.

If not already started, start the VisualAge IDE.

Select the program elements that you want to export. For this example, select the **COM.ibm.ivj.examples.vc.todolist** package.

Select **Export** from the File menu, as shown in Figure 8.1.

The Export SmartGuide appears with the **Java Files** radio button selected. Depending on the type of program elements that you selected, some radio buttons might not be available as seen in Figure 8.2.

Select the **Class Files** radio button.

Select the **Next** button to specify the directory to export your .class files.

As shown in Figure 8.3, ensure that the **Create package subdirectories** radio button is selected, then select the **Browse** button to open a file dialog.

Use the file dialog, shown in Figure 8.4, to locate the target directory: the directory where you want to place your exported .class files. For this example, create a subdirectory under C:\ called **myexports**. Use the New Folder button in the top right-hand corner of the file dialog to create a new folder named myexports.

Close the file dialog by clicking the **OK** button and clicking the **Finish** button on the Export SmartGuide. VisualAge exports the .class files for the classes in the selected package to the C:\myexports directory.

Later in this chapter we will discuss how to run applets outside the builder. To run the ToDoList applet, you can use the Sun JDK *appletviewer* tool. You

Figure 8.1 Exporting byte-code.

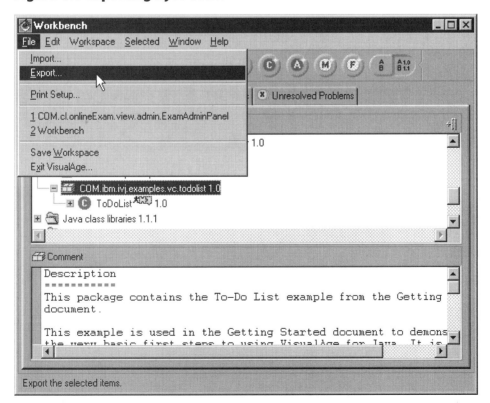

> **NOTE**
>
> Because you selected the **Create packages sub-directories** radio but-
> ton, VisualAge created a directory for each part of the package name. If
> the directories already exist, the export function reuses the existing direc-
> tories. For example, the package you exported (COM.ibm.ivj.exam-
> ples.vc.todolist) created the directory tree under C:/my exports as shown
> in Figure 8.5.

must supply an HTML file with an applet tag. Refer to Running Applets Outside
of the IDE, later in this chapter, for more information.

Exporting Java Source (.java Files)

When building beans, applets, or applications in VisualAge for Java, the source
code is stored in the repository. To share the source code with developers that use
tools other than VisualAge for Java, you must export to the file system in the
form of **.java** files.

Figure 8.2 Export SmartGuide: byte-code.

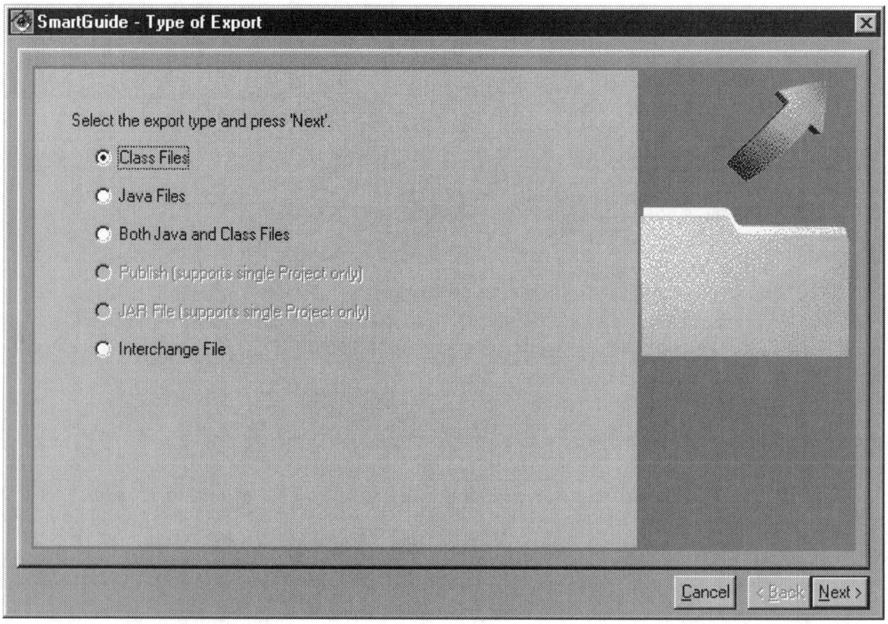

Figure 8.3 Export to Files options: byte-code.

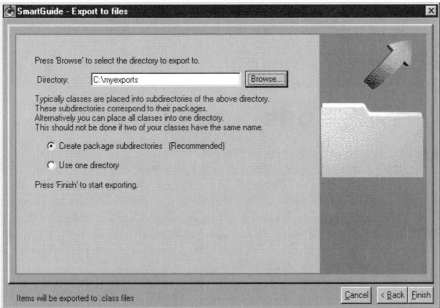

Why Export Java Source

In order to share Java source code (including beans) outside of VisualAge for Java or with other code maintenance systems, you must export the source files (.java files) to

Figure 8.4 File dialog.

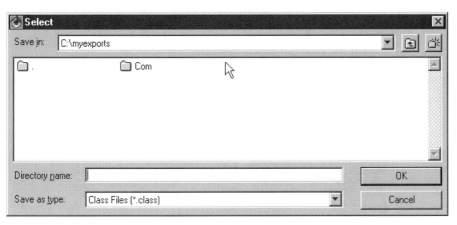

Figure 8.5 Directory structure for a package.

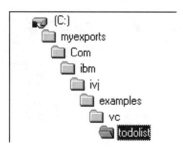

the file system. Exporting Java source (.java files), and Java archive (.jar) files are the only mechanisms for sharing source with non-VisualAge users and tools.

Java source files can be reimported into the VisualAge for Java repository. Additionally, these .java files can be given to other VisualAge for Java developers for importing. When .java files are imported, the VisualAge for Java IDE creates another edition of the class, stores the source code into the repository, and compiles the byte-code in the workspace.

An important consideration when exporting to .java files is the use of the Visual Composition Editor. Java source files do not contain VisualAge for Java connection information. Classes built with the Visual Composition Editor should not be exported as .java files if they are to be shared with other VisualAge for Java developers.

When exporting Java source code as .java files, you can export projects, packages, classes, and interfaces. Classes and interfaces with unresolved problems may also be exported as .java files. You may not export individual methods or classes that were previously imported as .class files.

An Example of Exporting Java Source

An IBM-supplied sample, COM.ibm.ivj.examples.vc.todolist, can be used to demonstrate how to export Java source (.java files) from VisualAge. This sample is found in the **IBM Java Examples** project.

If VisualAge is not already started, start the IDE.

Select the program elements that you want to export. For this example, select the **COM.ibm.ivj.examples.vc.todolist** package.

Select **Export** from the File menu, as shown in Figure 8.6.

The Export SmartGuide appears with the **Java Files** radio button selected as seen in Figure 8.7. Depending on the type of program elements that you selected, some radio buttons might not be available.

Select the **Next** button to specify the directory where you want the exported .java files to go.

Ensure that the **Create package subdirectories** radio button is selected as seen in Figure 8.8, then select the **Browse** button to open a file dialog.

Use the file dialog shown in Figure 8.9 to locate the target directory; the directory where you want to place your exported .java files. For the example, use the c:\myexports directory.

Close the file dialog by clicking the **OK** button and clicking the **Finish** button on the Export SmartGuide. VisualAge exports all of the .java files for the classes in the selected package to the C:\myexports directory.

> **NOTE**
>
> Because you selected the **Create package subdirectories** radio button, VisualAge creates (or reuses, if existing) a directory for each part of the package name. For example, the package you exported (COM .ibm.ivj.examples.vc.todolist) created the directory tree under C:\myexports as shown in Figure 8.10.

Figure 8.6 Exporting Java source code.

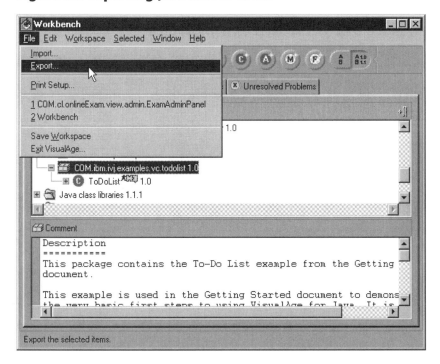

Figure 8.7 Export SmartGuide: source code.

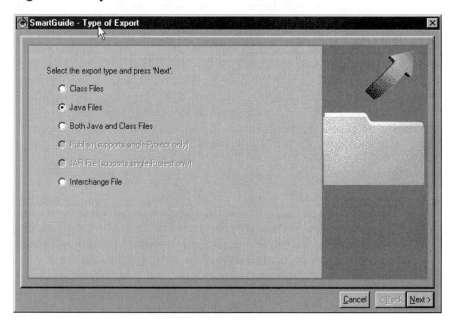

Figure 8.8 Export to Files options: source.

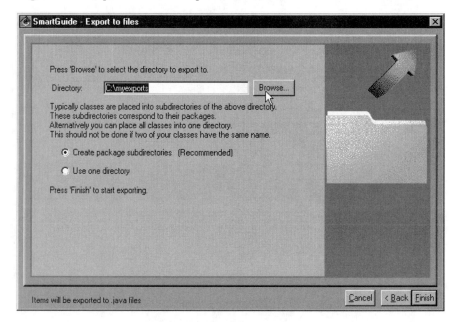

Figure 8.9 File dialog.

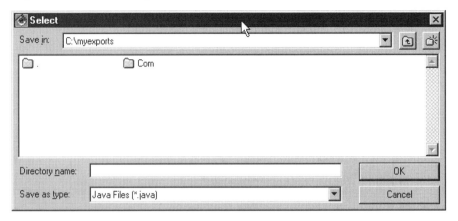

Java Archives (.jar Files)

JAR files, more precisely known as *Java Archives*, are new to the Java Development Kit 1.1 specification. JAR files enable you to package byte-code and resource files into a single, compressed file. Resource files are those files necessary for proper execution of your application or applet. Resource files include audio files, image files, video files and other files used by your applet or application.

Why Export Java Archives

In order to use the application, applet, or bean outside of the VisualAge IDE, you must export it to the file system. Exporting Java Archives, or .jar files, is an excellent choice for final deployment. By exporting your Java classes in a .jar file, your byte codes and resource files are compressed for performance and faster network transport. Exporting .jar files also enables you to export beans to give to colleagues.

Figure 8.10 Directory structure for a package.

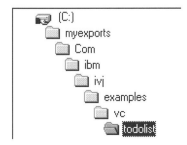

While JAR files are typically used to hold byte-code and resource files, you can put anything into a JAR file. If fact, you can use JAR files as portable source archives by exporting your code from VisualAge to .java files and using the JAR utility outside of VisualAge to assemble the JAR file.

A .jar file can be reimported into your VisualAge for Java workspace. The .jar files can also be given to other VisualAge for Java developers for importing. In fact, JAR files are the mechanism of choice for sharing beans with other developers.

When exporting byte-code as .jar files from VisualAge for Java, you can only export projects. You cannot export an individual package, class, interface, or method.

Exporting a Java Archive

A sample supplied with VisualAge for Java, sunw.demo.juggler.juggler, can be used for demonstrating how to export a Java Archive (.jar) file from VisualAge. This sample is found in the **Sun BDK Examples** project.

If VisualAge is not already started, start the IDE.

Select the project to export. For this example, select the **Sun BDK Examples** project.

Select **Export** from the File menu.

The Export SmartGuide appears with the **Java Files** radio button selected. Depending on the type of program elements that you selected, some radio buttons might not be available.

Select the **JAR File** radio button seen in Figure 8.11, then select the **Next** button.

Do not select any classes to be marked as beans at this point. Select the **Browse** button seen in Figure 8.12 to open a file dialog.

Use the file dialog to locate the target directory, the directory where you want to place your exported .jar files. For the example, use the **c:\MyExports** directory. Name the file **juggler.jar** (see Figure 8.13). Select the Juggler class to be marked as a bean and click the **OK** button on the file dialog, followed by the **Finish** button on the SmartGuide.

VisualAge exports all of the classes in the selected project to the C:\myexports\juggler.jar file. Exporting and compressing the .jar file takes some time. A message box informs you that the .jar file is being created seen in Figure 8.14.

The JAR file includes all the Java binary class files (.class files) for the project, all resources for the project, and a manifest file. The resources are from the project_resources directory for the project. VisualAge creates the manifest file and marks all classes selected in the bean list as JavaBeans.

Figure 8.11 Export SmartGuide: Java Archive.

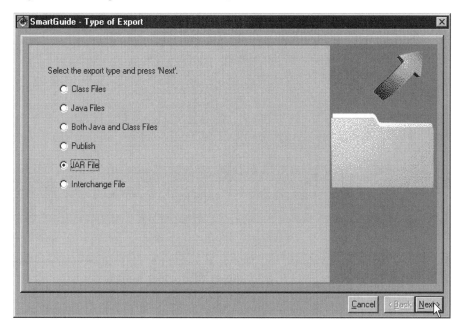

Figure 8.12 Export JAR file options.

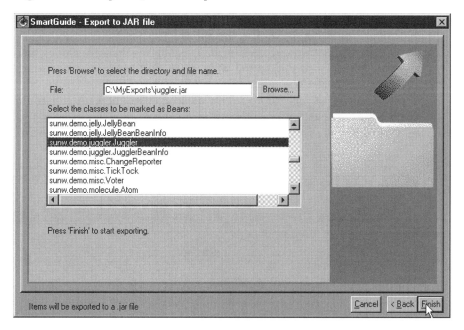

Figure 8.13 File dialog.

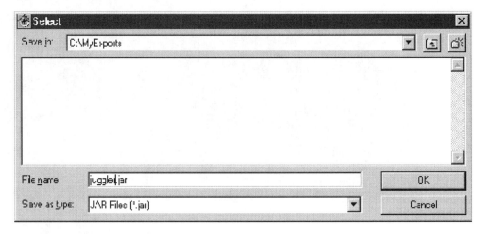

After exporting the .jar file, you need an HTML file to run the juggler object from the JAR file. Figure 8.15 shows the juggler.html file.

One way to help you write your HTML file when deploying your applet is to run the applet from within the VisualAge IDE. The VisualAge applet viewer prompts you for input and shows you HTML code for the *codebase*, *classpath*, *name*, *height*, and *width* attributes of the <applet> tag and for run-time parameters (<param> tag), as shown in Figure 8.16.

Figure 8.17 shows the running juggler applet. It will juggle the JavaBeans.

How VisualAge Uses Resource Files

VisualAge stores resource files in the file system. VisualAge does not store them in the repository or in the workspace. VisualAge creates a resources directory for each project you create. VisualAge does not create, edit, manage, or delete resource files for you. You must manage the project resources directory, subdirectories, and resource files. In the resources directory for a project, you can leave the files at one level or group them into subdirectories. If you

Figure 8.14 Exporting Archive message box.

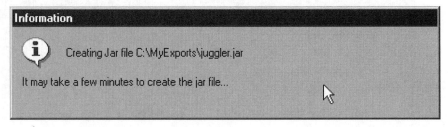

Figure 8.15 juggler.html file.

```
<HTML>
<HEAD>
<TITLE> Juggler </TITLE>
</HEAD>
<BODY>
Here is the output of my program:
<applet
      code="sunw.demo.juggler.Juggler" archive="juggler.jar"
      width=200 height=200 name="Hi There">
<param name=name value="Hi There">
</applet>
</BODY>
</HTML>
```

group them, your code must specify a path that is relative to the project's resources directory.

When you import a project from a JAR file, VisualAge extracts any resource files stored in the JAR file and copies them to the project's resources directory.

Figure 8.16 Running the applet in VisualAge.

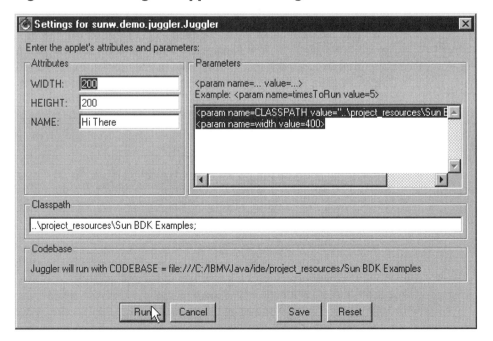

Figure 8.17 Juggler applet in applet viewer.

When you export a project as a JAR file, VisualAge copies the resource files from the project's resources directory and includes them in the JAR file with their directory structure intact.

When you run a program that uses resource files, the program can access resource files using several means:

- The **getResource**() method can be used to get resources. If the program specifies a ClassLoader, it can specify where to look for resource files. If the program does not specify a ClassLoader, it looks for resource files on the class path. If the program is an applet being run by the applet viewer, it looks for resource files first in the class path and then in the code base as specified in environment variables or HTML parameters.

- The **getSystemResource**() method can get system-level resources. The program looks for resource files on the class path.

- If the program is an applet, there are two ways to access resources, **getAudioClip**() and **getImage**(). The applet looks for resource files in the code base. If a bean inside the applet needs resource files, it looks for them in the bean's code base.

If you export the applet as a .class file and the applet uses resource files, you must copy the resource files to the directory where you export the applet files. If the applet uses resource files, they must be in the project_resources directory for the project that contains the applet class. Copy the resource files to the same directory where the exported applet class is located.

VisualAge Interchange Format (.dat Files)

VisualAge provides a common format for exchange of source code between multiple VisualAge for Java environments. This describes the same source management architecture used by many popular Smalltalk environments (VisualAge for Smalltalk, ParcPlace Smalltalk); the concepts are the same. **An interchange file is the only way to share visual connection information with other developers.** If you export a class built using the Visual Composition Editor as a .java or .jar file, you lose all of the Visual Composition (connections) information. To preserve the connection information, export the class to an interchange file.

You can export an entire project or individual packages in a format that can be imported easily into another VisualAge for Java workspace. Interchange files do not include resource files. The interchange file includes:

- Program elements (including project and package comments)
- Applet settings
- Information that the Visual Composition Editor uses (connections)

You can only export editions of entire projects or individual packages that have been versioned. However, these projects or packages may contain elements that have unresolved problems. You cannot export individual classes, interfaces, methods, or a project or package that is an open edition.

TIP

The resource files for the beans in a project are kept in a subdirectory with the Project's name. You need to copy these resource files and distribute them with the program. You should also backup the resource files in case of hardware problems.

Exporting an Interchange File

An IBM-supplied sample, COM.ibm.ivj.examples.vc.todolist, can be used for demonstrating how to export to an interchange (.dat) file from VisualAge. This sample is found in the **IBM Java Examples** project.

If VisualAge is not already started, start the IDE.

Select the program elements that you want to export. For this example, select the **COM.ibm.ivj.examples.vc.todolist** package.

Select **Export** from the Workbench File menu.

The Export SmartGuide appears with the **Java Files** radio button selected. Depending on the type of program elements that you selected, some radio buttons might not be available as seen in Figure 8.18.

Figure 8.18 Export SmartGuide: interchange file.

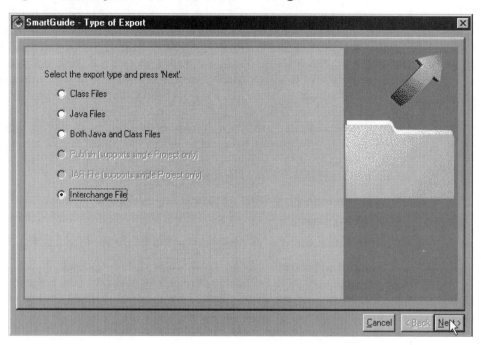

Select the **Interchange File** radio button.

Select the **Next** button and the **Browse** button to open a file dialog as shown in Figure 8.19.

Use the file dialog to locate the target directory, the directory where you want to place your exported .dat file. For this example, create a subdirectory under C:\ called **myexports**. The name of the interchange file is **ToDoList.dat**.

Close the file dialog by clicking the **OK** button and clicking the **Finish** button on the Export SmartGuide. VisualAge exports the .dat file for the classes in the selected package to the C:\myexports directory.

Publishing Programs

You publish a project from the workspace to export the byte-code and resource files for an entire project to the file system. Publish a project when you want to ship the project. The exported files include binary class files and all resource files. You cannot publish an individual package, class, interface, or method.

Figure 8.19 File dialog.

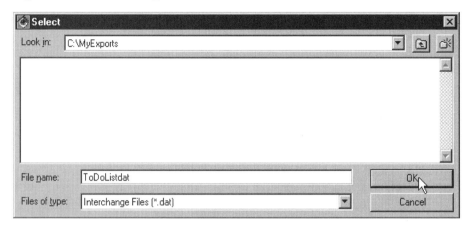

An Example of Publishing a Project

An IBM-supplied sample, COM.ibm.ivj.examples.vc.todolist, can be used for demonstrating how to publish a project in VisualAge. This sample is found in the **IBM Java Examples** project.

> If VisualAge is not already started, start the IDE.

> Select the program elements that you want to publish. For this example, select the **IBM Java Examples** project.

> Select **Export** from the File menu.

The Export SmartGuide appears with the **Java Files** radio button selected. Depending on the type of program elements that you selected, some radio buttons might not be available. Select **Publish** (Figure 8.20).

> Select the **Next** button to specify the directory to publish your project to and the Publish Project SmartGuide displays as seen in Figure 8.21.

> Use the file dialog seen in Figure 8.22 to locate the target directory, the directory where you want to place your published classes. For this example, create a subdirectory under C:\ called **myexports**.

> Close the file dialog by clicking the **OK** button and clicking the **Finish** button on the Export SmartGuide. VisualAge publishes the project to the C:\myexports directory.

Running Applets Outside of the IDE

When you export an applet, you need to export all of its dependent packages as well. You do not need to export the Sun Java class libraries; the web

Figure 8.20 Export SmartGuide: Publish.

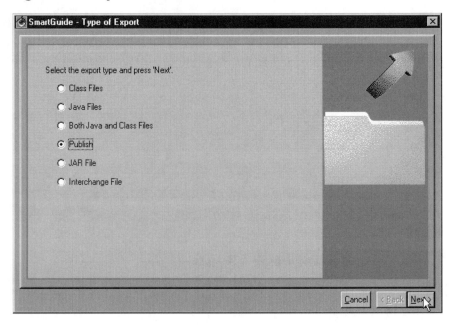

Figure 8.21 SmartGuide: Publish Project.

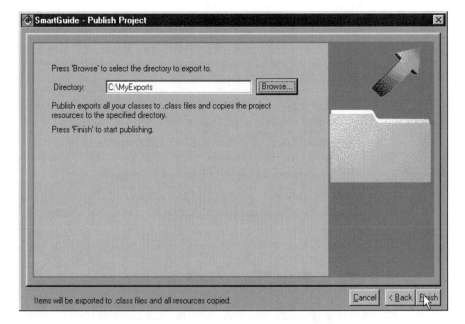

Figure 8.22 File dialog.

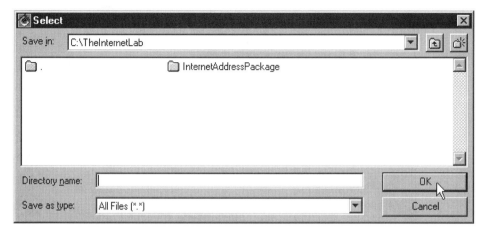

browser should include these. When you export .jar files or publish packages, VisualAge does not require you to find all the dependent classes. You must ensure that you have exported all dependent packages in order for you applet to work properly.

Additionally, you must ensure that all resource files used by the applet are placed in the appropriate directory. Exporting to a .jar file or using the publish option can help to ensure that resource files get put in the right place. However, these options only work if you have previously placed the resource files in the **project_resources** directory for the project that contains the applet class.

Making HTML Files

Deploying your applet requires you write an HTML file. You can use VisualAge to generate this for you. Run your applet from the VisualAge applet viewer. Select **tag** from the Applet menu to see the HTML code used for the applet viewer as seen in Figure 8.23.

The Applet HTML Tag window shows the basic HTML code you need to run your applet. You can cut and paste this code to a file. Figure 8.24 shows a listing of basic HTML required to run your applet.

If your applet is specified in a .jar file, remember that although a .jar file is compressed, the entire file is always downloaded. You need to ensure that you place only the items that need to be together in the appropriate .jar file, or your applet will download classes that are not needed. Exporting .class files provides your applet with what you need. However, the .class file is not compressed, and the browser must initiate a separate URL request to the server for each .class file.

Figure 8.23 Viewing HTML code for running applet.

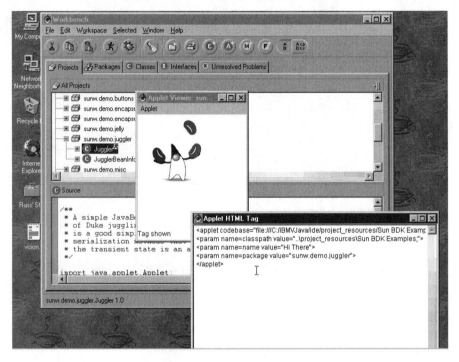

Figure 8.24 Basic HTML for running an applet.

```
<APPLET
    CODE = applet-filename
    WIDTH = pixel-width
    HEIGHT = pixel-height
    OBJECT = serialized-applet-filename
    ARCHIVE = comma-separated-jar-filename-list
    CODEBASE = applet-url
    ALT = alternative-text
    NAME = applet-name
    ALIGN = alignment
    VSPACE = pixel-vertical-margin
    HSPACE = pixel-horizontal-margin
>
<PARAM NAME = parameter VALUE = value>
<PARAM NAME = parameter VALUE = value>
. . .
alternate-text
</APPLET>
```

Tag	Description
APPLET	Specifies the applet to be loaded and run.
	If the applet viewer or web browser does not recognize Java applets, text after the ALT tag is displayed.
CODE	Required attribute specifies the .class file containing the applet class. Must be relative to the CODEBASE or the document URL.
CODEBASE	Optional attribute specifies the base URL of the applet. Should be a directory, not a file.
	If not specified, the URL of the document is used.
WIDTH	Required attribute specifies the initial width in pixels that the applet uses.
HEIGHT	Required attribute specifies the initial height in pixels that the applet uses.
OBJECT	Required attribute specifies the .class file containing a serialized applet class.
	Must be relative to the CODEBASE or the document URL
ARCHIVE	Optional attribute specifies a comma separated list of .jar files to be preloaded by the applet viewer or web browser.
	Must be relative to the CODEBASE or the document URL.
ALT	Optional attribute specifies alternative text to be displayed by a web browser that does not support Java applets.
VSPACE	Optional attribute specifies vertical margin in pixels.
HSPACE	Optional attribute specifies horizontal margin in pixels.
NAME	Optional attribute specifies the name of the applet instance.
ALIGN	Optional attribute specifies the alignment of the applet on the web page.

Running Applications Outside of the IDE

When you export the application .class files, you need to export all of the dependent packages as well. You do not need to export the Sun Java class libraries; the local Java VM will provide these. When you export .jar files or publish packages, VisualAge does not require you to find all the dependent classes. You must ensure that you have exported all dependent packages in order for your application to work properly.

If you do not publish the project that contains the application, or do not export the application as a .jar file, and if the application uses resource files, you must copy the resource files to the directory where you export the application files. If the application uses resource files, they are in the project_resources directory for the project that contains the application.

It is essential that the CLASSPATH environment variable be set to a default directory where your Java applications will run. When distributing the applications across the enterprise, you may want to create a batch file to set the CLASS-PATH variable for each application. Or you could use the '.' current directory indicator in your CLASSPATH to use the current directory as the starting point for finding the applications. You will also have to explicitly list each .jar file in your CLASSPATH.

Distributing Beans

Exporting JAR files enables you to share beans with other developers. When you create a .jar file, you receive the manifest file built for you by VisualAge or the JAR utility. Earlier, we exported a .jar file for the Sun Demo Examples project. The juggler.jar file had one bean marked for export. The **manifest.mf** file identifies the beans exported. Figure 8.25 shows a partial listing of this file and the bean marked in the export we did earlier.

To demonstrate sharing beans, you can reimport the juggler.jar file and place the juggler bean on the bean palette of the Visual Composition Editor.

Delete the **Sun BDK Examples** project from the workspace. You can re-load it later from the repository if desired. The errors found during the deletion will be fixed when we import.

Select the **MyProject** project and select **Import** from the Workbench's File menu.

Select the **JAR File (including resources)** radio button on the SmartGuide and **MyProject** in the text bean as seen in Figure 8.26.

Click the **Next** button and then the **Browse** button on the next window. Select the **C:\MyExports\juggler.jar** file from the file dialog and click the **Finish** button shown in Figure 8.27.

Enter the class name and category for the bean you want to add to the palette seen in Figure 8.28.

Figure 8.25 MANIFEST.MF file listing.

```
Manifest-Version: 1.0

Name: sunw/demo/juggler/Juggler.class
Java-Bean: True
Digest-Algorithms: SHA MD5
SHA-Digest: cJQCmvpQeDZVsPq7AHrhKPRVCKQ=
MD5-Digest: MoQ9yiRXseVv7FtUUUbBDQ==
```

Figure 8.26 Importing the juggler.jar file.

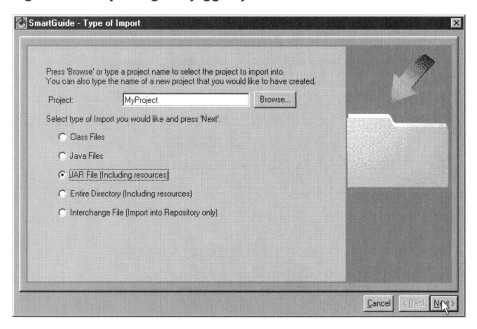

Figure 8.27 Import SmartGuide: Archive.

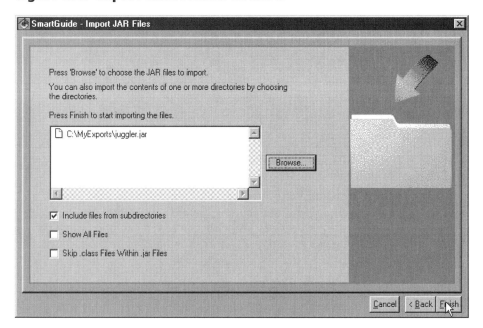

Figure 8.28 Category selection.

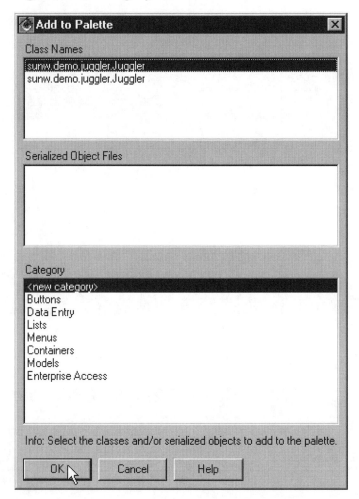

Next, enter **Demo** as the name for the new category and select the default radio buttons for the palette icons (Figure 8.29).

To see if the juggler bean is on the bean palette, create a new class as a subclass of applet and open the Visual Composition Editor. Scroll to the bottom of the categories and click the **Demo** category. Click the **juggler** bean and place it on the applet as shown in Figure 8.30.

Figure 8.29 New category specification.

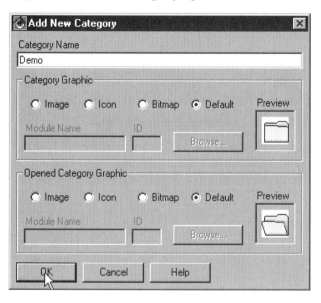

Figure 8.30 Bean on palette.

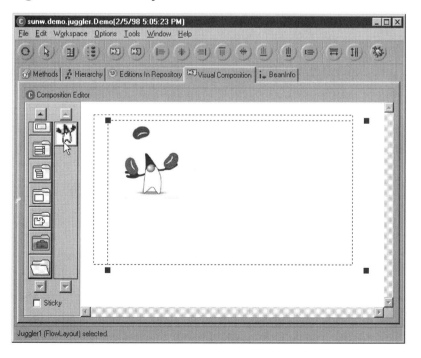

Summary

In this chapter, you learned how to export the various forms of source code and byte-code from the VisualAge repository to the file system. To do this you have:

- Exported a sample as .class, .java, .jar, and .dat (interchange format).
- Learned about resource files.
- Ran exported code both from a web page and as a stand-alone application.
- Learned what HTML tags are needed to test an applet.

Now that you can deploy your code in a variety of forms, you can share your beans, applets, and applications with colleagues. Deploying and testing your Java programs outside the development environment is an important step to completing the program.

BUILDING THE INTERNET
ADDRESS APPLET

9

What's in Chapter 9

Now that you have learned about the Visual Composition Editor and JavaBeans, you are ready to take advantage of object technology through visual layering and bean reuse. In this chapter, you will build a VisualAge Java applet that enters Internet address information for users and reformats the information in a list bean. In this chapter, you will learn how to:

- Build panels that can be layered to give the desired appearance and reused across applets and applications
- Promote bean features that can be accessed by other beans
- Use tear-off properties and Variables to simplify bean communications
- Use Factories to produce object instances visually
- Use CardLayout to simulate a notebook bean

VisualAge for Java enables you to extend object technologies through the visual programming of bean reuse across applets and applications. Building the Internet Address Applet shows how to reuse panels using layering, Factories and Variables. You develop the applet's model or domain classes, paint the user interface, connect the beans, and test the Java code by running it in the IDE. Figure 9.1 shows the first card in the running applet.

Figure 9.2 shows the second card in the running applet. In this chapter, you will build this applet using the CardLayout manager to manage the two cards. The cards contain GUI subbeans that you will build as separate beans. You will then use visual layering to combine the subbeans.

The **User Info** and **Additional Info** buttons enable the user to switch between two cards (or panels) to enter information about the Internet address. After typing information in the entry fields, the user can click the **Add** button to add the information to the list. When the user selects an item from the list, the information is placed in the corresponding text of the UserInfoPanel and AdditionalInfoPanel beans, respectively. When an item is selected in the list, information can be changed in the entry fields and updated with the **Update** button. Items can be deleted from the list when selected if the **Delete** button is clicked.

Figure 9.1 InternetAddressFinalApplet first panel.

The steps required to build the Internet Address Applet are:

1. Create a model, or the InternetAddress domain class, to hold information about the user's Internet address information.

2. Add bean properties to the InternetAddress class as well as constructors to create new InternetAddress instances.

3. Create the InternetAddress panels that contain the user interface for the applet.

4. Create the InternetAddressTestApplet class that contains the panels, model class, and other invisible beans of the applet.

5. Create the InternetAddressFinalApplet class that contains reused panels, model class, and other invisible beans to perform a final test of the applet.

Figure 9.2 InternetAddressFinalApplet second panel.

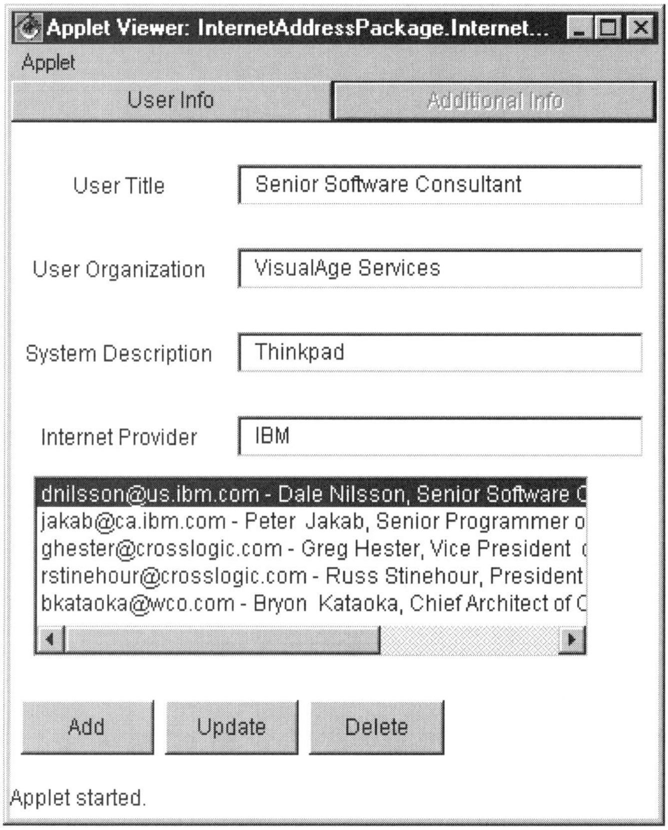

Creating the InternetAddress Class

The domain objects are a central part of your applet or application. These beans represent business objects and interface with GUI beans, broker beans, and controller beans. Domain objects are invisible beans that can run on the client or just as easily on the server. Start building the domain object with the following steps:

If you have closed VisualAge for Java, you need to restart it.

Select the My Project project in the Workbench.

VisualAge offers many ways to do the same task. You could use the tool bar to create the package; this time, you will use pop-up menus.

In the Workbench, click the right mouse button to add the new package. Select **Add package** from the pop-up menu.

Use the SmartGuide to enter the package name and click the check box to create a new package.

Now you are ready to create the InternetAddress class. The InternetAddress class contains information about the Internet address (state) and functions to get, format, and set Internet address information (behavior). It does not need to inherit behavior from any other classes, so its superclass is the Java Object class. Make the new class with the following steps:

Select InternetAddressPackage on the Workbench list and click the right mouse button to add the new class.

Select **New class/interface** from the pop-up menu. In the SmartGuide (as shown in Figure 9.3) enter **InternetAddress** as the class name.

Accept all other information as defaults and click the **Finish** button to enter additional information about the class.

VisualAge for Java generates the InternetAddress class and shows the new class in the package of the Workbench window displays as seen in Figure 9.4. If you are developing a number of classes, you can create all of them before defining

Figure 9.3 Class SmartGuide.

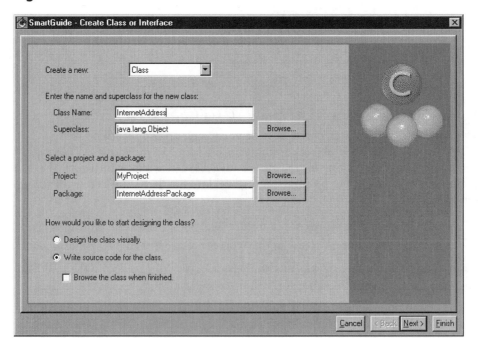

Figure 9.4 Class Browser.

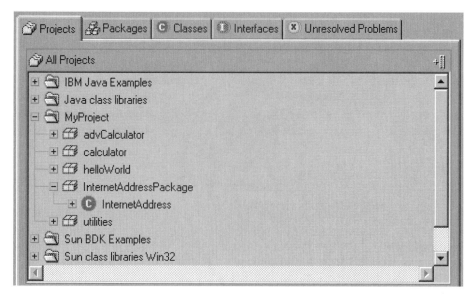

the features. The classes are displayed in the Workbench. You can add the features to each class. This method is very helpful when you are developing with a team. Each team member can work on completing his or her individual classes after the different classes are defined. For this program, you will develop the features for the InternetAddress class before creating the other classes needed for the applet.

Adding Bean Properties to the InternetAddress Class

Next, you need to add property and methods to the InternetAddress class to support communications to other beans as shown in Figure 9.5. Objects contain both fields and methods that access data and provide object behavior.

From the Workbench, move the mouse pointer over the InternetAddress class and click the right mouse button. Select **Open To** and then **Bean Info** as shown in Figure 9.6.

The browser for the bean appears and the BeanInfo tab is displayed.

From the InternetAddress BeanInfo page, place the mouse pointer in the features list, click the right mouse button, and select **New Property Feature**.

The SmartGuide-New Property Feature window appears, prompting you for information about the property being added. Type **firstName** as the property name and click the **Finish** button as seen in Figure 9.7.

Figure 9.5 InternetAddress class.

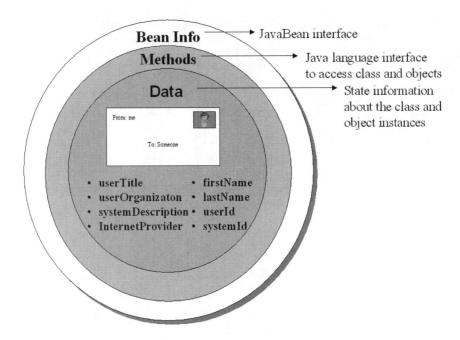

In the same way, add the following properties to the InternetAddress class:

lastName

userId

systemId

userOrganization

userTitle

systemDescription

internetProvider

You also need to create a method feature to format the userId, systemId, and user name for display purposes. Click the right mouse button over the features list and select **New Method Feature**.

From the SmartGuide-New Method Feature window, enter the method name and click the **Finish** button as seen in Figure 9.8.

Figure 9.6 BeanInfo page.

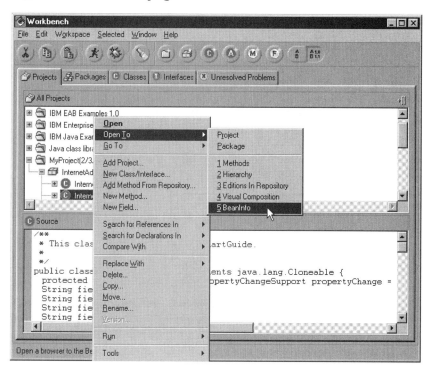

VisualAge for Java generates the method for you. Modify the generated getFormattedName() method to return a formatted string of the property features. The code to add is shown in bold face, as follows:

```
/**
 * Performs the getFormattedName method.
 * @return java.lang.String
 */
public String getFormattedName() {
/* Perform the getFormattedName method. */
  String fieldFormattedAddress = new String();
  try {
    fieldFormattedAddress = getUserId().trim() +
    "@" + getSystemId().trim() + " - " +
    getFirstName().trim() + " "
    + getLastName().trim() + ", " +
    getUserTitle().trim() + "
```

Figure 9.7 New Property SmartGuide.

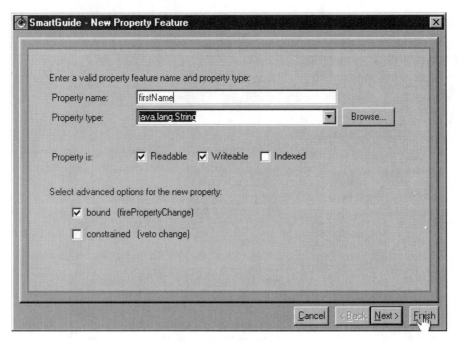

```
        of " + getUserOrganization().trim();
    } catch (java.lang.Throwable exception) {
        System.err.println("Exception creating
            formattedName");
    };
    return fieldFormattedAddress;
}
```

Figure 9.9 shows the BeanInfo page for InternetAddress.

InternetUserInfoPanel

InternetUserInfoPanel enables the user to enter the Internet user's first and last name, user ID, and system ID.

Making Constructors

Next, you will create base and default constructors for the InternetAddress class. A base constructor takes arguments and sets the state of InternetAddress properties. The arguments are Strings and need to be entered in the constructor declaration.

Figure 9.8 New Method Feature SmartGuide.

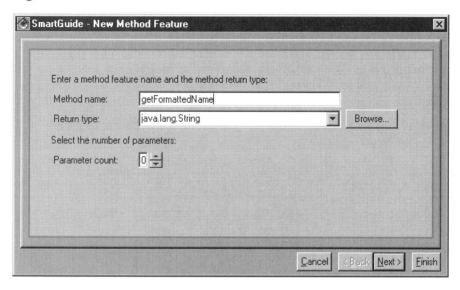

Figure 9.9 BeanInfo properties.

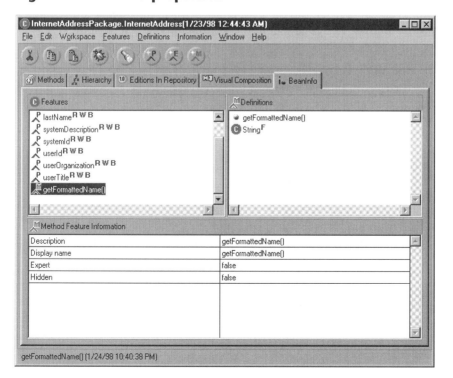

Go to the Methods page of the class browser. Start the New Method SmartGuide to create a base constructor for the InternetAddress class.

From the *Create a new* dropdown list, select the **Constructor**.

Enter fname, lname, uid, system, utitle, uorg, sysdescr, and iprovider as the parameters of type String inside the parentheses. The beginning of the declaration is as follows:

```
InternetAddress(String fname, String lname,...
```

Leave all the other default settings and press the Finish button to generate the constructor.

NOTE

It is a better OO design to pass an array of Strings or, better yet, an Object, rather than eight separate Strings, as parameters. If you add another String to the InternetAddress class, you will need a new constructor.

Adding Constructor Code

Add code to set the properties based on the constructor arguments. The code for the constructor follows. The code that you need to add is shown in bold face:

```
/**
 * This method was created by a SmartGuide.
 * @param fname java.lang.String
 * @param lname java.lang.String
 * @param uid java.lang.String
 * @param system java.lang.String
 * @param utitle java.lang.String
 * @param uorg java.lang.String
 * @param sysdescr java.lang.String
 * @param iprovider java.lang.String
 */
public InternetAddress ( java.lang.String fname, java.lang.String
lname, java.lang.String uid, java.lang.String system, java.lang.String
utitle, java.lang.String uorg, java.lang.String sysdescr,
java.lang.String iprovider) {
    setFirstName(fname);
    setLastName(lname);
    setUserId(uid);
    setSystemId(system);
    setUserTitle(utitle);
```

```
    setUserOrganization(uorg);
    setSystemDescription(sysdescr);
    setInternetProvider(iprovider);
}
```

Next, add a default (or no-argument) constructor. Using the New Method SmartGuide, provide the default constructor for the InternetAddress class. Add code to call the base constructor. The code you add follows in bold:

```
/**
 * This method was created by a SmartGuide.
 */
public InternetAddress ( ) {
this("", "", "", "", "", "", "", "");
}
```

The **toString**() method is required to return a formatted string of InternetAddress. The toString() method returns getFormattedName(). It is common to add a toString() method to convert object information into a Java String that can be used by other beans.

Creating User Interface Panels

Now that you have created the domain class, it is time to create the user interface for the applet. The InterfaceAddress Applet contains four panels that allow the user to enter Internet address information.

- **InternetUserInfoPanel** enables entry of user information.

- **InternetAdditionalInfoPanel** enables entry of additional information.

- **InternetFormattedInfoPanel** enables the selection of an address for update or deletion.

- **InternetButtonPanel** contains buttons that enable the user to add, update, and delete Internet address information from InternetUser-InfoPanel and InternetAdditionalInfoPanel in the InternetFormatted InfoPanel list.

InternetUserInfoPanel

InternetUserInfoPanel enables the user to enter the Internet user's first and last name, user ID, and system ID (Figure 9.10).

VisualAge Variables

VisualAge supports a special type of invisible beans called *Variable* beans. Variable beans are used to refer to specific instances of a certain type. In the Visual Composition Editor, a Variable bean dropped on the free-form surface next to

Figure 9.10 InternetUserInfoPanel.

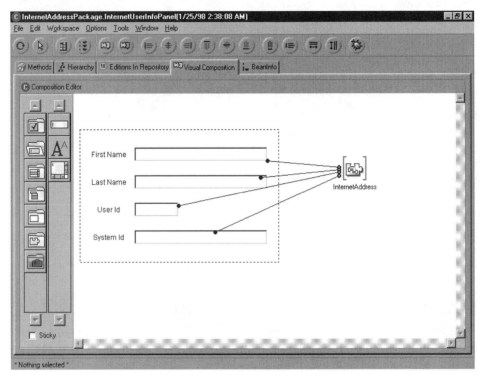

InternetUserInfoPanel will represent an instance of the InternetAddress class. In InternetUserInfoPanel, drop a Variable bean on the free-form surface:

 Click the Models icon from the left column of the beans palette.

 Select the Variable icon from the beans palette. The mouse pointer changes to a crosshair. Move the mouse pointer to the free-form surface and click the left mouse button to drop the Variable bean.

The Variable bean used for this panel represents the instance of the InternetAddress being worked upon by the user. The Variable bean's name is InternetAddress and its type, or class, is InternetAddress. Both the name and type can be set by placing the mouse cursor over the Variable bean and clicking the right mouse button. Selecting **Change Bean Name** and **Change Type** from the pop-up menu can be used to change the bean name and Variable bean type, respectively. The bean name can be any valid Java identifier, whereas the bean type must be a valid Java identifier and a valid class in the workspace.

The Variable's properties are connected to the TextField beans' text properties by property-to-property connections. The source of the connections is the Variable bean. These connections enable the InternetAddress, referred to by the Variable bean, to be updated when the user types information into the entry fields. The connections also enable the text in the entry fields to be updated when a new instance of InternetAddress is placed in the Variable.

Using the *This*

The *this* feature of the Variable should be promoted so the instance in the Variable can be accessed from InternetAddressApplet. Promote the *this* feature of the Variable bean with these steps:

Place the mouse pointer over the Variable bean and click the right mouse button. Select **Promote Bean Feature** from the pop-up menu.

Select the *this* property on the **Promote features from: InternetAddress** window as seen in Figure 9.11. After selecting the *this* feature, click the **Promote** button to promote the feature. This makes the feature public to other beans.

Click the **OK** button to close the window. Now the Variable can be accessed from the Applet or other beans.

You will use the GridBagLayout for the InternetUserInfoPanel. Set the Layout Manager for the panel as follows:

Click the left mouse button to select the panel and click the right mouse button for the pop-up menu.

Select **Properties** and click the value box of the *layout* property.

Select **GridBagLayout** and close the window.

The GridBagLayout can prove challenging when you are adding beans to a Panel or Frame. You have already used it in the Advanced Calculator, so this is another chance to practice with this powerful Layout Manager. When you add Labels and TextField beans to the Panel, GridBagLayout groups the beans in the center of the Panel. Either set the component beans' GridBag constraint weights or gain needed vertical space between rows of beans by inserting a blank label between each row.

In order to get the right size and position for the TextField, set properties with the following steps:

Click the left mouse button on the UserIdText bean and click the right mouse button for the pop-up menu. Select **Properties**.

UserIdText should show only eight characters of input. Set the UserIdText bean's *column* property to 8.

InternetUserInfoPanel's GridBagConstraints *anchor* property should
be West. To set this, select the *constraints* property from the Panel's
property sheet and select **West** for the *anchor* property, as shown in
Figure 9.12.

Promote the *text* properties of the TextFields to make them accessible to
other beans.

Save this Panel bean so you can use it later.

The next step is to continue developing components and create
InternetAdditionalInfoPanel.

InternetAdditionalInfoPanel

InternetAdditionalInfoPanel enables the user to enter the Internet user's title, the
user's organization, the system description, and an Internet provider. Create

Figure 9.11 Promote Bean Feature window.

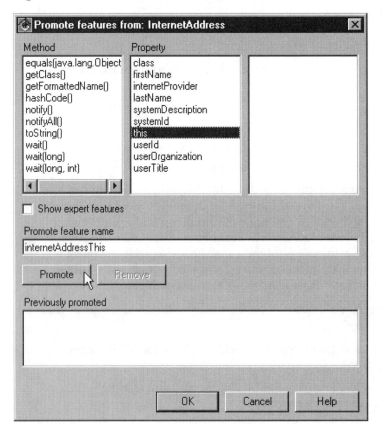

Figure 9.12 InternetUserPanel properties.

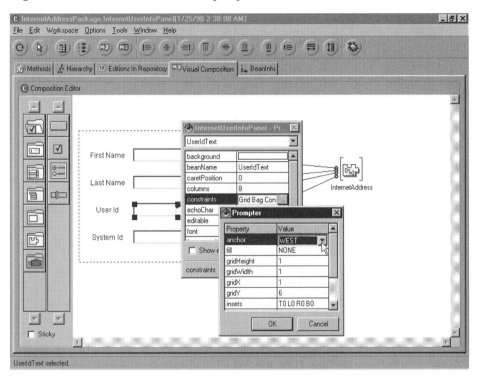

InternetAdditionalInfoPanel as seen in Figure 9.13 with the following beans and properties:

- GridBagLayout to manage the position of the GUI beans.
- Label and TextField beans to enable entry of the user title, the user organization, a system description, and the Internet service provider. These TextFields should have column *width* properties of 30. The *text* properties of the TextFields must be promoted so they are accessible from the Applet.
- A Variable to represent the instance of the InternetAddress being worked on by the user. The Variable should have a type of InternetAddress and a bean name of InternetAddress. The *this* feature of the Variable should be promoted.
- Connections between the source InternetAddress Variable properties and the target *text* properties of the TextFields. The specific connection events used are significant.

Figure 9.13 InternetAdditionalInfoPanel.

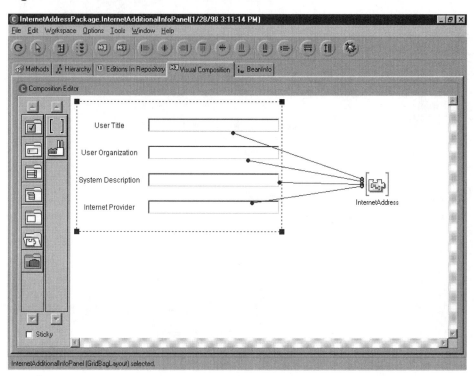

After visually programming the Panel, save your work and continue to the next section, where you create InternetFormattedInfoPanel. If you need any help working with GridBagLayout, setting bean properties, creating a Variable, or making the necessary connections, review the work you did for InternetUserInfoPanel.

InternetFormattedInfoPanel

InternetFormattedInfoPanel, seen in Figure 9.14, formats the information entered on the InternetUserInfoPanel and InternetAdditionalInfoPanel and displays the formatted information in a list. Items in the list are selectable by the user for possible update or deletion. The items of the list are Strings. When the applet is opened or when an Internet address is added, updated, or deleted, the **refreshListBoxItems**() method is called to place the Strings in a Vector. Code for this method follows:

```
/**
 * This method was created by a SmartGuide.
```

```
    */
public void refreshListBoxItems ( ) {

  getInternetAddressListBox().removeAll();

  // iterate thru the Vector and set the items of
  // the list box
for (int i = 0; i <
    getInternetAddressesVector().size(); i ++){
        getInternetAddressListBox().
            add(getInternetAddressesVector().
            elementAt(i).toString());
    }
return;
}
```

When the user selects an item in the list, the **selectInternetAddressListItem()** method is called to place the selected item into the CurrentInternetAddress

Figure 9.14 InternetFormattedInfoPanel.

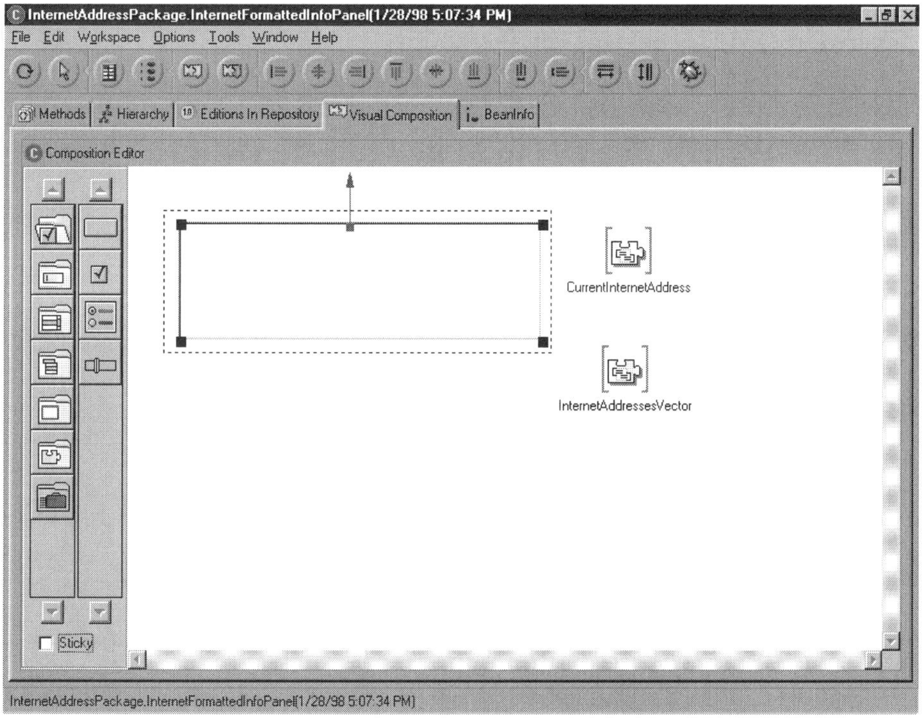

Variable. When this event happens, each of the fields will be copied to a Java Vector that holds the items for the list. Create this method as follows:

> Create a new method in the BeanInfo page named **selectInternetAddressListItem ().**

> Add the following code to this new method:

```
/**
 * This method was created by a SmartGuide.
 */
public void selectInternetAddressListItem ( ) {
// set the current InternetAddress properties
// based on the list item selected
int i = getInternetAddressListBox().getSelectedIndex();
if (i >= 0) {
  InternetAddress vectorIntAddr =
  (InternetAddress)getInternetAddressesVector().
      elementAt(i);

  InternetAddress currentIntAddr =
  (InternetAddress)getCurrentInternetAddress();
  currentIntAddr.setFirstName
    (vectorIntAddr.getFirstName());
  currentIntAddr.setLastName
    (vectorIntAddr.getLastName());
  currentIntAddr.setUserId
    (vectorIntAddr.getUserId());
  currentIntAddr.setSystemId
    (vectorIntAddr.getSystemId());
  currentIntAddr.setUserTitle
    (vectorIntAddr.getUserTitle());
  currentIntAddr.setUserOrganization
  (vectorIntAddr.getUserOrganization());
  currentIntAddr.setSystemDescription
  (vectorIntAddr.getSystemDescription());
  currentIntAddr.setInternetProvider
  (vectorIntAddr.getInternetProvider());
  }
return;
}
```

InternetFormattedInfoPanel contains two Variables. **CurrentInternetAddress** represents the current Internet address being worked upon by the user.

InternetAddressesVector represents a Vector of all InternetAddress objects added and modified by the user as seen in Figure 9.14.

When the user selects an item in the list, the itemStateChanged event is signaled and the **selectInternetAddressListItem**() method is called. This is an event-to-script connection. The script is a class method that you can call or create from a SmartGuide. Make this connection as follows:

Point the mouse at the Listbox and bring up the connection menu.

Select the **itemStateChanged** event as the source.

Move the mouse to the free-form surface and press the left mouse button. Select the **Event to Script...** menu item.

The Event to Script dialog displays the connection properties, as shown in Figure 9.15. Select the **void selectInternetAddressListItem**() script from the list box and click the OK button to complete the event to script connection.

When the user updates the InternetAddress item selected in the list, the **updateInternetAddress**() method is called, as follows:

```
//**
 * This method was created by a SmartGuide.
 */
public void updateInternetAddress ( ) {
// set the vector InternetAdress properties
// based on the curent internet address
int i =
 getInternetAddressListBox().getSelectedIndex();
if (i >= 0) {
  InternetAddress vectorIntAddr =
  (InternetAddress)getInternetAddressesVector().
   elementAt(i);
  InternetAddress currentIntAddr =
  (InternetAddress)
  getCurrentInternetAddress();

 vectorIntAddr.setFirstName
  (currentIntAddr.getFirstName());
 vectorIntAddr.setLastName
  (currentIntAddr.getLastName());
 vectorIntAddr.setUserId
  (currentIntAddr.getUserId());
 vectorIntAddr.setSystemId
  (currentIntAddr.getSystemId());
```

```
vectorIntAddr.setUserTitle
  (currentIntAddr.getUserTitle());
vectorIntAddr.setUserOrganization
  (currentIntAddr.getUserOrganization());
vectorIntAddr.setSystemDescription
  (currentIntAddr.getSystemDescription());
vectorIntAddr.setInternetProvider
  (currentIntAddr.getInternetProvider());
 }
return;
}
```

InternetButtonPanel

Create **InternetButtonPanel,** which contains buttons for add, update and delete. This Panel is used to contain the buttons in the shape and size required to fit in the South border of the applet (see Figure 9.16).

Be sure to promote the *actionPerformed* event for each of the buttons. Promoting the event makes the feature available to other beans.

Select a Button with the left mouse button and click the right mouse button for the bean's pop-up menu. Select **Promote Bean Feature;** then select the *addPBAction.actionPerformed* event and click the **Promote** and **OK** buttons as shown in Figure 9.17.

Figure 9.15 itemStateChanged connection.

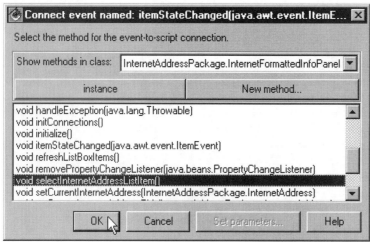

Figure 9.16 InternetButtonPanel.

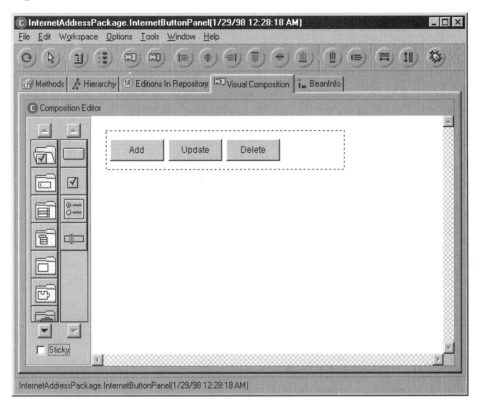

NOTE

It is very common to use a Tab GUI bean to get the look of a notebook. The Tabs blend into each card of the notebook for a seamless look. The AWT V1.1 class library does not include a Tab GUI bean, so we will use a Button. There are many Tab GUI beans available from bean providers on the web.

Testing the InternetAddress Panels

The applet will be tested in two steps. At this point, you can test to see if the InternetUserInfoPanel and the InternetFormattedInfoPanel work together. Figure 9.18 shows the end result of the applet test.

Figure 9.17 Promoting actionPerformed.

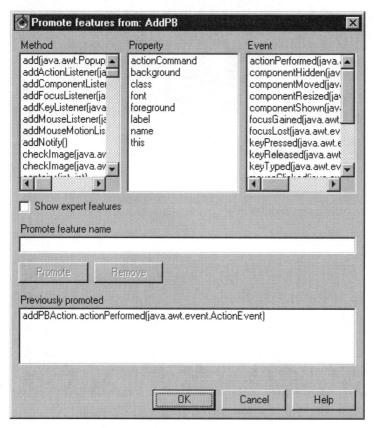

InternetAddressTestApplet uses BorderLayout as follows:

- InternetButtonPanel is in the South border cell.
- InternetUserInfoPanel is in the North border cell.
- InternetFormattedInfoPanel is in the Center border cell.

Figure 9.19 shows the Visual Composition Editor for InternetAddress TestApplet. Table 9.1 describes its Variables and beans.

After dropping the Panels on the Applet, and the Variables and beans on the free-form surface, you will make connections between these beans. Next, connect the Panel Variables to the Applet Variables with the following:

Connect the promoted *CurrentInternetAddress* feature of InternetUserInfoPanel to the CurrentInternetAddress Variable on the free-form surface of the Applet.

Connect the CurrentInternetAddress Variable on the free-form surface of the Applet to the promoted *CurrentInternetAddress* feature of InternetFormattedInfoPanel.

Connect the InternetAddressesVector Variable's *this* property to the promoted *this* property of InternetAddressesVector.

Make connections to initialize the Panel and Applet TextFields and Variables:

Connect the Applet's *init()* event to the InternetAddress() constructor of InitialInternetAddressObjectFactory.

Connect the *this* property of the CurrentInternetAddress Variable to the *this* property of InitialInternetAddressObjectFactory.

Now make the connections required to add an InternetAddress instance to the list of InternetFormattedInfoPanel. The event-to-method connections construct

Figure 9.18 InternetAddressTestApplet.

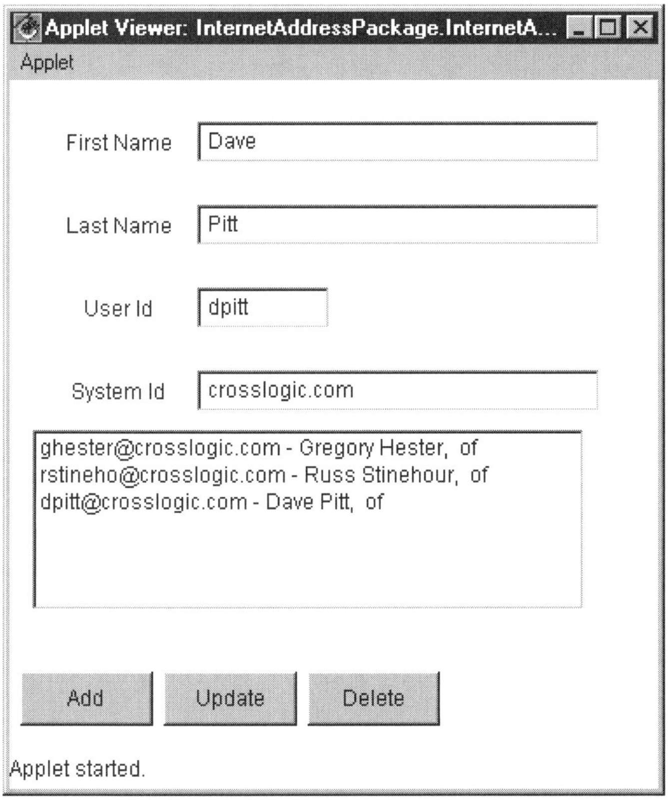

Figure 9.19 InternetAddressTestApplet in the Visual Composition Editor.

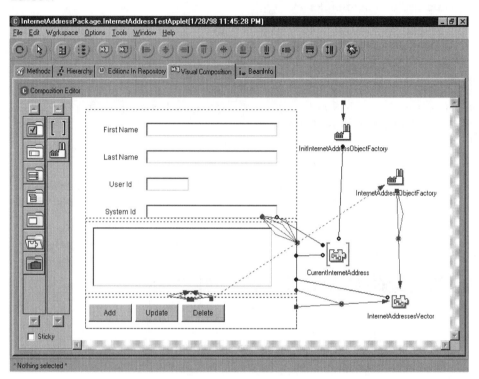

Table 9.1 Variables and Beans for InternetAddressTestApplet

Variable/Bean	Description
CurrentInternetAddress	Variable that references the instance of the InternetAddress being entered by the user
InternetAddressesVector	Vector that contains a collection of InternetAddress instances
InitialInternetAddressObjectFactory	Factory used to generate an initial instance of InternetAddress
InternetAddressObjectFactory	Factory used to generate an instance of InternetAddress when user adds an InternetAddress to the list

a new instance of InternetAddress and refresh the list's contents. The constructor uses the TextFields' *text* properties as parameters. Then add the instance generated by the InternetAddressObjectFactory constructor to the InternetAddressesVector:

Connect InternetButtonPanel's *addPBAction.action* event to the InternetAddress(java.awt.String, java.awt.String, java.awt.String, java.awt.String, java.awt.String, java.awt.String, java.awt.String, java.awt.String) constructor of InternetAddressObjectFactory.

Connect the promoted *text* properties of InternetUserInfoPanel to the String parameters of the previous connection.

Connect InternetButtonPanel's *addPBAction.action* event to InternetFormattedInfoPanel's refreshListBoxItems() method.

Connect the *this* event of InternetAddressObjectFactory to the InternetAddressesVector Variable's addElement(java.lang.Object) method.

Connect the *this* property of InternetAddressObjectFactory to the *obj* parameter of the previous connection.

Make the connections to delete an entry in the InternetFormattedInfoPanel list and refresh the list:

Connect InternetButtonPanel's *deletePBAction.action* event to InternetAddressesVector's removeElementAt(int) method.

Connect InternetButtonPanel's *deletePBAction.action* event to InternetFormattedInfoPanel's refreshListBoxItems() method.

Connect InternetFormattedInfoPanel's *ListBoxSelectedIndex* property to the *index* property of the previous connection.

Make the connections to update and refresh the InternetFormattedInfoPanel list:

Connect InternetButtonPanel's *updatePBAction.action* event to InternetFormattedInfoPanel's updateInternetAddress() method.

Connect InternetButtonPanel's *updatePBAction.action* event to InternetFormattedInfoPanel's refreshListBoxItems() method.

Your test applet is now complete. Save your work and run the applet from the Visual Composition Editor. After you are satisfied with the results of your applet, close the applet viewer. Then you will be ready to build the final applet, using all of the panels you have created.

Creating InternetAddressFinalApplet

The InternetAddressFinalApplet demonstrates the following:

- Reuse of Panel beans
- Use of CardLayout

Figure 9.20 shows the applet running from the VisualAge Java applet viewer.
InternetAddressFinalApplet reuses all of the beans, panels, and Variables found
in InternetAddressTestApplet. Other Panels are used for the CardLayout, with the
InternetAdditionalInfoPanel, to enable the user to enter data about the user and system. CardLayout is used to alternate among a deck of Panels.

CardLayout

CardLayout arranges components in a linear depth sequence similar to a notebook. Each component forming the deck is called a *card*. You add components to
the CardLayout parent, and VisualAge adds them to the top of the deck, making
the first bean the bottom card. To move through the deck or to perform tasks on

Figure 9.20 InternetAddressFinalApplet.

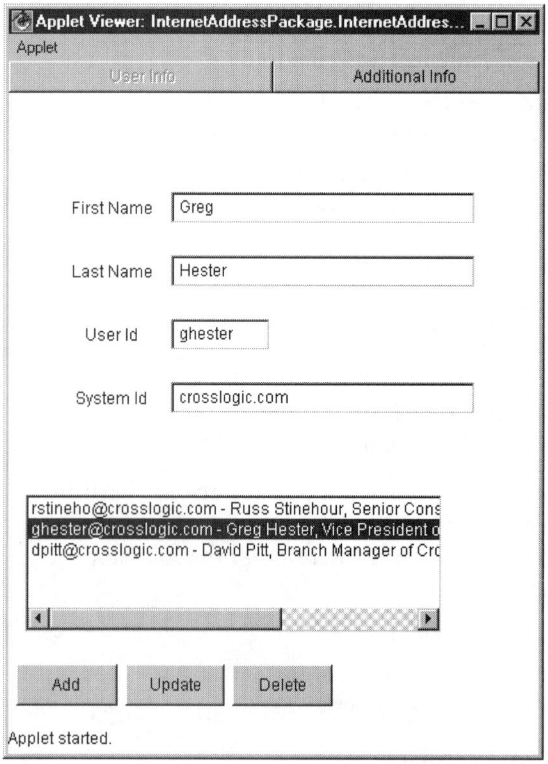

the covered cards in the beans list, select **Switch To** from the pop-up menu for the Panel containing the CardLayout.

Using CardLayout

To get access to the LayoutManager interface directly, follow these steps:

Drop a Variable on the free-form surface to the right of the CardLayout Container.

Change the type of the Variable to CardLayout.

Connect the *layout* property of the container bean to the *this* property of the Variable. Then connect to features of the Variable bean.

Before you can use CardLayout, you must build the Panel through the layering of other Panels to obtain the appearance of the Applet. Figure 9.21 shows the reuse and layering of Panels to achieve the desired appearance.

Figure 9.21 Panel reuse and layering.

InternetAddressFinalApplet Layering

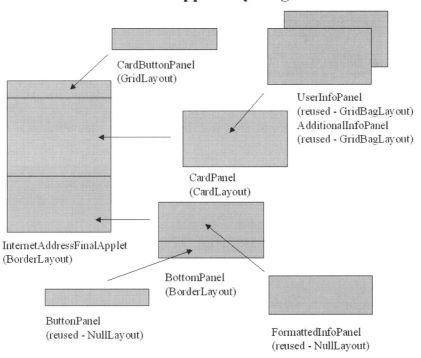

Panels can be created as separate beans or they can be created on the applet's free-form surface. Table 9.2 describes each of the Panels.

After building the Panel layers for the InternetAddressFinalApplet, it is time to connect the beans. Figure 9.22 shows the Visual Composition Editor for InternetAddressFinalApplet.

In the Visual Composition Editor, InternetAddressFinalApplet looks very much like InternetAddressTestApplet. All of the same Variables and invisible beans from the InternetAddressTestApplet appear on InternetAddressFinalApplet's free-form surface. There is one additional Variable and a few additional connections to discuss:

The CardLayout of CardPanel switches the card of the Panel. Add the CardLayout Variable to the free-form surface and connect the *layout* property of CardPanel to the *this* property of the CardLayout Variable.

Additional connections are required to switch to the first card when the **User Info** button is clicked. The userPBClicked() script is called to enable and disable the buttons when **User Info** is clicked:

Connect the *userInfoPBAction.action* event to the first(java.awt.Container) method of the CardLayoutManager.

Connect the *this* property of CardPanel to the *parent* property of the previous connection.

Connect the *userInfoPBAction.action* event to the userPBClicked() script as shown in Figure 9.22 of InternetAddressFinalApplet.

Table 9.2 Panel Descriptions

Panel Name	Description
InternetAddressFinalApplet	Primary bean. Uses BorderLayout with CardButtonPanel in the North, CardPanel in the Center and Bottom panel in the South.
BottomPanel	Built on InternetAddressFinalApplet's free-form surface. Uses BorderLayout with ButtonPanel in the South and FormattedInfoPanel in the Center.
ButtonPanel	Reused InternetButtonPanel.
FormattedInfoPanel	Reused InternetFormattedInfoPanel.
CardButtonPanel	Built on InternetAddressFinalApplet's free-form surface. Uses GridLayout. Used to switch between the CardLayout Panels.
CardPanel	Used to hold cards. Uses CardLayout.
UserInfoPanel	Reused InternetUserInfoPanel.
AdditionalInfoPanel	Reused InternetAdditionalInfoPanel.

Figure 9.22 InternetAddressFinalApplet in the Visual Composition Editor.

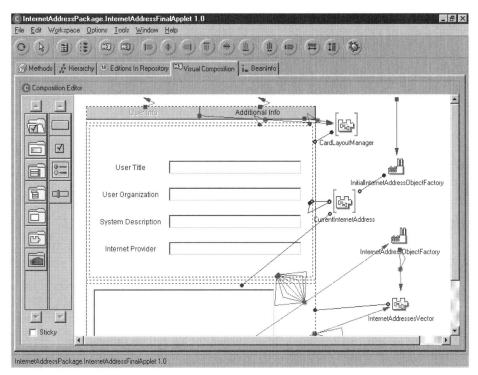

Connections are required to switch to the last card when the **Additional Info** button is clicked. The additionalPBClicked() script is called to enable and disable the buttons when **Additional Info** is clicked:

Connect the *additionalInfoPBAction.action* event to the last(java.awt.Container) method of CardLayoutManager.

Connect the *additionalInfoPBAction.action* event to the additionalPBClicked() script of InternetAddressFinalApplet. Code for this method follows:

```
/**
 * This method was created by a SmartGuide.
 */
public void additionalPBClicked ( ) {
  getUserPB().setEnabled(true);
  getAdditionalPB().setEnabled(false);
  return;
}
```

Connect the *userInfoPBAction.action* event to the userPBClicked() script of InternetAddressFinalApplet. Code for this method follows:

```
/**
 * This method was created by a SmartGuide.
 */
public void userPBClicked ( ) {
  getUserPB().setEnabled(false);
  getAdditionalPB().setEnabled(true);
  return;
}
```

If you have problems building this applet, you can load the answers version of the applet. This visual program has a lot of connections, and many of them are critical to the applet's successful completion.

Testing the InternetAddressFinalApplet

Let's test the applet and see how it works. Save these changes and test the applet with the following:

Press the Test button on the tool bar of the Visual Composition Editor to generate and run the applet. When the applet starts, it looks like Figure 9.23.

Enter data in the first page as shown in Figure 9.23. You can use the Tab key to move from field to field.

Press the **Additional Info** button and the second card displays as shown in Figure 9.24.

Enter sample data in the TextFields. Add the new InternetAddress to the list by pressing the **Add** button. The new InternetAddress displays in the Listbox.

Add other InternetAddresses in the list.

Update some data for one of your entries in the list. Notice how the selected item in the Listbox fills the TextFields with the appropriate data.

Delete a selected item in the Listbox.

When you are finished testing the applet, close it.

This applet demonstrates an example of how to use the CardLayout manager. It has many common features that you would expect to see in a program. There are a variety of ways you could have implemented this applet, and there are a few improvements that could be made to it. However, the applet does the job that is required and it is time to learn more new features of VisualAge for Java.

Figure 9.23 Testing the first card.

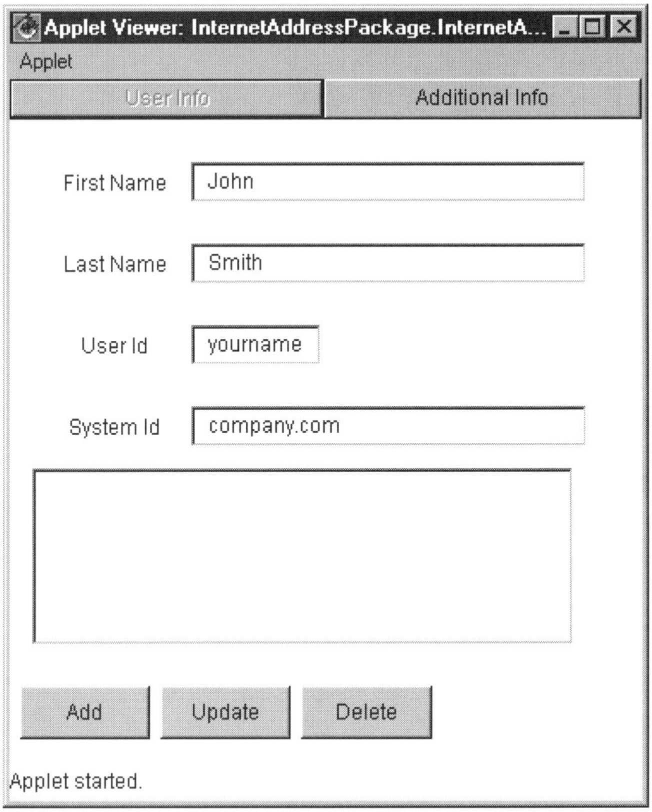

Summary

In this chapter, you have built a more complex applet using the Visual Builder and some new AWT GUI beans. This chapter showed you how to:

- Reuse Panels to test your Applet connections before you completed the final Applet.
- Use CardLayout with Panels to achieve a notebook appearance, helping you maximize window real estate.
- Use Variables to represent object instances, helping you pass an object from one Panel to another.
- Layer Panels to mix layouts, giving your Applets the appropriate size and position.
- Use Factories to generate instances of your domain class, minimizing code and simplifying your application.

Figure 9.24 Testing the second card.

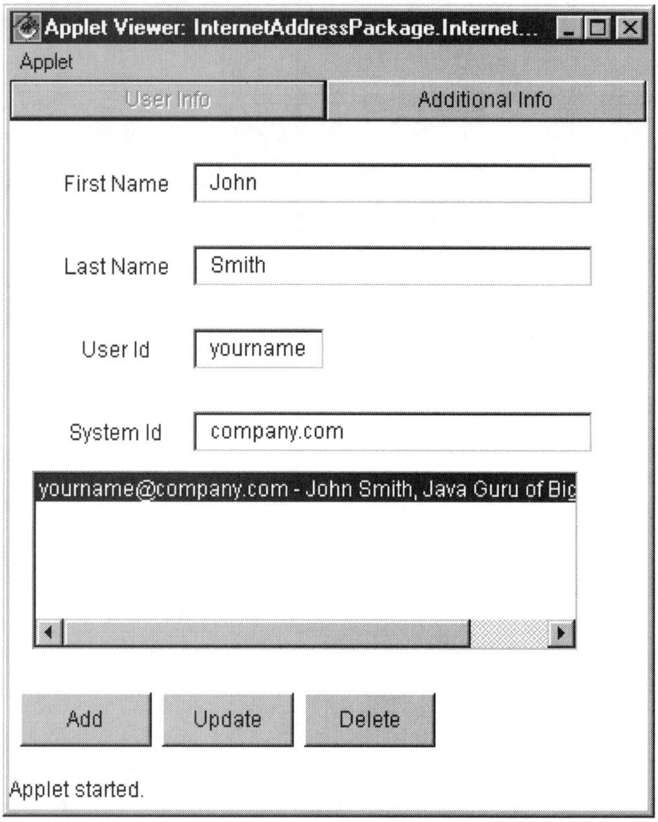

It is good to know how to use the CardLayout, because it is a common user interface container that can be used in many of your Java programs. The use of Factory Objects and Variables is essential for you to benefit from the Visual Builder. Finally, the usage of feature promotion will help you implement better OO Java programs.

THE REMINDER APPLICATION

What's in Chapter 10

In this chapter, you learn about several new beans available in the Java JDK 1.1. You will build a Reminder application that uses many new beans and techniques, both in visual and conventional programming. Some areas covered are:

- Menus
- Submenus
- Embedded beans
- CheckboxGroup
- Radio buttons
- TextArea
- Hashtable
- Event-to-script connections
- File dialog

This chapter also covers adding on-line help to an application. You will enable your application to:

- Select a web browser
- Display HTML help

In this chapter, you start a totally new application. Because you are building on the material already covered in this book, the instructions are described in less detail. For example, instead of giving you step-by-step details on how to add a bean to the Visual Composition Editor, the instructions direct you to add, or drop, a certain bean. By now, you should be able to locate a bean in the beans palette, select it, and drop it in the correct place. You should also be getting used to making connections. The convention used to describe connections consists of the source bean name, the source feature in parenthesis, an arrow, the target bean name, and the target feature in parenthesis. The following connection is an example of this convention:

```
pbClose (actionPerformed) → myWindow (dispose)
```

This connection translates to mean "connect the **pbClose** Button's **actionPerformed** event to the **myWindow** Frame's **dispose** method". When the feature of the bean needed for the connection could be ambiguous, it is clearly specified whether it is a method, property, or event.

Using Embedded Beans

This chapter introduces a key concept in VisualAge for Java called *embedded beans*. This technique uses the power of object-oriented technology to build custom visual and nonvisual components that can be used and reused in many applications.

Embedded beans can encapsulate complex behavior and present a simplified user interface, exposing only the interface components that are necessary to make the bean perform its function.

Requirements for the Reminder Application

This application saves and retrieves information that can be related to six categories and provides the functions of a reminder list, as shown in Figure 10.1.

When the user selects a radio button, the information related to that selection is displayed in the input/output area. The user can edit the text displayed. The input/output area is implemented using a **TextArea** bean.

Figure 10.1 Reminder application.

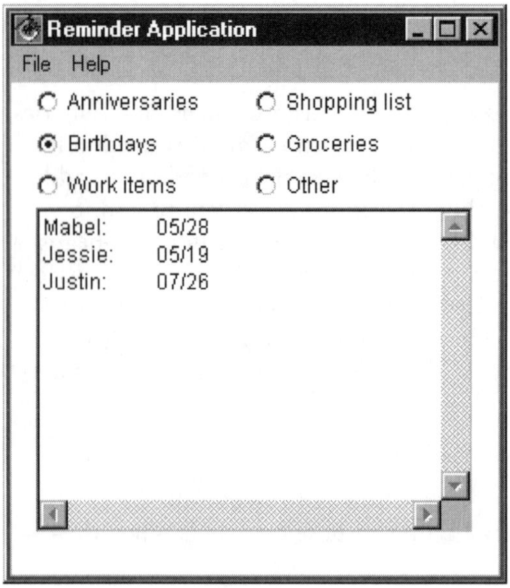

Figure 10.2 Menu bar.

The first radio button is preselected when the application starts, and the text area displays the information associated with that button. When a different radio button is selected, the current text in the text area is saved, and the text associated with the newly selected radio button is displayed in the text area. When the user exits the program, the current text in the text area is saved.

Data persistence is provided by the **ReminderHashtable** invisible bean. This bean is a subclass of the **Hashtable** class from the JDK 1.1 class library. You will define and complete this bean later in this chapter.

The application has a menu bar with the structure pictured in Figure 10.2.

Clear removes the contents of the text area; it can also be accessed using the Ctrl-Shift-C key combination.

The program can be ended by selecting **Exit** or by pressing the Ctrl-Shift-X key combination. At exit, any information displayed on the text area is associated with the currently selected radio button and saved.

Help is provided by bringing up a web browser displaying the appropriate HTML file. In this manner, help text is contained in a separate file, which can eventually be translated to other languages. Its contents can be changed without affecting the application code.

Depending on the operating system you are running, the Reminder application might have access to a pop-up menu associated with the text area to perform editing functions like **Cut, Copy,** and **Paste** upon the contents of the text area. This function is part of the built-in behavior of the peer control used to implement the TextArea bean in Windows.

Constructing the Reminder Application

You will start building the Reminder application from the bottom up. Below are the beans you will construct and later assemble:

- RadioButtonManager
- RadioButtonPanel

- ReminderPanel
- ReminderApp

You could build the whole application in one layer: starting with a Frame, laying out the components directly on it, and making connections to invisible beans to complete the project. This is usually not a good idea. By building finely grained beans, you can achieve a much higher level of maintainability and reuse. Smaller beans enable you to encapsulate function and to present a cleaner public interface to users of beans you create.

RadioButtonManager

RadioButtonManager is the bean responsible for handling a group of radio buttons. Its main purpose is to track the currently selected radio button and the one that was selected previously. This is very important for the Reminder application.

Remember from the spec that when a radio button is selected, the current contents of the text area must be saved and associated with the button that was previously selected. This capability is not readily available with the standard AWT beans, therefore, you will create your own bean with that capability.

The Java JDK does not provide radio buttons as a distinct class, or bean. To get the radio button look and behavior of mutual exclusive selection, you use multiple **Checkbox** beans and associate them in a group by means of a **CheckboxGroup** bean.

Each Checkbox bean has an attribute called CheckboxGroup, which is accessible through the getCheckboxGroup() and setCheckboxGroup() methods. Once a Checkbox is associated with a CheckboxGroup, its appearance changes to that of a radio button. Any other Checkbox beans associated with the same CheckboxGroup behave as a group of radio buttons, where only one can be selected at a time.

The CheckboxGroup bean can be queried to discover which is the currently selected radio button (really a Checkbox bean in disguise), by invoking the getCurrent() or the getSelectedCheckbox() methods. Both these methods return a Checkbox object.

Some of the behavior we need for the RadioButtonManager bean, like finding out which is the currently selected button, already exists in the CheckboxGroup bean. It makes sense that our bean should subclass, or inherit from, CheckboxGroup.

When to Use Radio Buttons

Radio buttons are used when you need to select one and only one option from a group of choices. Radio buttons are always used as a group of two or more choices; although each radio button is a separate control, clusters of radio buttons behave as a single control.

You should never use a single radio button to give the user a binary choice. The **Checkbox** bean should be used for that purpose. If multiple selections are enabled in a group of choices, you should also use Checkbox beans.

Creating the RadioButtonManager Bean

You will now create a new bean, **RadioButtonManager**, by following these steps:

Create a new package in the My Projects project called **reminder.**

Create a new class in the reminder package named **RadioButtonManager**. Make its superclass **java.awt.CheckboxGroup**. Select the **Write source code for the class** radio button. Press the **Finish** button to create the class.

Open a browser for the new class. Select the BeanInfo page.

Add two **java.lang.String** properties. Name them *previousKey* and *currentKey*. Ensure they are **readable, writeable** and **bound**. These properties will supply the keys necessary to access the Hashtable containing the information related to each radio button.

Switch to the Methods page and add a new method called **setCurrent**. This public method should return void, be synchronized, and take one parameter of type **java.awt.Checkbox** (call the parameter **newCurrentBox**). This method overrides setCurrent() in the superclass; it gets called by the Java VM every time a new radio button is selected. Overriding this method gives you a chance to act upon this event before the superclass does. In our case, we use this opportunity to save the previously and currently selected button's bean names to use as keys later on.

Add the highlighted code below to the generated setCurrent method:

```
/**
 * This method was created by a SmartGuide.
 * @param box java.awt.Checkbox
 */
public synchronized void setCurrent(
        java.awt.Checkbox newCurrentBox)
{
   // if any button was selected before
   if(getCurrent()!= null)
   {
      // if the newCurrentBox is different than
      //the current box
      if(newCurrentBox != getCurrent())
      {
```

```
            //set the previous name to the current
            //box's name
            setPreviousKey(getCurrent().getName());

            // let superclass do its thing
            // this call sets the current check box
            // to the newly selected button
            super.setCurrent(newCurrentBox);

            // now save the current button's name
            // in the currentKey property
            setCurrentKey(getCurrent().getName());
         }
      }
      // first time through
      else
      {
         super.setCurrent(newCurrentBox);
         setCurrentKey(getCurrent().getName());
      }
   return;
}
```

That is all there is to RadioButtonManager. By adding a couple of properties and overriding the setCurrent() method, you have created an invisible bean that not only knows when a radio button is selected but also remembers the previously selected radio button.

Because the *previousKey* and *currentKey* properties are bound, they will signal property-change events when their values change. Later on, you will use these events in the ReminderPanel bean as triggers to save and restore the contents of the text area.

RadioButtonPanel

RadioButtonPanel will hold a group of six radio buttons and the RadioButtonManager invisible bean. Together, they will provide you with a composite bean to represent the reminder categories available to the program. Follow these steps to code the new class:

Start by creating a new class in the reminder package. Call this class **RadioButtonPanel.** Make its superclass: **java.awt.Panel.** Select the **Design the class visually** radio button. Press the **Finish** button to create the class.

The Visual Composition Editor opens with a Panel on the free-form surface. Select the Panel and bring up its property sheet. Set the **layout** of the Panel to **GridLayout.** Set the layout to two columns and three rows.

From the Buttons category folder, drop six **Checkbox** beans on to the Panel. You may use **Sticky** if you wish. Name the Checkbox beans **cb1** through **cb6**.

Drop a **RadioButtonManager** bean onto the free-form surface. Because this bean is not in the bean palette, you press Ctrl-B, or select **Add Bean** from the Options menu. Name this bean **rbMgr**. Ensure that the **Class** radio button is selected as seen in Figure 10.3.

Make the following connection between rbMgr and each of the check box beans:

```
rbMgr (this) → cb# (checkboxGroup)
```

Change the labels of each of the check box beans to make up categories of things you want to reminders. Figure 10.4 shows a proposed set of labels, and also the connections from the previous step.

Notice that even though the check boxes are associated in a group by rbMgr, a CheckboxGroup, they still do not appear as radio buttons. This is because the association occurs dynamically when the RadioButtonPanel bean gets initialized.

You can actually run this bean by pressing the Test button. You are able to run this bean, even though it is a Panel, because the Visual Composition Editor generated a main() method for this bean, which instantiates the necessary components and then inserts the Panel in a Frame. This is done to help you test your beans quickly and to aid in the iterative development process. Press the Test button now and run the Panel. It should look like Figure 10.5. The check boxes now have the appearance of radio buttons and behave properly, where only one button can be selected at any one time.

Figure 10.3 Adding RadioButtonManager.

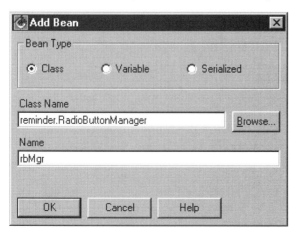

Figure 10.4 RadioButtonPanel completed.

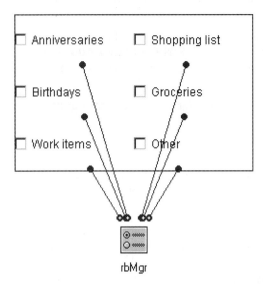

rbMgr

There is only one more thing to do before you can consider this part complete. As you remember from the spec, the first radio button in the group needs to be selected when the Reminder application starts up. This can be accomplished in several ways. To ensure that the timing is right and that all components of the application have been constructed before selecting the first radio button, you will use an event generated by the frame in the ReminderApp. The event is called windowOpened; it will trigger the connection to select the button. The connection will be (do not attempt this connection yet):

```
reminderFrame (windowOpened) → cb1 (setState)
```

Figure 10.5 Running RadioButtonPanel.

The problem is that because the RadioButtonPanel is embedded in another bean, its features are encapsulated and not accessible. You need to make the setState() method of **cb1** visible in the next level of composition. As you learned before, this is accomplished by promoting the required features or, if required, the entire bean.

Promote the setState() method of **cb1** by following these steps:

Click on the **cb1** check box to select it. Right-click to bring up its pop-up menu. Select **Promote Bean Feature.**

From the Method list, select **setState(boolean).** Accept the proposed name of **cb1SetState(boolean)** by pressing the **Promote** button.

Press **OK** to complete the promotion. Refer to Figure 10.6.

Promote the **previousKey** and **currentKey** properties of rbMgr:

Click on the rbMgr bean to select it. Right-click on it to bring up its pop-up menu. Select **Promote Bean Feature.**

From the Properties list, select **previousKey.** Accept the proposed name of **rbMgrPreviousKey** by pressing the **Promote** button.

Repeat the steps above and promote the **currentKey** property; accept its name as **rbMgrCurrentKey.**

Save and close the Visual Composition Editor for the RadioButtonPanel bean and proceed by building the next bean.

ReminderPanel

The next step is to create the ReminderPanel bean. This bean will encapsulate most of the function needed for the Reminder application to work as specified.

The ReminderPanel is composed of a RadioButtonPanel, a TextArea and a **ReminderHashtable** bean. You should be familiar with the first two beans. The ReminderHashtable is an specialization of the **java.util.Hashtable** class, which is part of the standard JDK 1.1.1.

ReminderHashtable

The **java.util.**Hashtable bean implements a collection class that provides you with a way to match a key to a value. You may know a hash table by other names like a map, a dictionary, or a table. The implementation of Hashtable is really not important; what is important is to know that it provides a means of storing key/value pairs in a Java program.

A Hashtable has methods such as get() and put() to manipulate its contents. Normally, when a value requested by the get(Object key) is not found in the Hashtable, a null object is returned. For the Reminder application, this is not the required behavior.

Figure 10.6 Promoting the setState() method.

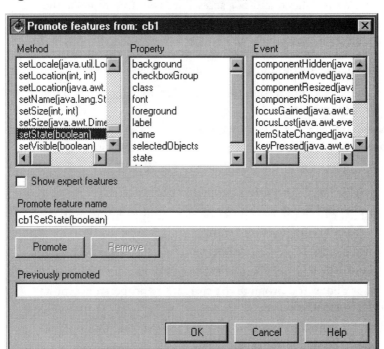

Think about it: What is the appropriate action if a category, for which no reminders have yet been entered, is selected? Clearing the contents of the text area to indicate no match is the right thing to do.

The ReminderHashtable extends Hashtable and overrides the get() method to return an empty String if the Hashtable returns null. Setting the text of the text area to an empty string clears it.

Start by creating a new class in the reminder package. Call this class **ReminderHashtable.** Make its superclass: **java.util.Hashtable.** Select the **Write source code for the class** radio button. Press the **Finish** button to create the class.

Ensure that you are in the Methods page of the browser and add a new method called **get.** This public method should return **java.lang.Object,** be synchronized, and take one parameter of type **java.lang.Object** (call the parameter **key**). This method overrides **get** in the superclass. Overriding this method gives you a chance to intercept the call before the superclass executes it. In our case, we use this opportunity to call the superclass' **get** method and examine the returned object. If it is null, we return an empty string object.

Add the highlighted code below, to the generated get method:

```
/**
 * This method was created by a SmartGuide.
 * @return java.lang.Object
 * @param key java.lang.Object
 */
public synchronized Object get( Object key) {
    // call the superclass' get method
    Object result = super.get(key);

    // if value not found for key, return an
    // empty String
    if(result == null)
        return (new String(""));
    // else return the found object representing
    // the found value for the key
    else
        return result;
}
```

The ReminderHashtable bean is now ready to be used in the ReminderPanel, which you will build next.

The ReminderPanel is built as a subclass of **java.awt.Panel**. As mentioned earlier, this panel is used to combine a RadioButtonPanel, a TextArea, and a ReminderHashtable. Build the ReminderPanel by following these steps:

Start by creating a new class in the reminder package. Call this class **ReminderPanel**. Make its superclass: **java.awt.Panel**. Select the **Design the class visually** radio button. Press the **Finish** button to create the class.

The Visual Composition Editor opens with a Panel object on the free-form surface. Select the Panel and bring up its property sheet. Set the layout of the panel to **BorderLayout**.

Add a RadioButtonPanel to the North of the border layout on panel. Call it **rbPanel**.

From the Data Entry category, drop a TextArea bean into the center of the border layout on the panel. Call it **reminderText**.

Add a ReminderHashTable to the free-form surface. Call it **theTable.** Your Visual Composition Editor should look like Figure 10.7.

Figure 10.7 All components in place.

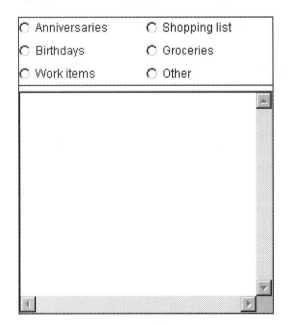

theTable

Make the following connection:

```
rbPanel (rbMgrPreviousKey) → theTable (put)
```

It is important to understand what this connection does and when it executes. As you recall, when you created the *previousKey* property in the RadioButtonManager, you designated it as a bound property. All bound properties fire *propertyChanged* events when their value changes. In our case, the value of *previousKey* changes every time a new radio button is selected by the user. You coded this behavior in the setCurrent() method of the RadioButtonManager bean.

From the spec, you know that every time the user selects a new radio button, the current reminder in the text area must be saved and associated with the previously selected radio button. Using the event generated when *previousKey* changes value is just what you need to put the value of the text area into the reminder Hashtable. The connection above does just that.

The previous connection calls the method:

```
Object put( Object key, Object value)
```

As you can see, it requires two parameters, the key and the value to be stored in the Hashtable. These parameters are readily available. Make the following property-to-parameter connections:

```
rbPanel (rbMgrPreviousKey)  →  connection (key)
reminderText (text)  →  connection (value)
```

The three connections above save the contents of the text area to the Hashtable every time the *previousKey* property changes. This is only half of what you need. Make the following connections to get the contents of the Hashtable every time the *currentKey* property changes and place the result in the text area. The *currentKey* property is used as the key to retrieve the correct value from the Hashtable. Connect:

```
rbPanel (rbMgrCurrentKey)  →  theTable (get)
```

This connection requires one parameter, the key to be used to retrieve the stored value in the Hashtable. This parameters is readily available. Make the following property-to-parameter connections:

```
rbPanel (rbMgrCurrentKey)  →  connection (key)
connection(normalResult)  →  reminderText(text)
```

The last connection is used to apply the return value of the Object get(Object key) method to the contents of the text area. If the key was not found, an empty string is placed into the text area. This produces the effect of clearing its contents. You coded this behavior in the get() method of the ReminderHashtable bean. Once

Figure 10.8 Connections completed.

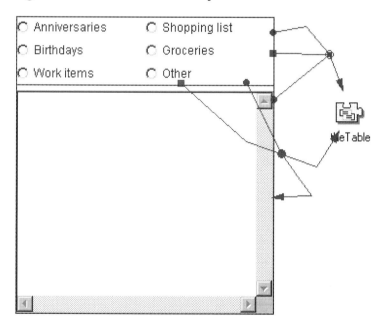

you have completed all the above connections, your Visual Composition Editor should look very much like Figure 10.8.

Run this panel to test the function you have completed so far. You should be able to select categories with the radio buttons, enter text in the input area, switch back and forth between radio buttons, and have the correct text displayed in the text area for each of the reminder categories.

You have made connections to save the contents of the text area to the Hashtable. There is also a requirement to save the text in the text area when the program exits. To accomplish this task, create a new method called **saveCurrentCategory**.

> Ensure that you are in the Methods page of the browser and add a new method called **saveCurrentCategory**. This public method should return void, be synchronized and take no parameters.

> Add the highlighted code below to the generated method:

```
public synchronized void saveCurrentCategory()
{
    gettheTable().put(getrbPanel().
      getRbMgrCurrentKey(),
      getreminderText().getText());
    return;
}
```

This method is written in a single line of code, which chains a few method calls to other beans in ReminderPanel to perform the put method on the Hashtable. This method will be used later from the ReminderApp bean.

Double Promotion

The last thing to do before proceeding to the ReminderApp is to promote the **cb1SetState** method from the RadioButtonPanel bean again. As you remember, this method was promoted when you built that bean. That promotion made the method visible in this bean. If you want it to be visible at the next level, the ReminderApp, you must promote it again.

Promotions only increase the visibility of a feature one level at the time. If necessary, features must be re-promoted to propagate them to higher level beans.

This is not necessarily a bad thing; it forces the developer to verify that a feature is required to be visible at the next level of usage. This prevents the public interface of complex beans from becoming cluttered.

Select the rbPanel bean, click the right mouse button, and select **Promote Bean Feature**. From the Method list, select **cb1SetState(boolean)**. Change the proposed name of **rbPanelCb1SetState(boolean)** to **cb1SetState(boolean)**. This will keep the same name from level to level of promotion.

In the next section, you will add the ReminderPanel to a Frame so it can be run as a stand-alone Java application. You will also add function to implement the part of the specification dealing with initialization and persistence.

ReminderApp

Most of the features required for the Reminder Application already exists in the ReminderPanel bean. According to the spec, the features that still need to be implemented include:

- Select the first category when the program starts.

- Provide persistence for reminders between program invocations.

- Ensure that when the program closes no information is lost.

- Add a main menu bar with File and Help menu items.

The ReminderApp is a subclass of **java.awt.Frame**. The frame is used to hold a ReminderPanel bean and a menu bar. It also has the necessary logic to save the Hashtable and to start another process where a web browser containing the help system will run.

Start by creating a new class in the reminder package. Call this class **ReminderApp.** Make its superclass: **java.awt.Frame.** Select the **Design the class visually** radio button. Press the **Finish** button to create the class.

The Visual Composition Editor opens with a Frame object on the free-form surface. Select the Frame and bring up its property sheet. Set the layout of the panel to BorderLayout. Set the *title* property to **Reminder Application.**

Add a ReminderPanel bean to the center of the border layout on the frame. Call it **reminderPanel.** Placing a bean in the center of a border layout causes that bean to expand in all directions. When there are no other beans in the periphery, the bean in the center touches the border of the frame. In most cases, this does not look very good. To provide a margin, drop a Label bean on each of the West, East, and South areas of the border layout of the Frame. Erase the label of each of the Label beans. The Visual Composition Editor should look like Figure 10.9.

Make the following connection to select the first category radio button when the window opens:

```
ReminderApp (windowOpened event) → reminderPanel (cb1SetState)
```

The connection will appear dashed as it needs to know whether to set the state to true or false. Double-click the connection, press the **Set parameters** button, and set the *state* parameter to true. Press **OK** twice to complete the operation.

The *windowOpened* event happens only once in the life of a Frame, when it first opens. This makes it a good event to trigger the selection of the first category. The next two connections deal with the application closing. It is important that these connections execute in the right order. They are all triggered by the

Figure 10.9 Reminder Application.

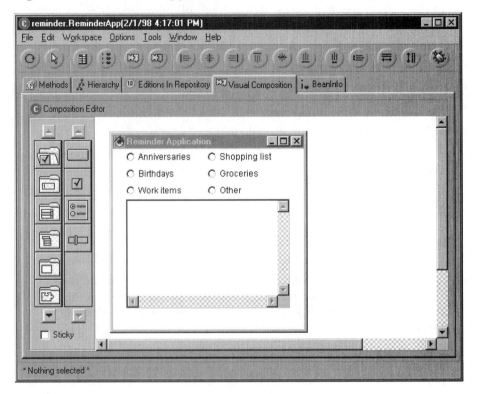

windowClosing event. This event happens only once in the life time of a Frame, just before it closes. Connect:

```
ReminderApp (windowClosing event) → reminderPanel (saveCurrentCategory)
```

The next connection is automatically created by the Visual Composition Editor when a new class subclassing from Frame is created. Make sure it exists and was not deleted by mistake. If missing, make it again.

```
ReminderApp (windowClosing event) → ReminderApp (dispose)
```

ReminderApp, in the connections above, refers to the actual Frame bean on the composition surface.

Run the ReminderApp to see how it behaves so far. When the application starts, the first radio button should be selected. You should be able to select other categories and add text for them. Switching back and forth between categories should properly save and recall the correct text.

Adding Persistence

The only problem is that when you close the application and then start it up again, your reminders are gone. This is because you have not made any provisions for saving the reminders in a nonvolatile type of storage.

To make the reminders persist, you have a variety of choices, some more portable than others. You could:

- Read and write to a flat disk file
- Use the operating system's registry
- Use .ini files
- Serialize the Hashtable

Serialization is the Java way of providing persistent storage. It is easy to do because the language was designed with it in mind. Java can serialize a Java bean by storing its type and its state. Later on, the serialized data can be used to reconstruct the bean and restore its original state.

Every Java language book that covers version 1.1 and above has a section about this subject, so we will not spend any time on the internal mechanism that makes serialization possible. Any bean that implements the **java.io.Serializable** interface can be serialized.

Serialized beans are stored as binary files and are treated as resources. That means that a Java program using serialized beans must be able to find and access these files. By convention, serialized bean files have an extension of **ser**. There are no conventions regarding the location of files containing serialized beans. In this project, you will store the serialized ReminderHashtable in the same directory as the class files.

The **java.io.ObjectOutputStream** and **java.io.ObjectInputStream** classes provide the writeObject() and readObject() methods to store and retrieve serialized objects.

This version of VisualAge for Java does not handle serialized beans very gracefully. VisualAge is a consumer of serialized beans, but not a producer. That is not to say that you cannot produce, or create and store, serialized beans; you can and you will. What it means is that producing serialized beans is not an automated process, and there are no SmartGuides to help you along to create them.

While in the Visual Composition Editor, you cannot use a serialized bean that does not already exist; the tool will not create that very first instance for you. This is a chicken-and-egg situation. You need an existing serialized object before you can use it, but you cannot create it easily inside the tool when you need to use it. We will show you a couple of ways to deal with this problem.

Using Serialized JavaBeans

As mentioned before, you cannot drop a serialized bean on the free-form surface of the Visual Composition Editor unless you already have one to refer to. When you try to use a serialized bean, the Visual Composition Editor asks you for its file name. You cannot just create an empty file with the right name because the visual builder will actually open the file to find out what type of bean it contains. You need a way to create a file containing a legitimate serialized bean.

First Approach

Open the Visual Composition Editor for the ReminderPanel bean. You will add a serialized ReminderHashtable bean to replace the one already there. Once it is on the free-form surface, you will move the connections from the existing bean (**theTable**) to the new serialized bean, delete the original bean, and rename the new bean to **theTable**.

Select **Add Bean** from the Options menu.

Press the **Serialized** radio button and notice how the **Class Name** entry field becomes the **File Name** entry field. Pressing the **Browse** button enables you to look for the file containing the bean shown in Figure 10.10. The problems is that the bean doesn't exist yet, so you can't find it. Press the **Cancel** button.

This approach will show you how to create a serialized bean of the type you need (in your case, a ReminderHashtable bean) outside the Visual Composition Editor. This is not as hard as it sounds.

From the main menu, open a Scrapbook window and enter the code shown below. Make sure that the first line, where the **outFile** object is created, is typed all in the same line in the Scrapbook. (This line is spread over several lines in the book because of space constraints.) There should be no spaces anywhere between the quotes defining the string with the path and file name.

Figure 10.10 Adding a serialized bean.

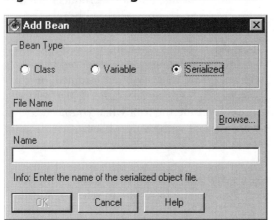

Make sure you use the drive letter of where VisualAge for Java is installed in your system to make up the correct path to store the bean.

Make sure that the **reminder** directory exists under **My Project**; if it doesn't, create it before running the code in the Scrapbook. Select all of the code and press the Run button.

```
java.io.FileOutputStream outFile =
new java.io.FileOutputStream(
    "D:\\IBMVJava\\Ide\\project_resources\\
    My Project\\reminder\\table.ser");

java.io.ObjectOutputStream outStream = new
    java.io.ObjectOutputStream(outFile);

reminder.ReminderHashtable ht = new
    reminder.ReminderHashtable();


outStream.writeObject(ht);
```

The directory used to create the FileOutputStream is where VisualAge for Java expects the resources and serialized beans to be for the **reminder** package in the **My Project** project.

Now you have an empty ReminderHashtable serialized bean ready to be brought into the Visual Composition Editor. Return to the Visual Composition Editor and add **table.ser** to the free-form surface by following these steps:

From the Options menu, select **Add Bean**.

Press the **Serialized** radio button. Press the **Browse** button and find the table.ser file. Name the bean **newTable**. Press the **OK** button as shown in Figure 10.11.

NOTE

Even though you named the bean in the Add Bean dialog, the Visual Builder will not use the name. You will need to change the bean name once it is added to the free-form surface.

Now you have two ReminderHashtable beans on the free-form surface, **theTable** and **newTable**. Because these two beans are of the same type, you can move the connections from **theTable** to **newTable**. Select the connection, drag the ending point from one bean to the other. Move the two connections now.

The original ReminderHashtable, **theTable**, is no longer needed. Delete it.

Figure 10.11 Adding a serialized ReminderTable bean.

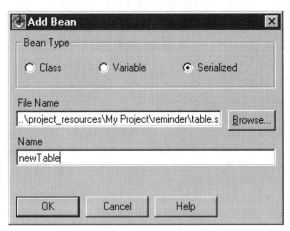

Rename **newTable** to **theTable**. This keeps the references to **theTable** in the other components of the program valid.

Promote the *this* property of **theTable**. This enables you to refer to the Hashtable from ReminderApp in order to save any changes when exiting the program. Name the promoted feature **theTable**.

Save the bean. From the File menu, select **Save Bean**.

There is one other thing to think about. If you look at the gettheTable() method just created, you will see how a new instance of ReminderHashtable is created from the serialized bean file. But what happens if the file is not found at run time? This is a normal and expected condition, especially the first time the program is run. Also, the user might erase this file if he or she wants to start over again.

The generated code does not handle this situation at all. Add the highlighted code below to the gettheTable() method to handle the situation where the file doesn't exist and the bean could not be created. In this case, an exception is thrown and the catch clause creates a new ReminderHashtable.

```
/**
 * Return the theTable property value.
 * @return reminder.ReminderHashtable
 */
/* WARNING: THIS METHOD WILL BE REGENERATED. */
public ReminderHashtable gettheTable() {
   if (ivjtheTable == null) {
      try {
         java.lang.Class iiCls = Class.forName
```

```
      ("reminder.ReminderHashtable");
    java.lang.ClassLoader iiClassLoader =
      iiCls.getClassLoader();
    ivjtheTable =
      (reminder.ReminderHashtable)
      java.beans.Beans.instantiate(
      iiClassLoader,"Reminder\\table");
    // user code begin {1}
    // user code end
    } catch (java.lang.Throwable ivjExc) {
      // user code begin {2}
      ivjtheTable = new
        reminder.ReminderHashtable();
      // user code end
      handleException(ivjExc);
    }
  }
  return ivjtheTable;
}
```

Save the gettheTable() method and test the program. It should still behave as before. That is to say, it will still not save your reminders when you exit. To get the program to do that, you need to write a bit of code in the ReminderApp bean.

Now you have a choice. If you can't wait to get this part of the program completed, go ahead to the next section, Saving the ReminderHashtable. However, if you continue reading, you will learn a second way to instantiate serialized beans in the Visual Composition Editor, without having to create one in the Scrapbook first.

Second Approach

This approach uses a variable; you will learn about variables in detail in the next chapter. For now, suffice it to say that a variable is not a bean in itself; it is a reference to an already existing bean of the same type. For those of you with C++ experience, a variable is very similar to a pointer, but Java has no pointers.

To iterate once more on the ReminderPanel bean, follow these steps and replace the serialized ReminderHashtable bean with a variable of the same type:

From the Options menu, select **Add Bean**.

Press the **Variable** radio button. Set the **Interface/Class** entry field to **reminder.ReminderHashtable**. Name the bean **newTable**. Press the **OK** button as shown in Figure 10.12.

Once again, you have two ReminderHashtable beans on the free-form surface, **theTable** and **newTable**. Notice that the icon representing **newTable** is enclosed in brackets; this is to signify that it is variable and

Figure 10.12 Adding a ReminderTable variable.

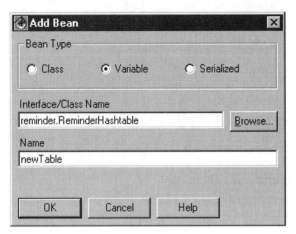

not a concrete bean. Because these two beans are of the same type, you can move the connections from **theTable** to **newTable**. Select the connection, drag the ending point from one bean to the other. Move the two connections now.

The serialized ReminderHashtable, **theTable,** is no longer needed. Delete it.

Rename **newTable** to **theTable**. Doing so keeps references to **theTable** in the other components of the program valid.

Promote the *this* property of **theTable**. This will enable you to refer to the Hashtable from ReminderApp in order to save any changes when exiting the program. Name the promoted feature **theTable**.

Save the bean. From the File menu, select **Save Bean**.

Examining the generated code reveals the gettheTable() method does not do much.

```
/**
 * Return the theTable property value.
 * @return reminder.ReminderHashtable
 */
/* WARNING: THIS METHOD WILL BE REGENERATED. */
public ReminderHashtable gettheTable() {
   // user code begin {1}
   // user code end
   return ivjtheTable;
}
```

This is because a variable needs to be set programmatically. Its initial value is set to null and must be assigned to refer to another object of the same type at the appropriate time in the program. Notice that the code generator assigned the name **ivjtheTable** to the variable.

Add the highlighted code below to the gettheTable() method to attempt to load a serialized ReminderHashtable bean or create a new one if the load fails. The newly created bean is then assigned to the **ivjtheTable** variable.

```
/**
 * Return the theTable property value.
 * @return reminder.ReminderHashtable
 */
/* WARNING: THIS METHOD WILL BE REGENERATED. */
public ReminderHashtable gettheTable() {
   // user code begin {1}
   if(ivjtheTable==null) {
     try{
       String userDir =
         System.getProperty("user.dir");
       String beanLocation = userDir +
         "\\reminder\\table.ser";
       java.io.FileInputStream istream = new
         java.io.FileInputStream(beanLocation);
       java.io.ObjectInputStream p = new
         java.io.ObjectInputStream(istream);
       ivjtheTable =
         (ReminderHashtable) p.readObject();
         istream.close();
     }
     catch(Exception e){
       ivjtheTable = new
         reminder.ReminderHashtable();
     }
   }
   // user code end
   return ivjtheTable;
}
```

This code is simpler than it appears; the first two lines determine the fully qualified path from which to read the serialized file. The first line gets the **user.dir** property from the System object. This returns the directory from where the program was started, which is usually the root directory of the *classpath*. From there, you add the package and file names **\\reminder\\table.ser**. The result is the string, **beanLocation**, which corresponds to the file's location.

Once you have the fully qualified name of the serialized object's file, open a FileInputStream using the beanLocation string. With the FileInputStream, you create an ObjectInputStream. Finally, use the readObject() method to read and reconstruct the object, which is cast to a ReminderHashtable and assigned to the ivjtheTable variable.

If, for any reason, any of the steps above throws an exception, create a new ReminderHashtable so that the program can continue executing.

Saving the ReminderHashtable

The specifications for the Reminder program dictate that when the program exits, the reminders need to be saved.

Because you already have the code to read a serialized bean, the easiest way to save the reminders is to serialize the ReminderHashtable.

The trigger to save the reminders is the **windowClosing** event. As explained earlier in this chapter, this event only happens once in the lifetime of a Frame, just before it closes.

Ensure you are in the Visual Composition Editor for the ReminderApp. Connect:

```
ReminderApp (windowClosing event) →
free-form surface (Event to Script...)
```

As before, ReminderApp in the connection above refers to the actual Frame on the free-form surface. An event-to-script connection brings up the Event-to-Script window. In this window, you can connect to any method in the class. You can also create a new method as shown in Figure 10.13. Press the **New method** button.

You are now in a SmartGuide that will facilitate creating a new method in the ReminderApp class. Call it **saveTable**: It should return void and accept no parameters. It should be private and synchronized as shown in Figure 10.14. Press the **Next** button to continue with the SmartGuide.

The next page of the SmartGuide appears. In this page, you can define any exceptions this method throws as shown in Figure 10.15. Add an java.io.IOException to the list of exceptions. Press the **Finish** button.

The Event-to-Script window returns. Select the saveTable() method and press the **OK** button to complete the connection.

Switch to the Methods page of the browser and select the saveTable() method. Enter the highlighted code below to complete the code necessary to serialize and save the ReminderHashtable:

```
/**
 * This method was created by a SmartGuide.
 * @exception java.io.IOException The exception
```

```
* description./
private synchronized void saveTable( ) throws
        java.io.IOException {
  String userDir =
    System.getProperty("user.dir");
  String beanLocation = userDir +
    "\\reminder\\table.ser";

  java.io.FileOutputStream outFile = new
    java.io.FileOutputStream(beanLocation);
  java.io.ObjectOutputStream outStream = new
    java.io.ObjectOutputStream(outFile);
  outStream.writeObject(
    getreminderPanel().gettheTable());

  return;
}
```

This code is very similar to that of the second approach to load a serialized bean.

The first line gets the **user.dir** property from the System object. This returns the directory from where the program was started, which is usually the root directory of the *classpath*. From there, you add the package and file names: **\\reminder\\table.ser**. The result is the string, **beanLocation** , which corresponds to the file's location.

Figure 10.13 Event-to-Script window.

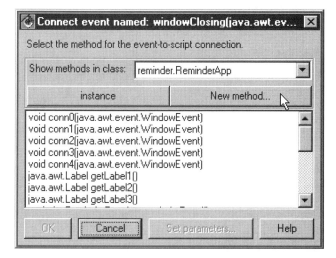

Figure 10.14 Adding the saveTable method.

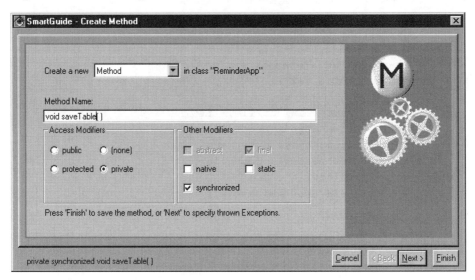

Once you have the fully qualified name of the serialized object's file, you open a FileOutputStream using the **beanLocation** string. The FileOutputStream is used to create an ObjectOutputStream. Finally, you use the writeObject() method to serialize and store the ReminderHashtable object.

Figure 10.15 Adding to the exceptions list.

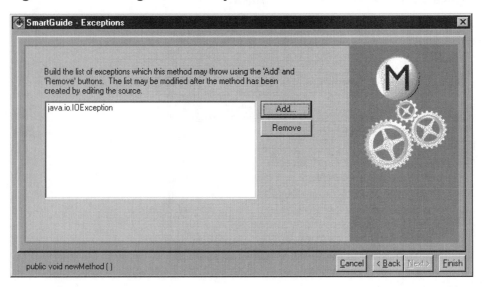

Exiting the Application

While running in the VisualAge for Java environment, a connection from the *windowClosing* event to the Frame's dispose method is enough to exit the program.

Once you deploy your application and depending on the VM you are running under, you might find that calling dispose() does not close your window. In this case, you need to drop a **System** bean on the free-form surface and name it **System**. Then make the following connection:

```
ReminderApp(windowClosing event) → system(exit)
```

Once the connection is made, double-click on it, to set its properties. Press the **Set Parameters** button and set the *status* parameter to 0. This is the exit code of the program.

TIP

When you set the parameter to the default value, the Visual Builder does not recognize the change and the connection line remains dashed. If you want to turn the dashed green line into a solid line, you need to:

   Open the property editor for the connections and set the parameter to a nondefault value.

   Close the property editor to save the change, then reopen the property editor and set it back to the default value.

All connections and coding are now complete. The Visual Composition Editor for the ReminderApp bean should look like Figure 10.16.

If you have been keeping track of the connections from the ReminderApp Frame to various methods, you know that there are four actions triggered by the *windowClosing* event. It is very important that these connections execute in the right order; otherwise, you might be disposing the window before you save the table.

Select the ReminderApp frame, right-click, and from the pop-up menu, select **Reorder Connections From**. This brings up the Reorder Connections window. In this window, you can drag and drop connections to alter the order in which they fire. Make sure that your order is the same as that of the connections in Figure 10.17.

NOTE

Drag and drop connections just like you do any object in the Visual Builder. You point the mouse at the connection you want to move, press and hold down the left mouse button, then drag the connection to the desired position and release it.

Figure 10.16 Connections complete.

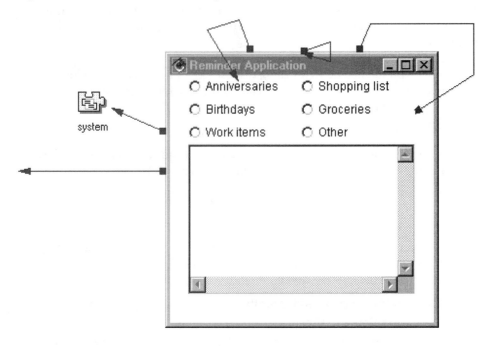

   Congratulations! You have finished the first phase of the Reminder application. At this point you should test it and make sure that reminders are saved and restored properly when you exit and restart the program. Once you are happy that it is working fine, you should version the package.

Figure 10.17 Verifying the connection order.

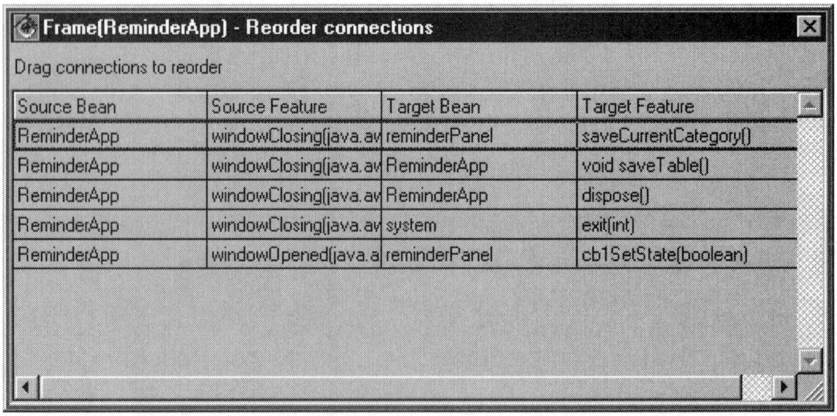

Source Bean	Source Feature	Target Bean	Target Feature
ReminderApp	windowClosing(java.av	reminderPanel	saveCurrentCategory()
ReminderApp	windowClosing(java.av	ReminderApp	void saveTable()
ReminderApp	windowClosing(java.av	ReminderApp	dispose()
ReminderApp	windowClosing(java.av	system	exit(int)
ReminderApp	windowOpened(java.a	reminderPanel	cb1SetState(boolean)

Frame(ReminderApp) - Reorder connections

Drag connections to reorder

After versioning, you may want to go back to the ReminderPanel bean and try the alternate persistence approach.

Running Outside the IDE

You may also be interested in trying to run the program outside the VisualAge for Java environment. If so, export your package to a directory in your *classpath*. Choose the option to **Create package subdirectories** in the second screen of the **Export SmartGuide** as shown in Figure 10.18.

Before you can run the program outside VisualAge, you must install the JDK 1.1, available free from java.sun.com/products/index.html. If you are thinking of shipping stand-alone Java applications, you should know that Sun does not allow the JDK to be shipped with your applications You must instead ship the Java Runtime Environment (JRE). It is available from the same URL.

To see what your CLASSPATH environment variable is set to, open a command window and at the prompt type: **echo %classpath%**. If the reply is **ECHO is on** or you do see any directories listed, your *classpath* is not set. To temporarily set it, enter at the command prompt: **set classpath=.;d:\javabook\classes** or to another directory where you want to start saving the files for your projects.

Multiple directories can be set in the *classpath* and must be separated by the directory separator used in your operating system. In Windows and OS/2, use the

Figure 10.18 Exporting the reminder package.

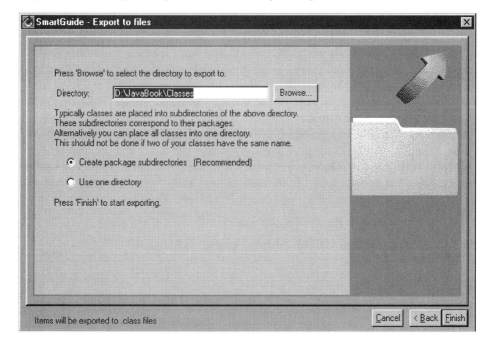

semicolon (;). It is also a good idea to start the *classpath* with a period (.) denoting the current directory. The directory to which you exported the files from VisualAge should be listed in your *classpath*.

Permanently setting the *classpath* is done differently depending on your operating system. In Windows95 and OS/2, you enter the above in your autoexec.bat file. In Windows NT, you use the Environment object from the Control Panel's System folder.

Once the JDK is installed and your *classpath* set, switch to the same directory to which you exported the package from VisualAge. At the command prompt, type **java reminder.ReminderApp**. This command assumes you have entered the JDK's **java.exe** location in your PATH statement. If not, you have to fully qualify the previous command.

If you have the JRE installed, you can start the program by entering the following command at the prompt:

jre -cp d:\javabook\classes reminder.ReminderApp

This command assumes you have entered the JRE's **jre.exe** location in your PATH statement. If not, you have to fully qualify the previous command.

The JRE ignores any *classpath* you might have set. The *classpath* is defined with the command line parameter **-cp d:\javabook\classes**.

This will start the Java VM and load and run the ReminderApp class. You should see the program's main window appear.

The file, **table.ser**, containing the ReminderHashtable will be in the same directory as the other class files for the program.

Adding Menus

The next function to implement in the Reminder program is the main menu bar and submenus for the application. The menus for this application are not very complex in structure and will serve as an introduction to the mechanics of building menus in VisualAge for Java.

Open the ReminderApp bean in the Visual Composition Editor. Beans for assembling menus can be found in the bean palette in the **Menus** category.

From the Menus category, select a **MenuBar** bean and drop it on the Frame. The result is that a menu bar is added below the title bar of the frame window. An icon representing the first **Menu** object is added to the free-form surface. The icon is connected to the menu bar item of the same name. This is not a connection that can be selected or changed; it is fixed. You can only add one MenuBar bean to a Frame.

Complete the menu for the application by following these steps:

Open the properties window for the **Menu** and change the following properties

- actionCommand to **miFile**
- beanName to **miFile**

- name to **miFile**
- label to **File**

 Drop two **MenuItem** beans on top of the File menu. Open the property sheet for the first menu item and change the following:

- actionCommand to **miClear**
- beanName to **miClear**
- name to **miClear**
- label to **Clear**
- shortcut to Ctrl-Shift-C

   Open the property sheet for the second menu item and change the following:

- actionCommand to **miExit**
- beanName to **miExit**
- name to **miExit**
- label to **Exit**
- shortcut to Ctrl-Shift-X

 Drop a **MenuSeparator** bean between the two menu item beans you just added.

   Drop a second **Menu** bean on top of the menu bar. Open its property sheet and change the following:

- actionCommand to **Help**
- beanName to **miHelp**
- name to **miHelp**
- label to **Help**

   Drop one **MenuItem** bean on top of the Help menu. Open its property sheet and change the following:

- actionCommand to **miGeneralHelp**
- beanName to **miGeneralHelp**
- name to **miGeneralHelp**
- label to **General help**
- shortcut to Ctrl-Shift-H

The ReminderApp should look like Figure 10.19. Note that, to reduce the complexity of the following figures, the already existing connections have been hidden.

As you may have noticed, the shortcut keys do not appear beside the menu items in the Visual Composition Editor. This is done to conserve space on the free-form surface. When you run the program, they appear. Press the Test button to see what the menus look like at run time.

Menu items, like buttons, generate *actionPerformed* events when selected. Therefore, making connections to menu items is very simple.

Sometimes, making even very simple connections is not the right design choice.

The **Exit** menu item must perform the same functions as closing the window. As you recall, there were four connections required to properly save and close the application. This means those four connections must be duplicated, this time originating from the **miExit** menu item. A better design would be to add a method, or script, to perform all the necessary clean-up in one place. Connect:

```
miExit (actionPerformed event) → free-form surface (Event to Script...)
```

Figure 10.19 Menu structure.

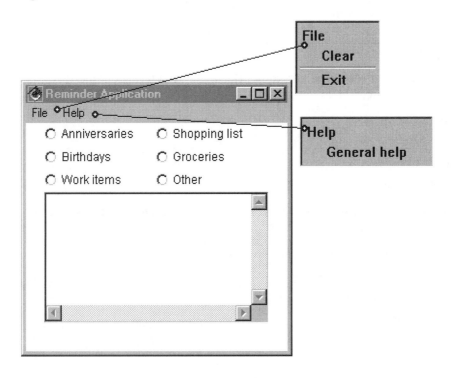

Press the **New method** button on the Event-to-Script window. Create a new private method. Call it **cleanUp;** it should return void and accept no parameters. Press the **Finish** button and complete the connection by selecting **cleanUp** from the instance methods list. If you need more details, refer to where you added the **saveTable** method earlier in this chapter.

Switch to the Methods page of the browser and add the highlighted code to the cleanUp method:

```
/**
* This method was created by a SmartGuide.
*/
private void cleanUp ( )
{
    getreminderPanel().saveCurrentCategory();

    try {
        this.saveTable();
    } catch (java.lang.Throwable ivjExc) {
        handleException(ivjExc);
    }

    this.dispose();
    System.exit(0);
    return;
}
```

Delete the four connections from the Frame's windowClosing event, as they are replaced by the `cleanUp()` method.

Connect:

```
ReminderApp (windowClosing event) →
free-form surface (Event to Script...)
```

Select the cleanUp() method from the list.

This is much cleaner design and a good example of how a little hand-coding can replace a lot of connections. In this case, we saved six connections. This code will not only perform better, but it will also remove some complexity from the Visual Composition Editor display. See Figure 10.20 with no hidden connections.

Activating Clear

The next function to implement is the one to clear the text area using the option in the main menu.

Figure 10.20 Simplified connections.

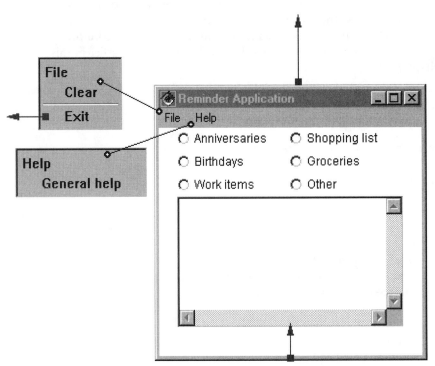

Because the TextArea bean does not have a clear method, you will use the setText(java.lang.String) method, passing as a parameter an empty string. As you remember, the text area is part of the ReminderPanel bean, and as such, its features are encapsulated in the bean and not accessible in the ReminderApp.

Open the Visual Composition Editor for the ReminderPanel bean. Select the text area and promote the **setText()** method. Overwrite the proposed name of the promoted feature and make it **setTextArea(java.lang.String)**. Save the bean. Back in the Visual Composition Editor for the ReminderApp, connect:

```
miClear(actionPerformed) → reminderPanel(setTextArea)
```

Notice that the connection is dashed, indicating that a parameter is needed. Double-click the connection, and in the property sheet for the connection, press the **Set parameters** button.

The next window enables you to enter a constant parameter to be passed to the setTextArea(java.lang.String t) method (see Figure 10.21). You want to pass an empty string, so you do not need to enter anything in the **Value** entry field. Do not enter anything; press **OK** and **OK** again to close the previous window. The

Figure 10.21 Entering constant parameter.

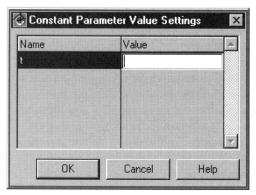

connection remains dashed even though you attempted to enter the required parameter. If you save the bean and look at the generated code, you will see:

```
getreminderPanel().setTextArea(new
    java.lang.String());
```

This will do what you want: set the text in the text area to an empty string. However, it is not a good idea to leave a dashed connection in the visual builder, as it indicates (falsely, in this case) that something is missing.

To make the connection solid, you must enter something in the Value column of the window and press **OK** to accept it. Right away, press the **Set parameters** button again and delete what you previously typed, effectively leaving an empty string in the Value column. Press **OK** and **OK** again to close the previous window. Now the connection is solid. The generated code in this case looks a little different but still performs the same function:

```
getreminderPanel().setTextArea("");
```

Test the application again and verify that the text in the input area clears when selecting **Clear** from the File menu. It should also work when you press the shortcut key Ctrl-Shift-C.

At this point, it is probably a good idea to create a new version of the reminder package.

Activating Help

Adding basic help to an application is not very hard to do. Adding context-sensitive help is another story. Unlike other programming languages, Java does not support accessing the operating system's help subsystem. Perhaps this is due to the fact that once you bring up an HTML page, you can use it for browsing other

HTML help pages, as if you were browsing a local web site that contains the help for the program.

You will implement basic help for the ReminderApp. Selecting **General help** from the Help menu will start a web browser in another process. The browser will start in the Help's home page for the program.

The most complex part of coding this implementation is determining where the browser is installed. Different operating systems offer different services to find out which is the default browser installed in the system.

Most of these services are used through operating system APIs and must be accessed by native Java methods. One must first determine which operating system the program is running under using the System.getProperty("os.name") static method. Then choose the appropriate way to determine the default browser for that operating system. This implementation is beyond the scope of this book.

In the ReminderApp, the user will tell the program which browser to use. The program will remember this information by storing it in the ReminderHashtable, which is already persistent.

Start by dropping another **MenuItem** bean on top of the Help menu, below the General help menu item already there. Open its property sheet and change the following:

- actionCommand to **miBrowser**
- beanName to **miBrowser**
- name to **miBrowser**
- label to Browser setup

From the **Containers** category, drop a **FileDialog** bean on the free-form surface somewhere close to Help menu. Name this bean **fileDialog**. Open the property sheet and set:

- file to *.exe
- modal to **true**
- title to Select web browser executable

Make the following connections:

```
miBrowser (actionPerformed) → fileDialog (show)
miBrowser (actionPerformed) → fileDialog (dispose)
miBrowser (actionPerformed) → free-form surface (Event to Script...)
```

In the Event-to-Script dialog now showing, create and select a new private method called **setBrowser,** which returns void and takes two **java.lang.String** parameters. Name the parameters *directory* and *fileName.*

From fileDialog, connect as parameters to the previous connection:

```
fileDialog (directory) → connection (directory)
fileDialog (file) → connection (fileName)
```

Save the bean.

This step makes up a fully qualified path to your web browser and stores it in the ReminderHashtable. Switch to the Methods page of the browser. Select the setBrowser() method and add the highlighted code:

```
/**
 * This method was created by a SmartGuide.
 * @param fileName java.lang.String
 */
private void setBrowser (
        java.lang.String directory,
        java.lang.String fileName)
{
    if(fileName != null)
    {
        getreminderPanel().gettheTable().
            put("browserLocaction",
            directory + fileName);
    }

    return;

}
```

You might be wondering how this sequence of connections works. The first connection between miBrowser and the show() method of the file dialog does just that; it makes the file dialog appear. Because it is modal, the call to show() does not return until the file dialog is closed, either by pressing the **Cancel** or the **OK** button. At that point, the call returns and the dispose() method executes, removing the file dialog from the screen. Next, the call to setBrowser() executes, getting its parameters from the file dialog. If the **Cancel** button was pressed, the *file* property of the file dialog is null.

In the setBrowser() method, the *directory* and *fileName* parameters are concatenated and saved in the Hashtable using a key of **browserLocation**. Because the Hashtable is serialized and saved when the program exits, we have a way of remembering this setting.

You could add a number of improvements to this simple implementation. For example, you could disable **General help** until the browser setup is done. Or better still, when the user selects **General help** for the first time, you could invoke the setBrowser routines to do the initial setting. We have chosen the approach you just implemented because it shows all the steps necessary to accomplish the task. We leave these refinements as an exercise to the reader.

Finally, the application is ready to display HTML help. All that is left to do is to make one connection and a few lines of code. Follow these steps to complete the ReminderApp:

Connect:

```
miGeneralHelp (actionPerformed) →
free-form surface (Event to Script...)
```

In the Event-to-Script window now showing, create and select a new private method called **showHelp**, which returns void and takes no parameters.

Save the bean.

The showHelp() method checks to see if a browser location has been set. If the query to the Hashtable does not return an empty string, the fully qualified path to the help home page is constructed and concatenated with the fully qualified path name to the browser. Then the Runtime.exec() method is called to start a new process, invoking the browser and passing as a parameter the starting HTML page.

Switch to the Methods page of the browser. Select the showHelp()method and add the highlighted code:

```
/**
 * This method was created by a SmartGuide.
 */
private void showHelp ( ){
  String browser =
    (String)getreminderPanel().
    gettheTable().get("browserLocation");
  if (browser.equals("") == false)
  {
    try
    {
      String userDir =
        System.getProperty("user.dir");
      String helpFile = " " + userDir +
        "\\reminder\\reminderHome.html";
      Runtime.getRuntime().exec( browser +
        helpFile);
    }
    catch (java.io.IOException e) {}
  }
```

```
    return;
}
```

You can test most of the ReminderApp in the VisualAge for Java environment. However, when it comes to starting the process to show the help screen in the web browser, you will find that VisualAge does not do it. We are not sure whether to call this a bug or a design decision. But do not fear: When you deploy the application, it will run as expected.

In the Workbench, select the reminder package and export the Java classes to the same directory you did earlier in the chapter. When asked, choose to overwrite the existing files.

Before you continue, take a minute to copy the .html, .gif, and .jpg files from the reminder directory in the CD-ROM to the same directory where you exported your class files.

Open a command window and type **java reminder.ReminderApp**. This starts the program running. If you have not yet set the browser information, you should do that now by selecting **Browser setup** from the Help menu. The system's file dialog will come up. Find the location of your browser and press **OK** as shown in Figure 10.22.

Figure 10.22 Setting the web browser.

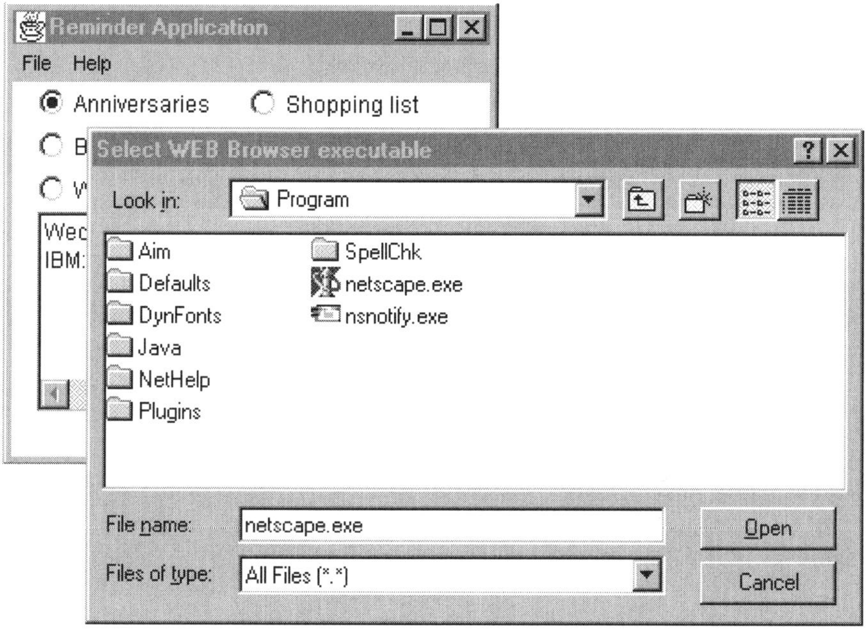

Figure 10.23 Displaying help in browser.

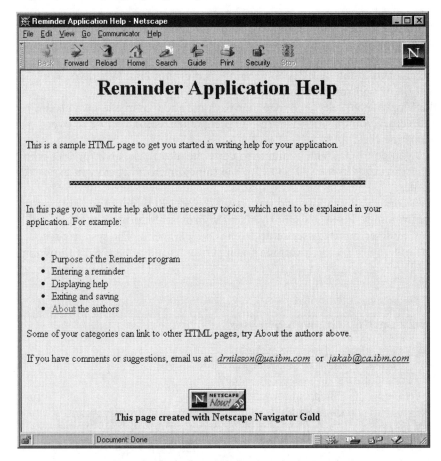

Now that the program knows which web browser to use, go ahead and select **General help** from the Help menu. The selected browser should come up displaying your help home page as shown in Figure 10.23.

Summary

A lot of new concepts were covered in this chapter. You built a new application from the ground up. In this chapter, we covered:

- Menus
- Submenus
- Embedded beans
- CheckboxGroup

- Radio buttons
- TextArea
- Hashtable
- Event-to-script connections
- File dialogs
- Displaying HTML Help

All of these beans and features give you a broader knowledge of Java programming and prepare you for making your own programs.

ADVANCED TOPICS

11

What's in Chapter 11

This chapter covers a number of topics. You have learned most of the basic functions in VisualAge for Java. Now it's time to investigate some of the more advanced topics. This chapter covers:

- Exploring the Data Access Builder, which is a component in the Enterprise edition
- Making user-generated events to use in your Java programs
- Understanding visual design patterns that are unique to the Visual Composition Editor
- Looking at the JDK V1.2 changes, focusing on new and improved GUI beans

Now that you have mastered the basics, you are ready to look at more extensive use of Java. Each section has a different focus and provides something for everyone. This first section focuses on how to use the Data Access Builder, which is not included in the Entry edition provided on the CD-ROM. If you have the Enterprise edition, you can follow along. If you do not have the Data Access Builder, it is very helpful to review this section to understand how to map relational data to objects.

Enterprise Edition

The VisualAge for Java Enterprise edition provides several tools for hooking your application or applet to relational data, CICS transactions, C/C++ code, and remote methods by using Remote Method Invocation (RMI). These tools are integrated into the VisualAge IDE and are available from pop-up menus.

The Enterprise Access Builder for Data (referred to as the *Data Access Builder*, or the DAB) is an application development tool that you can use to create data access classes customized for your existing relational database tables. These Data Access classes (which are beans) can be used directly in your Java programs, or they can be used with the Visual Composition Editor to create GUI programs. The Data Access Builder also generates executable code as Test Access Classes that you can run to perform database access testing with the generated code.

The CICS Access Builder generates a COMMAREA bean and associated classes that enable your Java client program to remotely access CICS transactions written in COBOL.

The C++ Access Builder generates access beans and associated classes that enable your Java program to access C++ services that reside in a .dll. You can generate code and develop your application entirely from the command line, or you can import your access beans into the IDE and create and test the client. The C++ Access Builder reads C++ header files and generates beans representing the classes written in C++. It also generates a make file to construct the C++ .dll.

The RMI Access Builder takes advantage of the Remote Method Invocation mechanism defined in the Java Language specification. The RMI Access Builder enables you to generate distribution code from the application code contained in a source bean. Once the distribution code has been generated and you have created your client program, you can deploy your source bean as a server bean and access it remotely using the services of RMI.

Exploring the Data Access Builder

This section focuses on using the Data Access Builder to create beans and add customized SQL statements to those beans. Additionally, this section discusses the generated AccessApp for testing generated beans to data access.

The generated beans provide the ability to add new rows, update a specific row, delete a row, and select rows from a table using a complex WHERE clause. The DAB generates a bean to represent a row in a table as well as support classes for selection and key management. The DAB maps each column of the table to a property in the generated bean. Also, the DAB enables you to omit columns, perform minor data transformations, and generate methods with custom SQL statements on the bean. Additionally, the DAB can map database views and can be used to create JavaBeans based on a table-join.

The first step to using data from a relational database is to generate the necessary beans to access the data. To support this need, the Enterprise edition provides additional menus to access the enterprise tools. The following sections give examples of using these tools.

In order to complete the samples in this section, you must have the VisualAge for Java Enterprise edition installed. The Entry edition in the CD-ROM, which came with this book, does not have the capability to build and complete this project. Additionally, the sample utilizes DB/2 as the database. If you are using ODBC or Oracle, the same SAMPLE database can be found in those products and, as such, used similarly with VisualAge for Java. To summarize, in order to use the Data Access Builder, you need:

Access to a database product.

There must be a database defined with some data in it.

Authority to connect to the database.

Load the JDBC (Java Database Connectivity) drivers, provided by the database supplier, into VisualAge for Java.

> **NOTE**
>
> The database supplier ships JDBC as .jar or .zip files. After you install DB/2, you will find x:\Sqllib\java\db2java.zip. Copy this file to the same directory as a .jar file. Go to the Workbench and import the .jar file into the repository. This will load and compile a lot of classes, so be prepared for a coffee break.

Generating Data Access Beans

This sample walks you through the creation of beans for data access using the DAB. As a part of this sample, you will create a new project and package in order to organize the generated code. Start the sample with the following steps:

If VisualAge is not already started, start the IDE (Enterprise Edition).

Create a project named **My DAB Example**.

Create a package in the My DAB Example project named **my.dab.example**.

Select the package and click the right mouse button. As shown in Figure 11.1, select **Data Access** from the Tools menu; then select **Create Data Access Beans**.

The Data Access Builder appears as in Figure 11.2.

> **TIP**
>
> If the Data Access Builder cannot connect to the database, there are two things you can try. First, make sure the database is started. You can enter db2start at a command prompt. Second, make sure you are logged on the system. If you are using Windows95, logon when the system starts (and not press the Esc key). If you are using WindowsNT, start the *DB2 Security Server* from the Services icon in the Control Panel.

Select the package name and click the right mouse button. Select **Map Schema** from the pop-up menu as shown in Figure 11.3.

A SmartGuide then guides you through the mapping of the schema. The first panel of the mapping SmartGuide is shown in Figure 11.4. This

Figure 11.1 Starting the Data Access Builder.

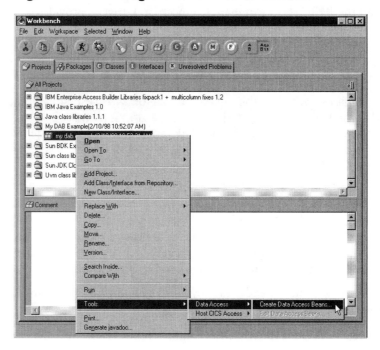

Figure 11.2 First Data Access Builder window.

Figure 11.3 Starting the schema mapper.

Figure 11.4 Mapping SmartGuide.

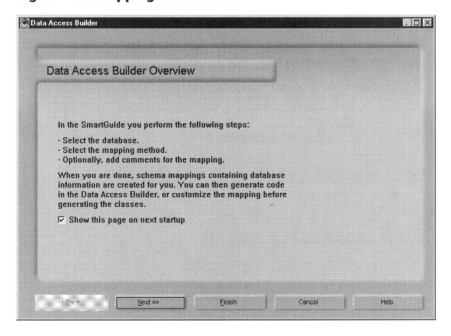

panel provides some instructions on how to proceed. Press the **Next** button to continue to the next page.

Once you have started the mapping SmartGuide, you must specify the database source and the database. Select **DB/2** as your database source and the SAMPLE database as the database. To specify the mapping method, select **By selecting database tables or views** as shown in Figure 11.5. Press the **Next** button to continue to the next page of the SmartGuide.

Next, specify the tables that you wish to map. Press the **Get Tables** button to retrieve a list of all tables in the database. Then select the Department and Employee tables as shown in Figure 11.6. Press the **Next** button to continue to the next page of the SmartGuide.

The last page of the SmartGuide enables you to enter a schema mapping description. Type in any description you want to have added to the generated beans. Then press the **Finish** key to complete the mapping as shown in Figure 11.7.

The Data Access Builder window can now show schema mappings under the package name, as shown in Figure 11.8.

Figure 11.5 Mapping selection of database.

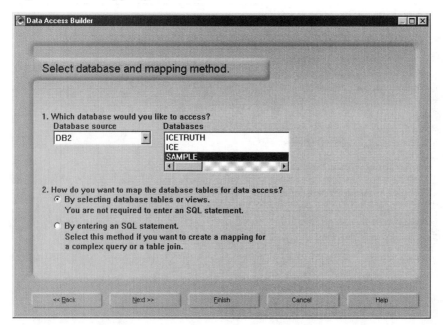

Figure 11.6 Selecting tables.

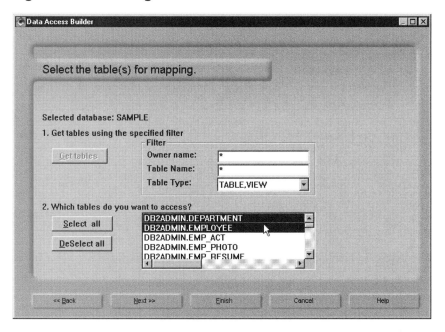

Figure 11.7 Schema description.

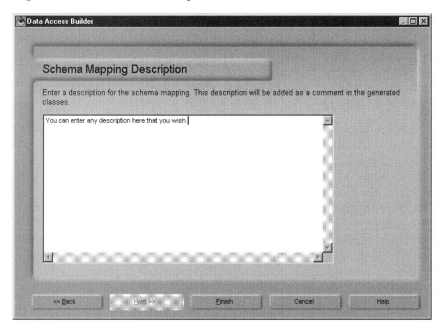

Figure 11.8 Schema mapping.

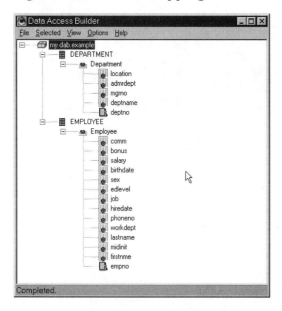

The icons used in the schema mapping have the following meanings:

 Database table.

 Bean representing a row in the database table.

 A property of the bean.

 A property that has been marked as a data identifier. Database keys are automatically marked as data identifiers.

You can select any of the icons and, using the right mouse button, obtain a pop-up menu containing actions that can be performed on the item. For each of the above icons, you can access its properties. For others, such as the bean, you can add customized SQL statements.

Now that the access beans have been created in the DAB, you must save them to the IDE. This action generates the Java code to support the selections made in the DAB for the bean. From the File menu, select **Save and Generate All** to save the beans to the associated package as shown in Figure 11.9.

Saving and generating can take some time. The progress indicator is shown in Figure 11.10. Be patient; it is better for VisualAge to generate this JDBC code than for you to have to type it.

After the code has been generated and saved to the IDE, close the DAB window. From the File menu, select **Exit.** If you then expand the my.dab.example

Figure 11.9 Save and Generate All option.

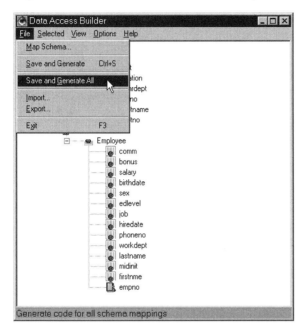

package, you will see that the DAB has created several classes for both the Department and Employee tables as shown in Figure 11.11.

Note that there are several classes generated to support access to the Department table. Each class is named with the bean name assigned from the DAB as the first part of the name. Some of these classes are provided for access, while others are provided for the test access application.

Figure 11.10 Saving and Generating progress indicator.

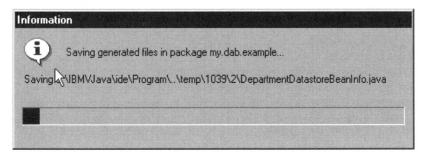

Figure 11.11 DAB-generated classes.

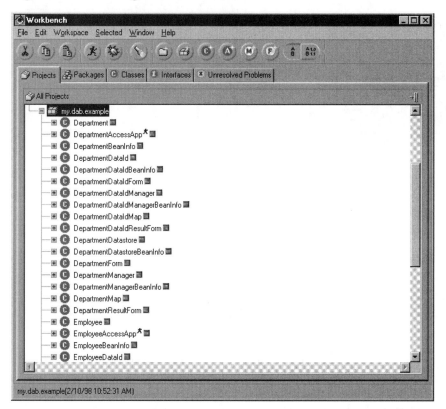

Access Classes

The access classes are generated to provide the ability to access the database with operations such as add, read, update, and delete. The descriptions in Table 11.1 use the classes generated from the Department table in the SAMPLE database. Note that for each of the classes in the table, a corresponding BeanInfo class is also generated to define the JavaBeans interface for the bean.

Test Access Application Classes

The test access application classes are generated to provide the ability to immediately test your access to the database using the generated beans. You can run the test access application as either a Java application or an applet. The descriptions in Table 11.2 use the classes generated from the Department table in the SAMPLE database.

Table 11.1 Access Class Descriptions

Class Name	Description
Department	Defines get and set methods for properties mapped to a table. Methods for type conversion are also defined in this class. Additionally, add, delete, and update methods are found in this class. An instance of this class can be thought of as a row in the table.
DepartmentDataId	For schemas with data identifiers (keys as defined on the table or assigned data identifiers), this class is used in the delegation model to supply the get and set methods for the data identifiers.
DepartmentDataIdManager	For schemas with data identifiers (keys as defined on the table or assigned data identifiers), this class is used in the delegation model to supply select and cursor control similar to the Manager class.
DepartmentDataIdMap	For schemas with data identifiers (keys as defined on the table or assigned data identifiers), this class is used in the delegation model to define the basic row-to-object mapping for the data identifiers.
DepartmentDatastore	Provides connect and disconnect functionality to the database, as well as rollback and commit behavior. This class is a subclass of DatastoreJDBC.
DepartmentManager	Provides select, fetch, and cursor control capabilities over the table.
DepartmentMap	Defines the basic row-to-object mapping specifications for all properties. For data identifiers, this behavior is delegated to the DataIdMap class.

Using the Generated Data Access Beans

Once you have generated beans for accessing your database, test the access by running the DAB generated test access application. From this application, you can retrieve all records and display them, fetch one record at a time, or perform update, add, and delete operations on the database table. The following steps guide you through connecting to the database, selecting all records, and fetching records one at a time.

If VisualAge is not already started, start the IDE (Enterprise edition).

In the previously created My DAB Example project and the my.dab.example package, select the class **DepartmentAccessApp**.

Table 11.2 Test Access Application Class Descriptions

Class Name	Description
DepartmentAccessApp	Driver class for the test access application. You can run this class as either a Java application or as an applet.
DepartmentDataIdForm	A Panel subclass that displays all of the data identifiers for a particular department.
DepartmentDataIdResultForm	A Panel subclass that displays a multicolumn list with all data identifiers in it for all departments.
DepartmentForm	A Panel subclass that displays all properties for a particular department.
DepartmentResultForm	A Panel subclass that displays a multicolumn list with all columns for the department table for all departments.

Run this class as an application by clicking on the Run button at the top of the Workbench window. The window shown in Figure 11.12 appears. This window contains several panels, which are accessed through the buttons at the top of the window.

Type in an appropriate user ID and password and then press the **Connect** button to connect to the database.

When you have successfully connected to the database, click on the **Manager** button to show the DepartmentManager panel, shown in Figure 11.13. The open() action is selected.

Press the **Execute** button to perform the open action on the database.

Next, click on the **ResultForm** button to show the DepartmentResultForm panel as shown in Figure 11.14. From this panel, press the **Fill** button to select all records from the Department table and display them in the ResultForm.

To fetch the records one by one, go to the DepartmentCursor panel by pressing the **Cursor** button. A panel with a value for each field appears as shown in Figure 11.15.

Press the **Reopen** button to reposition the cursor at the beginning of the table.

Next, press the **Fetch Next** button to fetch the next record. Subsequent fetches return the next record until the last record has been fetched.

Close the window to end the application.

Figure 11.12 Connecting to the database.

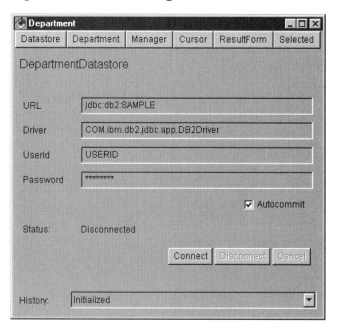

Figure 11.13 Opening the database.

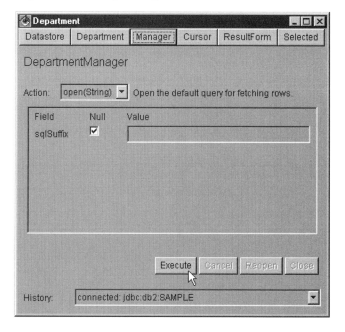

Figure 11.14 Selecting all items.

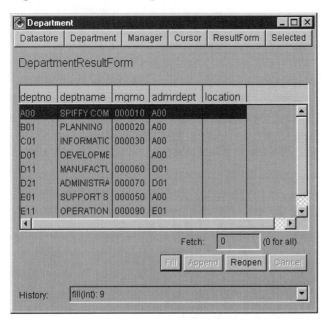

Figure 11.15 Fetching one item at a time.

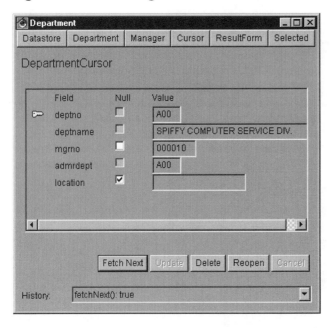

Adding a Custom Method to a Generated Bean

Many applications that access data need to perform other operations in the data layer on behalf of the domain or application layer. One such operation is to generate a unique key for use when adding a new record. A way to do this is to find the highest value for a key field in the database and then add 1 to that value. This guarantees a unique key. The SQL code to find the maximum value of Deptno in the Department table would be:

```
SELECT MAX(DEPTNO) FROM DB2ADMIN.DEPARTMENT
```

Note that DB2ADMIN is the user ID that owns the database (or high-level qualifier). Using the DAB, this select statement can be placed in a generated method for the generated bean, Department. The following steps guide you through adding this customized SQL statement to the Department bean as the getMaxId method.

If VisualAge is not already started, start the IDE (Enterprise edition).

In the previously created My DAB Example project, select the my.dab.example package and click the right mouse button. As pictured in Figure 11.16, select **Data Access** from the Tools menu. Then select **Edit Data Access Beans**.

Figure 11.16 Editing data access beans.

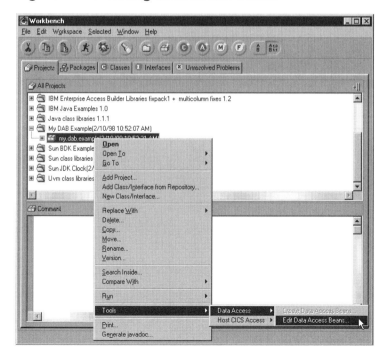

The Data Access Builder window appears with the previously created beans for Department and Employee in the window. Select the **Department** bean and click the right mouse button for the pop-up menu; select **Methods** as shown in Figure 11.17.

The methods with customized SQL statements are displayed as shown in Figure 11.18. Press the **Add** button in the center of the window to add the getMaxId method.

The Add Customized SQL Statement window appears. In the SQL statement area, type the select statement as shown in Figure 11.19. Then press the **Validate** button to validate the SQL. If there are no errors, the **Validate** button is disabled. If errors occur, a window appears with a descriptive message. Make the corrections and try again.

Next, change the method name to **getMaxId** and select parameter1. Change the **Map To** radio button to **Return Value** so that the method returns the maximum ID as a return value. Leave the return type as **String**.

Figure 11.17 Open customized SQL methods.

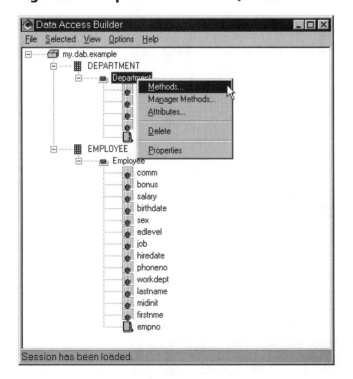

Figure 11.18 Customized SQL methods.

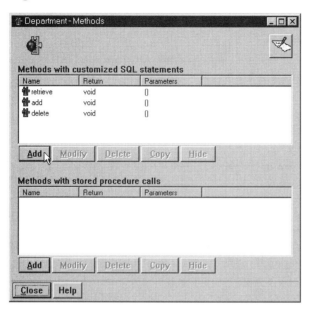

Figure 11.19 Adding customized SQL.

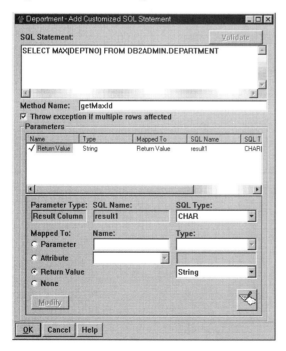

Press the **Modify** button to commit the change on the parameter; then press the **OK** button to save the changes and close the window. Notice that the getMaxId method has been added to the list of Customized SQL methods, as shown in Figure 11.20.

Close the Methods window, do a **Save and Generate All** from the DAB File menu, and close the DAB window.

Lastly, look at the Department class in the Workbench and notice that the getMaxId method has been added to the class as shown in Figure 11.21.

Data Access Builder Summary

As you can see, the Data Access Builder makes it much easier to work with relational databases.

User-Generated Events

In Chapter 5, we briefly discussed user-generated events. User-generated events are common in object-oriented design, especially when implemented using visual programming techniques.

Events generally indicate that a component in a program has reached a certain state or that a certain externally generated action has taken place. Events

Figure 11.20 Customized SQL methods with getMaxId added.

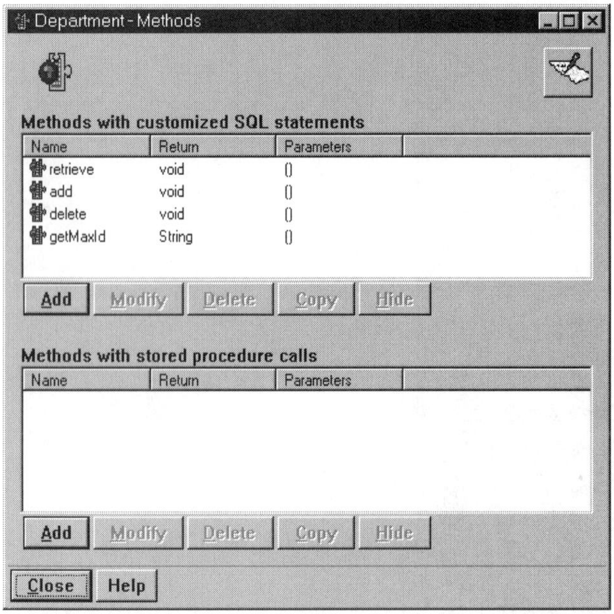

Figure 11.21 Resulting the getMaxId method.

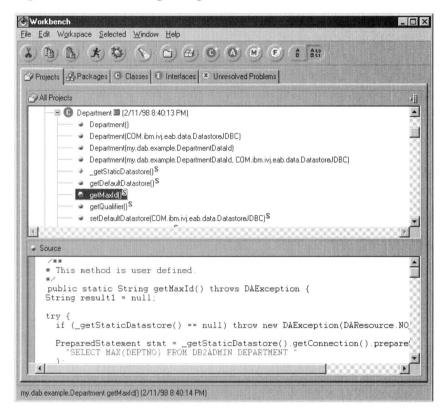

usually happen at an unpredictable moment in time. It is not necessary for the program to wait for the event to occur. However, when the event does occur, the program should be notified and respond appropriately.

Events should not be confused with exceptions, even though on the surface, they appear quite similar. Exceptions have a completely different execution path and occur as the result of an error. Once an exception is thrown, the calling stack of the program is unwound until some component handles the exception in a catch block or the program abnormally terminates. In contrast, if an event is signaled and no component is listening for it, nothing happens.

Types of Events

Events are said to be *raised* or *signaled*. Some examples of events that are signaled by Java AWT classes are:

- key
- mouse

- focus
- propertyChanged
- text

Create your own events to satisfy the needs of your program or component. For example, if you had a bean that represented a disk file, it should raise an end-of-file event to signal that there is no more data to be read. If the bean representing a fuel tank changes state to almost-empty, an event should be fired to turn on a light and warn the driver to get some fuel.

The Java event model in version 1.1 and above is said to be delegation-based. In the delegation model, there are event sources and event listeners. Listeners are responsible for registering their interest in an event with the source of the event. When the event occurs, the source informs all listeners, which can then act on the event according to their own needs. Most Java 1.1 language books in the market explain the delegation event model in detail, so we won't duplicate that effort in this book.

Making Your Own Events

Implementing your own events in VisualAge for Java is very simple, because the tool generates all classes necessary to define the event and multicast it to its listeners. Once an event is defined in VisualAge, it can be used by any class in the current image. When connecting an event to a method, VisualAge generates the code necessary to register the target class as a listener and to handle receipt of the notification.

Bank Account Example

The best way to understand how VisualAge for Java makes it so simple to create and use your own events is to create an example applet and study the generated code. We will keep the applet trivial and concentrate on explaining the creation and use of the event.

The sample applet represents a bank account. The account has a balance. You can withdraw and deposit into the account. When the balance reaches 0, the balance display changes its background color to red. While the balance is 0 or above, the background is white.

The instructions to build this sample will be short and to the point. By now, you should be able to follow these steps, short as they are, and successfully complete the applet.

AccountView

Start by creating a new package under the My Project project. Call the package **userEventSample**. Create the account view bean by following these steps:

Create a new class called **AccountView** subclassing java.awt.Applet. Design the bean visually.

Use a GridBagLayout on the applet.

Drop two Label beans on the applet. Change the labels to **Account balance:** and **balance here**. Name the last Label bean **lblBalance**.

Drop a Panel on the free-form surface. Set its layout to FlowLayout.

Drop two Buttons onto the Panel. Name them **pbWithdraw** and **pbDeposit**, change their labels to **Withdraw $10** and **Deposit $10** respectively.

Drag the Panel onto the Applet. Your AccountView bean should look similar to Figure 11.22.

AccountModel

The account model consists of two methods, withdraw() and deposit(). They subtract or add $10 from the balance, respectively. You could get fancier and let the user define the amount of the transaction, but the object of this exercise is to build a quick and easy sample to explain user-created events. Follow these steps to build the account model bean:

Create a new class; call it **AccountModel**. Its superclass is java.lang.Object.

Open the browser for AccountModel and switch to the BeanInfo page.

Add a new *int* property. It should be readable, writeable, and bound. Call it **balance**.

Figure 11.22 AccountView bean.

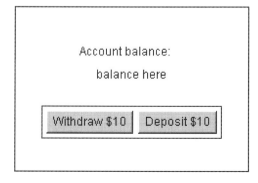

Add two methods that return void and take no parameters. Call them **withdraw** and **deposit**.

Switch to the Hierarchy page of the browser and select the AccountModel class in the Class Hierarchy pane. To change the initial value of the balance to $100, switch to the Source pane and change:

```
int fieldBalance = 0; to
int fieldBalance = 100;
```

Select withdraw() from the Methods pane and add the following highlighted line to the method:

```
public void withdraw() {
/* Perform the withdraw method. */
setBalance(getBalance() - 10);
return;
}
```

Select deposit() from the Methods pane and add the following highlighted line to the method:

```
public void deposit() {
/* Perform the deposit method. */
setBalance(getBalance() + 10);
return;
}
```

Connect the Beans

Open the Visual Composition Editor for the AccountView bean. Drop an AccountModel bean on the free form surface. Call it **account.** Connect the following:

```
account (balance) → lblBalance (text)
pbWithdraw (actionPerformed) → account (withdraw())
pbDeposit (actionPerformed) → account (deposit())
```

So far, the AccountView bean should look like Figure 11.23.

Save and test the program. The starting balance should be 100, and you should be able to make deposits and withdrawals to the account. When the account reaches 0 and goes negative, nothing happens.

AccountOverdrawnEvent

Now you will add a new event interface to handle the special situation caused when the account balance goes below 0.

Figure 11.23 Connections so far.

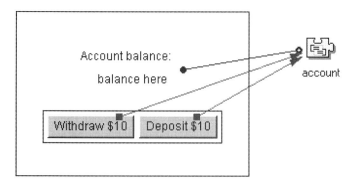

With the browser for the AccountModel bean opened, switch to the
BeanInfo page.

 You might be tempted to press the New Event Set feature button. It is used
when you want the bean to be the source of an existing event, like an action
event.

When creating a new event, one that doesn't already exist in the image,
you need to select **New Listener Interface** from the Features menu. This option
is also available from the pop-up menu in the Features pane. Create a new listener
interface by following these steps:

Select **New Listener Interface** from the Features menu. The New Event
Listener SmartGuide appears as shown in Figure 11.24.

Enter the name of the event you are creating, in this case, **account-
Overdrawn**. By convention, event names start in lowercase. The
SmartGuide suggests the names for the following interface and classes:

• Event listener interface

• Event object class

• Event multicaster class

These names are derived from the event's name and usually make sense
and can be accepted as they are. Press the **Next** button.

The next page of the SmartGuide appears as shown in Figure 11.25. On
this page, you enter the name of the listener method that will be called by
the multicaster when the event occurs. This method will be implemented by
every class who listens for this event. Enter **handleAccountOverdrawn** and
press the **Add** button.

Figure 11.24 New Event Listener SmartGuide.

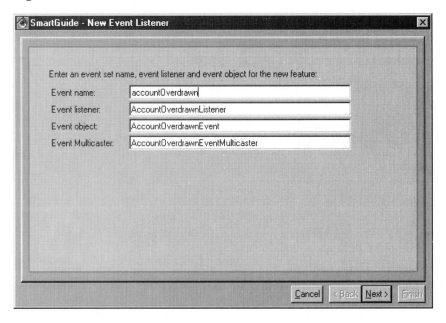

Figure 11.25 Entering a listener method name.

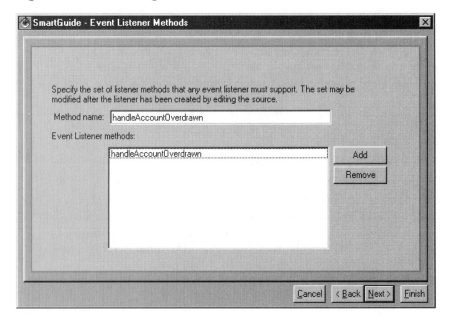

Press the **Finish** button.

Switch to the Methods page of the browser and note the methods created:

- addAccountOverdrawnListener()
- removeAccountOverdrawnListener()
- fireHandleAccountOverdrawn()

The first two methods are used by the listeners to add and remove themselves to the list of interested objects. The last method is used in this bean to indicate that the account is overdrawn.

Switch to the setBalance() method and add the highlighted code to signal the accountOverdrawn event when the balances dips below 0:

```
public void setBalance(int balance) {
  /* Get the old property value for fire property
     change event. */
  int oldValue = fieldBalance;
  /* Set the balance property (attribute) to the
     new value. */
  fieldBalance = balance;
  /* Fire (signal/notify) the balance property
     change event. */
  firePropertyChange(" balance" ,
    new Integer(oldValue), new Integer(balance));

  if( fieldBalance < 0)
    fireHandleAccountOverdrawn(
      new AccountOverdrawnEvent(this));

  return;
}
```

Open the Visual Composition Editor for the AccountView bean and make the following connection:

```
account (handleAccountOverdrawn) → lblBalance (background)
```

The connection is dashed because you need to define what color you want to set the background to. Double-click the connection, press the **Set parameters** button, and set the value to **red**.

Save and test the program. Press the **Withdraw $10** button several times until the balance becomes less than 0. The balance should now be shown with a red background.

How Events Work

Select the connection you just made and note its name. In our case it is **conn3**; depending on how you built the sample, it might be a different number in your case. Switch to the Methods page of the browser and find the conn3() method. This method is responsible for setting the background color of lblBalance:

```
getlblBalance().setBackground(java.awt.Color.red);
```

But when is conn3() called? If you look at the methods for the AccountView class, you will see that the handleOverdrawnAccount() method was created when you made the last connection. It is called on all objects registered as listeners of the accountOverdrawn event by the multicaster object. This method determines which object originated the event; if it is the **account** object, it triggers conn3. See the following code:

```
public void handleAccountOverdrawn(
    AccountOverdrawnEvent event) {
  // user code begin {1}
  // user code end
  if ((event.getSource() == getaccount()) ) {
    conn3(event);
  }
  // user code begin {2}
  // user code end
}
```

Event Listeners

If you look at the declaration for the AccountView bean, you will see that it implements the **userEventSample.AccountOverdrawnListener.**

```
public class AccountView extends Applet implements
    java.awt.event.ActionListener,
    java.beans.PropertyChangeListener,
    userEventSample.AccountOverdrawnListener
```

In the initConnections () method, the account object registers itself as a listener for the accountOverdrawn event:

```
private void initConnections() {
  // user code begin {1}
  // user code end
  getaccount().addPropertyChangeListener(this);
  getpbWithdraw().addActionListener(this);
  getpbDeposit().addActionListener(this);
```

```
    getaccount().addAccountOverdrawnListener(this);
    conn0SetTarget();
}
```

Summary of Events

As you can see, this is fairly complex mechanism. The good news is that you do not have to write any of the event's supporting classes or implement the listener interface by hand. A considerable amount of code was generated for you by the tool. All you had to do was decide on a name for the event, determine what condition should signal the event in your program, and write one line of code to actually signal the event.

Now that you have been exposed to creating and using user-generated events, go back and iterate on the AccountModel bean to add a new event interface called **AccountOK**. This event should be signaled when the account balance is no longer negative. Use this event in AccountView to turn the background color of lblBalance to white.

Visual Design Patterns

The Visual Composition Editor in VisualAge for Java utilizes the unique *construction from parts* paradigm. Most developers find the Visual Composition Editor very easy to use, especially because it generates a lot of the code needed for your program. However, you must write code in your programs, as you have seen throughout this book. When developing programs with the Visual Composition Editor, keep a healthy balance between drawing connections and writing code.

Just as with writing code, there are many ways to use connections. When you combine connections, the result is a visual design pattern. This section covers some of the many visual design patterns we have seen when using the Visual Composition Editor. With each pattern example, a small sample is provided to illustrate the pattern. Many of the patterns have performance considerations, so alternative patterns or suggestions are also provided.

GUI Connection Pattern

This pattern shows a common misuse of connections as shown in Figure 11.26. Using connections to set GUI beans functions properly, but it is very inefficient and creates visual clutter. Connections should be used for high-level functions.

This GUI connection pattern can be easily simplified by writing code. You can create a class method and call it as shown in Figure 11.27. The method could be called clearAll(); it would call the setter methods for each field. This reduces visual clutter, reduces the code size, and improves performance.

Figure 11.26 GUI connection pattern.

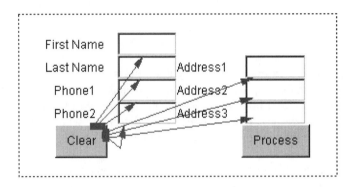

Aggregation Pattern

Sometimes you see a collection of invisible beans that have only one connection to another bean. This group of beans is highlighted in Figure 11.28. This pattern happens as programs evolve through the iterative development process.

The best way to solve this problem is to aggregate the invisible beans as shown in Figure 11.29. You need to create a new bean, move the components to the new bean, recreate the connections, and substitute the new aggregate bean for the discrete components previously used. What you have done, is create a composite invisible bean, which provides the function under the covers and simplifies the connections.

Circular Pattern

The circular pattern frequently occurs through iterative development, as shown in Figure 11.30. This sample is over-simplified. Some developers end up stringing

Figure 11.27 Simplifying the GUI connection pattern.

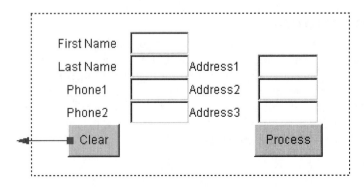

Figure 11.28 Aggregation pattern.

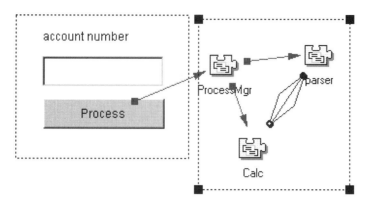

many beans together. If the beans use a lot of property-to-property connections, the program slows as all the connection methods are called. There are a number of ways to fix this pattern, all of which require some redesign and reimplementation. Be careful using property-to-property connections, because they usually signal events in both directions.

Monolithic Pattern

Some developers are used to writing procedural applications. When they start developing object-oriented applications using the Visual Composition Editor, they put the logic in the bean and call it from the user interface with connections similar to what is shown in Figure 11.31. This pattern is difficult to maintain, impractical for reuse, and is a good example of weak object-oriented programming. The solution for the design pattern is better use of invisible beans. Substitute Event to Script connections with invisible JavaBeans when you can reuse the function provided in the script.

Figure 11.29 Simplifying the aggregation pattern.

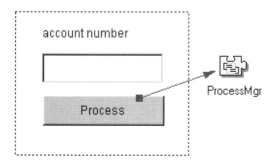

Figure 11.30 Circular pattern.

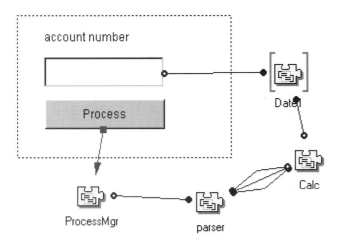

Tight Coupling Pattern

Some visual programs have a large number of property-to-property connections, as shown in Figure 11.32. This is not inherently bad, but it creates a very tight coupling of the beans. Also, depending on what is in the target bean, the pattern might also cause performance problems. One solution for this is to pass an object, an array, or a vector to the target bean. This solution is similar to the solution for the Diamond pattern and it is a much more flexible design.

Figure 11.31 Monolithic pattern.

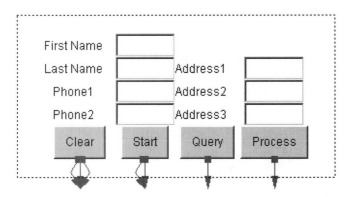

Figure 11.32 Tight coupling pattern.

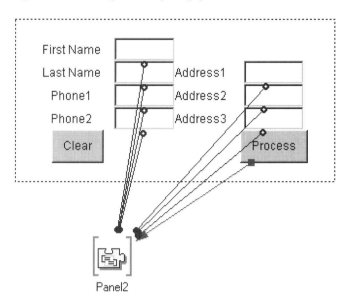

Diamond Pattern

An easily identified pattern is the Diamond, shown in Figure 11.33. This effect happens when you promote a large number of individual features in an embedded bean. When you connect a lot of these promoted features to another bean, the connection lines form a diamond shape.

Figure 11.33 Diamond pattern.

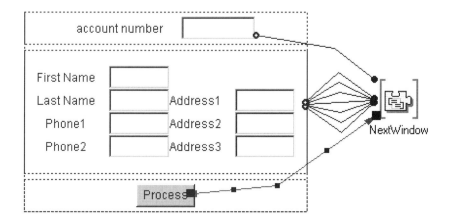

The Diamond pattern can be improved as shown in Figure 11.34. You can redefine the method to accept a parameter. You should also promote an aggregation of the properties, then you can pass an object, an array, or a vector to the target bean.

Visual Patterns Summary

The patterns discussed in this section frequently occur in visual programming, and it is good to be able to identify them and improve them as needed. With any fairly complex program, there are many different ways to implement the design. As mentioned in this section, the iterative development process causes programs to evolve. Each iteration should be reviewed so that design patterns that adversely affect the performance, maintainability, or extensibility of the program can be fixed.

A Tour of the Swing Toolkit

With JDK 1.2, Sun will release a new user interface tool kit called *Swing*. Its more formal name is the Java Foundation Classes (JFC). Swing offers a much better user interface framework and class library for building Java programs than the Abstract Windowing Toolkit (AWT) provides. Swing conforms to the JavaBeans specification and provides a plethora of new user interface beans. IBM will support Swing in the next release of VisualAge for Java. This section gives you a tour of the features provided in Swing by running through a Swing example application, SwingSet as shown in Figure 11.35.

Figure 11.34 Simplifying the diamond pattern.

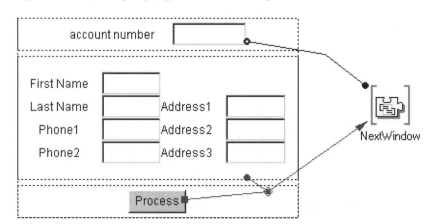

Figure 11.35 The SwingSet sample application.

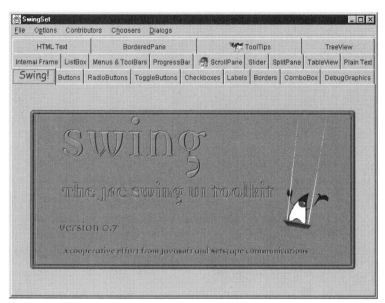

Combination Box

Combination boxes present lists of data from which an item can be selected. Swing provides read-only, editable, and custom combination boxes shown in Figure 11.36. Note that the custom combination box shown at the lower right contains a hierarchical list of items.

DebugGraphics

This sample shows a unique feature of Swing in the DebugGraphics tab, shown in Figure 11.37. Specify which beans to debug; when you repaint the panel, the area paints in slow motion. This can help in debugging your visual beans.

Tree View

With the tree view, you can display hierarchical data. The tree view doesn't actually contain the data; it's simply a view of the data. Figure 11.38 shows a sample of the tree view.

Look and Feel

One of the many important features found in Swing is the ability to change the look and feel of an application by making a single property change to a container. Figure 11.39 shows how the SwingSet application provides for changing look and feel.

Figure 11.36 ComboBox sample.

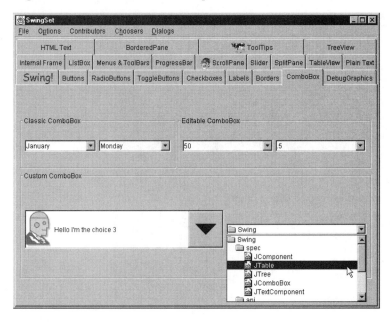

Figure 11.37 DebugGraphics sample.

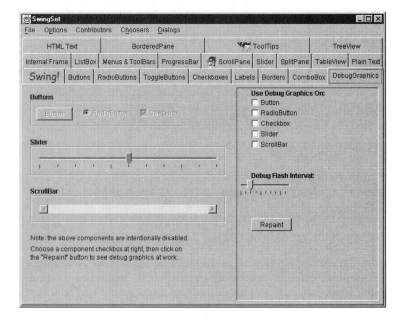

Figure 11.38 Tree view sample.

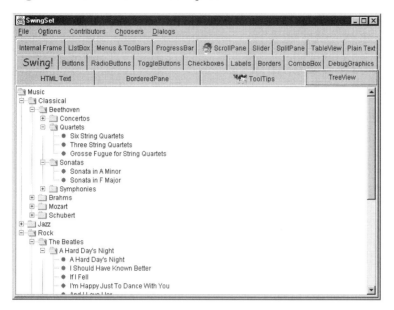

Figure 11.39 Switch to Motif look.

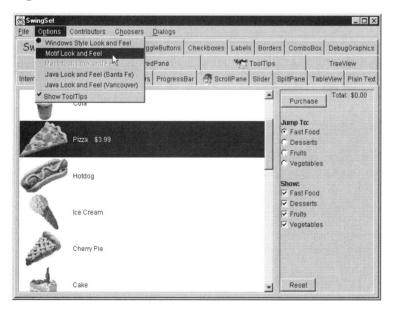

If the Motif look-and-feel option is chosen, the application is repainted to look and feel like a Motif application. Figure 11.40 shows the SwingSet application using the Motif look and feel. Notice that the radio buttons and check boxes have a much different look in Motif.

Other Swing Enhancements

Other Swing bean enhancements include:

Enhanced Push Buttons. Swing provides new push buttons that provide the ability to display both text and graphics in the push button. You can use the "rollover" property to change the button colors or graphic when the mouse floats over it.

Enhanced Radio Buttons. Swing provides new radio buttons that provide the ability to display both text and graphics in the radio button.

Enhanced Toggle Buttons. Swing has added enhanced toggle buttons. Swing supports toggle buttons that use animated images when a toggle button is selected.

Enhanced Check Box. Swing offers enhanced check boxes that support graphic images.

Enhanced Label. Swing offers the ability to provide text and graphics in a label.

Figure 11.40 Motif look and feel.

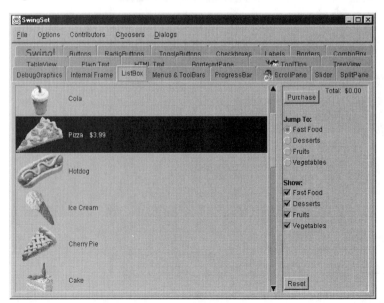

Borders. One area where the AWT is lacking is in providing borders to group related visual beans. Swing provides such borders.

Frame. Swing provides a mechanism to open a frame within a panel. The frame can be made to be closeable, iconifiable, and resizable.

Enhanced List Bean. Swing replaces the AWT list bean with a much enhanced list box that allows graphics to be displayed with text. Upon selection, you can change a line in the list box to show additional data or some other event.

Enhanced Menus and Tool Bars. Swing provides the ability to have menus and tool bars. You can use menu bars or pop-up menus, and menu items can contain text and graphics. Tool bars can be associated with a text area. A tool bar can be torn off of the window into its own window or placed on a different edge.

Progress Bar. The progress bar is used to mark the progress of a long running application or applet.

Sliders. Swing provides various sliders, both horizontal and vertical, that allow for tick marks and different slider buttons.

Split Pane. The split pane is used to divide two (and only two) Components. The two Components are graphically divided based on the look-and-feel implementation. The two Components can be resized interactively by the user.

Table View. The table view is a user interface component that presents data in a two-dimensional table format. The table view has many features that make it possible to customize its rendering and editing. However, the table view provides defaults for these features so that simple tables can be set up easily.

Plain text. Swing supports text that allows for the editing of a single line of text. It is intended to be source-compatible with the text field implementation provided by the AWT.

Summary

This chapter had four sections covering some advanced topics. You learned the following:

- How to use the Data Access Builder, which is a component in the Enterprise edition.

- How to make user-generated events to use in your Java programs.

- How to recognize different visual design patterns that are unique to the Visual Composition Editor, and some remedies for weak patterns.

- What GUI JavaBeans are in the JDK V1.2 and some of their new functions.

Wrapping Up the Book

After completing this book, you have learned many of the basic concepts used to implement good object-oriented Java applications. You have developed a number of well-designed and functional sample programs that cover a broad range of AWT GUI JavaBeans and business logic. You have learned how to use the many functions in VisualAge for Java to develop JavaBeans. Now you will have more confidence that you can produce good Java software using VisualAge for Java.

Programming is both a science and an art, and a good software professional should develop the best application possible under the constraints of the project. This means that experience and planning are key components to good software development. You need to budget time for iterating the design, testing, incorporating user feedback, adding error detection and correction, Help, and documentation. There is a lot more to application development than painting screens and making connections.

We hope you have enjoyed this book as much as we have enjoyed writing it.

RELATED PUBLICATIONS

Berg, Daniel J. 1998. *Advanced Techniques for Java Developers*. New York, NY: John Wiley & Sons, Inc.

Carrel-Billiard, Marc, and John Akerley. 1998. *Getting Started with VisualAge for Java 1.0*. Englewood Cliffs, NJ: Prentice Hall.

Chang, Daniel, and Dan Harkey. 1998. *Client/Server Data Access with Java*. New York, NY: John Wiley & Sons, Inc.

Daconta, Michael C. 1998. *Java 1.2 and JavaScript for C and C++ Programmers*. New York, NY: John Wiley & Sons, Inc.

Flanagan, David. 1997. *Java in a Nutshell, Second Edition*. Sebastopol, CA: O'Reilly & Associates, Inc.

Gosling, James, et al. 1998. *Java Programming Language, Second Edition*. Reading, MA: Addison-Wesley.

Horstmann, Cay S. 1997. *Practical Object-Oriented Development in C++ and Java*. New York, NY: John Wiley & Sons, Inc.

McGraw, Gary, and Edward Felten. 1996. *Java Security*. New York, NY: John Wiley & Sons, Inc.

Orfali, Robert, and Dan Harkey. 1998. *Client/Server Programming with Java and CORBA, Second Edition*. New York, NY: John Wiley & Sons, Inc.

Vanhelsuwe, Laurence. 1997. *Mastering JavaBeans*. Alameda, CA: Sybex.

Weiner, Scott and Stephen Asbury. 1998. *Programming with JFC*. New York, NY: John Wiley & Sons, Inc.

INDEX

A

abstract modifiers, 91
Abstract Windowing Toolkit. *See* AWT
    classes.
access classes, 310–311. *See also*
    Data Access Builder.
access modifiers, 144
AccessApp class, 302
actionPerformed events, 246, 248, 288–289
Add button, 227
add() method, 112, 170
Add Package SmartGuide, 33, 34, 68, 69
Add Project SmartGuide, 12, 33, 34, 67, 68
Adding Machine application, 65–71, 83–84
    adding logic to, 68, 88–109
    GUI beans in, 75–79
    invisible beans in, 88–95
    testing and debugging, 109–114
    user interface for, 68–92
AddionalInfoPanel, 254
Additional Info buttons, 227, 255
addListener() method, 87
Advanced Calculator applet, 141–142
    adding logic to, 167–176
    connections for, 172–182
    exception handling in, 182–191
    Layout Managers and, 148–150
    numeric-only TextField in, 192–197
    user interface for, 151–155
aggregation connection design
    pattern, 328, 329
<ALIGN> HTML tag, 221
alignment, setting, 53, 152–154. *See also*
    Layout Managers.
All Features option, 56, 107
<ALT> HTML tag, 221
anchor GridBag property, 148, 154, 155
Appearance options page, 28–29
Applet class, 32, 36, 41–43, 68, 69–70, 72
<APPLET> HTML tag, 212, 219–221
applets
    buttons and, 51–52

    display features of, 74
    GUI beans and, 31, 42–45, 46
    HTML files for, 219–221
    IDE, running inside of, 14–24
    IDE, running outside of, 217, 219–221
    paint method and, 18–20
    projects and packages for, 32–35
    running outside of IDE, 209–212
    saving, 45–46, 57
    security features of, 17–18
    version controls for, 20–22. *See also*
        JavaBeans.
appletviewer tool, JDK, 204
applications
    browser selection by, 294–296
    exiting, 285–286
    exporting, 287–288
    IDE, running inside of, 14–24
    IDE, running outside of, 221–225,
        287–288
    naming conventions in, 79–80
    serialized beans in, 275–288
<ARCHIVE> HTML tag, 221
Archives, exporting Java, 209–212
arrays, examining in Scrapbook, 125–126
attributes. *See* properties, JavaBean.
audio files, packaging, 209–211
automatic connection conversion, 174–175
Automatic version option, 21, 23
AWT classes, 7–8, 39–40, 42–60, 62–65,
    72–73, 98–99, 191, 319–320. *See also*
    GUI beans.
AWT Panel subclass, 155–158

B

bank account event example, 320–325
base constructors, 234
bean palette, 191, 222–225
BeanInfo class, 87–88, 99–104
BeanInfo page, 93, 96, 99–101,
    168–170, 231–234
beans. *See* JavaBeans.

Beans List window, 81–83
Behavior page, 29
bell() method, 127
bookmarks, 24
BorderLayout Manager, 72
borders, Swing improvement of, 337
BottomPanel, 254
bound check box, 97
bound properties, 86
breakpoints, setting, 134–135
Browse function, 36, 97
browsers, 17–18, 114–116, 294–296
ButtonPanel, 254
buttons, 51–52, 76, 77, 79–80, 155–158,
    264–267, 336
byte-code, exporting Java, 202–204, 205

C

C++ Access Builder, 302
CalculatorLogic bean, 68, 88–109
CalculatorView bean, 67–84, 88–92,
    95–114, 147–150
CardButtonPanel, 254
CardLayout Manager, 72, 252–256
CardPanel, 254
cards, 252
categories in Visual Builder, 39, 40
CD-ROM software, 5–8
    loading interchange file from, 128–132
check boxes, 97, 262–263, 336
Checkbox bean, 262, 263
CheckboxGroup bean, 262
CICS Access Builder, 302
CICS transactions, 301, 302
circular connection design pattern,
    328–329, 330
Class class, 100
.class files, 202–204, 214, 219, 221
Class/Interface browser, 92–94, 96, 167–170
Class Qualification window, 36, 37, 71
class repository, 4, 9, 11, 206
Class view, 10
classes, Java, 9, 10, 11–14, 41–43, 301,
    302, 310–311
    connections and, 53–56
    creating new, 68–71, 88–92, 229–231
    DAB generated, 310–311
    name conventions, 36, 70, 79–80
    versioning all in a package, 21–22
CLASSPATH variables, 222, 287–288
clear() method, 178–180, 291–293

clearing text areas, 178–180, 291–293
Clone window, 8
COBOL, CICS transactions and, 302
code, Java source, 32, 45–51, 58–60,
    111–113, 144–146, 221, 236–237. See
    also debugging tools, JavaBean.
<CODEBASE> HTML tag, 221
columns, DAB control of, 302–311
columns property, TextField, 151–152, 155
combination boxes in Swing, 333, 334
combining beans, 63
COMMAREA bean, 302
comments, viewing code, 59
Compare with option, 20
Component base class, 64
Component class, 64
composite beans, 62, 63
conn() method, 58–60
Connect option, 107
connections, 51–60, 105–109,
    259–260, 285, 286
    debugging of, 119–121
    exceptions and, 188–191
    exporting as .dat files, 215–216
    moving among beans, 172–176, 196–197
    visual design patterns and, 327–332
console, VisualAge for Java, 8, 119–121
constant parameters, 289–293
constrained properties, 86
construction from parts paradigm, 327
constructors, 234–237
Container class, 42, 64, 71–74, 155–160
context menu, 54
copy warning, 143–144
copying JavaBeans, 142–147
Create Class/Interface SmartGuide, 36, 37,
    70, 90, 230
Create Method SmartGuide, 282, 284
Create package subdirectory, 206–207
CurrentInternetAddress Variable, 244, 250
currentKey property, 264, 271
customizing Layout Managers, 73

D

DAB. See Data Access Builder.
.dat files, exporting, 215–216
data access beans, 301–318
Data Access Builder
    building classes with, 301–311
    managing databases with, 311–318
data access classes, 303–318

databases, DBA control of, 301–318
Date bean, 51–52, 53
dateLabel bean, 51, 53
DB/2, Data Access Builder and, 302–311
Debugger window, 8, 136
debugging tools, JavaBean, 8, 64–65, 117
   console and, 119–121
    Scrapbook and, 122–127
    source-level debugger and, 128–140
    System.out.printIn() and, 118
    uvm.tools.debugger and, 127–128
DebugGraphics tab in Swing, 333, 334
DebugSupport class, 127–128
default access modifier, 16, 144
default beans, VisualAge, 191
default constructor, 237
Definitions pane of BeanInfo page, 100, 101
Delay Before Lists Pop Out option, 29–30
Delete button, 227
deleting beans, 177
Department class, 311
DepartmentAccessApp class, 312
DepartmentDataId class, 311
DepartmentDataIdForm class, 312
DepartmentDataIdManager class, 311
DepartmentDataIdMap class, 311
DepartmentDataIdResultForm class, 312
DepartmentDatastore class, 311
DepartmentManager class, 311
DepartmentMap class, 311
DepartmentResultForm class, 312
deprecated AWT class methods, 62–63
Design the class visually option, 38, 70
development environment, integrated. *See*
    IDE, VisualAge.
diamond connection design pattern, 331–332
display names, 97–98
dispose() method, 285
Distribute horizontally icon, 53
divide() method, 172, 190
domain objects, 229–230
Double Click Opens option, 29
double-clicking options, 28–29
double promotion of beans, 272
drop zones, 158

E

editable property in read-only text fields, 79
editions, managing applet, 13, 20–21
Editions pane, 13
embedded beans, 260

Enterprise Access Builder for Data. *See* Data
    Access Builder.
Enterprise VisualAge for Java edition, 6, 11,
    31, 301–318
Entry VisualAge for Java edition, 4, 6–8, 11
errors, handling of, 13–14, 32, 143–144.
    See also debugging tools, JavaBean.
event icon, 96, 97
Event Listener Methods SmartGuide,
    323, 324
event listeners, 86, 87, 326–327
event-to-method connections, 105
event-to-property connections, 105
event-to-script connections, 105, 282–284,
    329, 330
Event-to-Script window, 282–283
events, 87, 110–111
   actionPerformed, 246, 248, 288–289
   user-generated, 318–327
   windowClosing, 274, 282, 285
   windowOpened, 266, 273–274
exception handling, 59, 87, 121–122,
    182–191, 282–284, 319
Exceptions SmartGuide, 282–284
executable class icon, 14
exiting applications, 285–286
expert features, 98–99
export options, file
   interchange files and, 215–216
   Java archives and, 209–212
   Java byte-code, 202–204, 205
   Java source code, 204–209
Export SmartGuide, 202, 204, 206–208,
    211, 215–217, 287
exporting applications, 287–288

F

factories, object, 249–251
features, JavaBean, 86–88, 92–104
   BeanInfo class and, 87–88, 99–104
   events, 110–111, 246, 248, 266, 273–274,
     282, 285, 288–289, 318–327
   methods, 9, 10, 49–51, 87, 104, 111–113,
     144, 169–170, 175–176, 179–180,
     232–234, 272, 315–318
   properties, 86, 95–104, 107–111, 149,
     151–154, 167–170, 333, 335, 336
   this, 239–240
   types, 86, 97, 103–104, 167, 168
Features pane of BeanInfo page, 99–100
fields. *See* properties, JavaBean.

file dialogs, 272
file format export options
    interchange files and, 215–216
    Java archives and, 209–212
    Java byte-code, 202–204, 205
    Java source code, 204–209
fill GridBag property, 148
filter() method, 198–200
FilteredTextField bean, 193–194
final modifiers, 91
float properties, 167–170
FlowLayout Manager, 72
focus events, 320
focus, setting with init(), 164–165
fonts, setting, 30–31, 44–45, 46
FormattedInfoPanel, 254
frames, 125–127, 262, 273–274, 285,
    288–289, 337
free-form surface, Visual Builder, 39, 40–41

G

generated Java code, viewing, 45–51,
    58–60, 144–146
get methods, 86, 97
Get Tables button, 306
getAppletinfo() method, 47
getAudioClip() method, 214
getCheckboxGroup() method, 262
getdateLabel() method, 59
getFormattedName() method, 233–234
getImage() method, 214
getMaxId() method, 316, 317, 318, 319
getResource() method, 214
getSystemResource() method, 214
gettheTable() method, 280–281
Graphical User Interface beans.
    See GUI beans.
GridBagConstraint class, 148–150, 152–154
GridBagLayout Manager, 72, 148–150,
    158–163
gridHeight GridBag property, 149
GridLayout Manager, 72, 75–76
grids, GridBag, 148
gridX GridBag property, 149
gridY GridBag property, 149
GUI beans, 38, 39, 41–43, 62–64
    connections, 52–53, 170–171, 327, 328
    copying, 142–147
    creating new, 36–38
    Layout Managers and, 75–77, 148–150

naming conventions, 78, 163–164
    packages and classes for, 68–71
    substitutions of, 194–195
    Tab, 247
    tab order and, 80–83
    TextArea bean, 260–261, 292
    TextField, 79, 151–155, 175, 192–200
    Visual Composition Editor and, 170–171
GUI connection design pattern, 327, 328

H

halt() method, 127
handleException() method, 47, 121–122
Hanoi applet example, 15–23
hardware requirements, VisualAge, 1–3
Hashtable class, 261, 262, 267–272, 282–284
<HEIGHT> HTML tag, 221
Hello World applet
    adding beans to, 41–43, 51–52
    GUI beans in, 36–38
    main() method in, 47, 49–51
    projects and packages in, 32–35
help features, adding to applications, 293–298
help, hover in Visual Builder, 39
hidden features, 98–99
Hide Tab Tags option, 82
Hierarchy view, 41, 42, 47, 58
hover help in Visual Builder, 39
<HSPACE> HTML tag, 221
HTML files
    for applets, 219–221
    help features and, 293–298
    Javadoc and, 114–115
    running juggler.jar with, 212, 213, 214

I

IBM Java Examples projects, 12–14,
    202–203, 206–207, 215–216
icons, VisualAge, 14, 24, 33, 36, 46, 53, 93,
    95, 96, 97, 124, 308
IDE, VisualAge, 8–10, 14, 16
    applets and, 14–24, 45–51, 57
    applications and, 14–24
    exporting code from, 201–217
    hardware requirements for, 2–3
    loading Java classes into, 11–14
    new packages and, 67–68, 69
    new projects and, 32–33, 34, 67–68. *See
    also* Workbench.

image files, packaging, 209–211
implements, 91
Import SmartGuide, 128, 129, 194, 223
import statements, 91
incremental compilers in VisualAge, 32
indexed properties, 86
init() method, 47, 48, 164–165
initial focus, setting, 164–165
InitialInternetAddressObjectFactory, 250
initializing applets, 18
inset GridBag property, 149, 154
inspect() method, 127, 128
Inspector window, 125–127
int properties, 167
intConnections() method, 326–327
integrated development environment. *See*
    IDE, VisualAge.
interchange files, 128–132, 215–216
Interface view, 10
Internet Address applet, 227–231, 251–257
    bean properties, adding, 231–234
    connections in, 248–251
    constructors in, 234–237
    panels and, 237–251, 254
InternetAdditionalInfo Panel, 237
InternetAdditionalInfoPanel, 240–242
InternetAddress class, 229–237
InternetAddressesVector, 245, 250
InternetAddressFinalApplet, 254
InternetAddressObjectFactory, 250
InternetButtonPanel, 237, 246–247
InternetFormattedInfoPanel, 237, 242–246
InternetUserInfoPanel, 234, 237–240
IntTextField bean, 192–200
invisible beans, 62, 64–65, 88–95, 229
    connections and, 105–109, 172–176,
        328, 329
    copying, 142–147
    creating new, 88–92
    features and, 92–104, 167–171
ipadx GridBag property, 149
ipady GridBag property, 149
iterative development method, 32, 328–329
ivjtheTable variable, 281

J

JAR files, 209–212, 219, 222–225
Java Archive files, 209–212, 219, 222–225
Java byte-code, 202–204, 205
Java classes. *See* classes, Java.

Java Database Connectivity drivers, 303
.java files, 192–193, 204–208
Java Foundation Classes, 332–337
Java HTML Help feature, 6, 293–298
Java modifiers, 16, 91
Java Object class, 230
Java Runtime Environment, 287
Java source code, 32, 45–51, 58–60,
    111–113, 144–146, 192–193, 204–208,
    221, 236–237. *See also* debugging
    tools, JavaBean.
Java types, 86, 97, 103–104, 167, 168
Java V1.0 and V1.1 classes, 62–63
JavaBeans, 44–51, 52–53, 62–65, 92–95,
    177, 191
    connections and, 51–60, 105–109,
        119–121, 172–176, 188–191,
        196–197, 215–216, 259–260, 285,
        286, 327–332
    copying, 142–147
    creating new, 36–38, 88–92
    debugging tools and, 8, 64–65, 117,
        118, 127–140
    distribution of, 209–212, 222–225
    embedded, 260
    events and, 86, 87, 110–111, 246, 248,
        266, 273–274, 282, 285, 288–289,
        318–327, 320–325
    features of, 85–88, 95–104, 231–234
    importing, 183–186
    Layout Managers and, 42, 53, 71–76,
        148–150, 158–163, 252–256
    methods and, 9, 10, 49–51, 86, 87, 104,
        111–113, 144, 169–170, 175–176,
        179–180, 232–234, 315–318
    naming conventions, 43–44, 70, 78,
        163–164
    new in JDK V1.2, 333–327
    promotion of, 267, 272
    properties and, 86, 95–104, 107–111, 149,
        151–154, 167–170, 333, 335, 336
    for relational databases, 303–318
    serializing, 275–288
    SQL statements and, 315–318
    switching, 194–195
    types and, 86, 97, 103–104, 167, 168
    Variable, 237–240
    Visual Composition Editor and, 105,
        170–171, 191, 222–225. *See also*
        GUI beans; invisible beans.
Javadoc, generating, 114–115

java.io.PrintStream class, 118
JDBC drivers, 303
JDK Version 1.1, 62
JDK Version 1.2, 332–337
JFC (Java Foundation Classes), 332–337
JRE (Java Runtime Environment), 287
juggler HTML file, 210, 212, 213, 214, 222–224

K

key events, 319
key/value pairs, 267–272

L

Label bean, 42–45, 46
labels
    alignment of, 152–153
    Label bean, 42–45, 46
    Swing enhancements of, 336
layering of Panels, 252–256
Layout Managers, 42, 53, 71–74, 149, 150
    BorderLayout, 72
    CardLayout, 72, 252–256
    FlowLayout, 72
    GridBagLayout, 72, 148–150, 158–163
    GridLayout, 72, 75–76
list beans, 337
listeners, event, 86, 87, 326–327
lists, IDE, 31
Lists page, 31
Log window option, 8
look-and-feel options in Swing, 333, 335, 336

M

main() method, 32, 47, 49–51, 114, 146–147
manifest.mf file, 222
Mapping SmartGuide, 303, 305, 306
MenuBar beans, 288–289
menus, 288–298, 337
message boxes for exceptions, 183–186, 188
Method view, 10
method with unresolved problems modifier, 16
methods, 9, 10, 49–51, 87, 104, 111–113, 144, 169–170, 175–176, 179–180, 232–234, 315–318

add(), 112, 170
addListener(), 87
bell(), 127
conn(), 58–60
dispose(), 285
divide(), 172, 190
filter(), 198–200
getAppletinfo(), 47
getAudioClip(), 214
getCheckboxGroup(), 262
getdateLabel(), 59
getFormattedName(), 233–234
getImage(), 214
getMaxId(), 316, 317, 318, 319
getResource(), 214
getSystemResource(), 214
gettheTable(), 280–281
halt(), 127
handleException(), 47, 121–122
init(), 47, 48, 164–165
inspect(), 127, 128
intConnections(), 326–327
main(), 32, 47, 114, 146–147
multiply(), 172
println(), 118, 120–121
readObject(), 275
refreshListBoxItems(), 242–243
removeListener(), 87
saveCurrentCategory(), 272
selectInternetAddressListItem(), 243–244, 245
setBrowser() method, 294–295
setCheckboxGroup() method, 262
setCurrent() method, 263–264
setDisplayName(), 98
setExpert() methods, 98
setHidden methods, 98
setLayout() method, 73
setShortDescription(), 98
setText() method, 59, 292–293
show(), 127
showException(), 191
showHelp(), 296
start(), 47, 48
subtract(), 172
System.out.printIn(), 118, 119, 120–121
updateInternetAddress(), 245–246
writeObject(), 275
methods icon, 96, 97
Methods page of class/interface browser, 93, 100

Methods pane in Debugger window, 136
Methods view, 47, 49, 58–59
minimizing connections, 179–180
modal behavior of Sticky function, 75–76
Model-View-Controller design, 61–62
modifiers, bean, 91
monolithic connection design
    pattern, 329, 330
Motif look-and-feel option, 333, 335, 336
mouse events, 319
moving JavaBean connections,
    172–176, 196–197
multiply() method, 172

N

Name each version option, 22, 23
<NAME> HTML tag, 221
naming conventions
    in application development, 79–80
    for buttons, 79–80
    for classes, 36, 70, 79–80
    for JavaBeans, 43–44, 70, 78, 163–164
    for packages, 33, 35
    for projects, 33
    for properties, 86
native modifiers, 16
New Class icon, 36
New Event Listener SmartGuide, 323, 324
New Method Feature SmartGuide, 104,
    232–234, 235, 236
New Package icon, 33
New Project icon, 33
New Property Feature SmartGuide, 97, 98,
    231, 234
null layout option, 42, 53, 73. *See also*
    Layout Managers.
numbers-only TextField beans, 192–200

O

object factories, 249–251
<OBJECT> HTML tag, 221
OKDialog bean, 183–184
old AWT class methods, 62–63
One name version option, 22, 23
online VisualAge documentation, 7–8
operating systems, compatible, 3–4
operation methods, calculator, 170, 172
OS/2 Warp Version 4.0, 3, 6

P

package subdirectory, 203, 204
packages, 9, 10, 32, 33–35, 67–68, 69,
    141–142
paint method, 18–20
palette, bean, 191, 222–225
panels, 19, 30, 41, 72, 155–160, 237–256,
    261–267, 337
parameters, 270–272, 289–293
ParcPlace Smalltalk, 215
patches for VisualAge, 4, 5
pbSetDate button, 52, 53
persistence, adding to applications, 275–288
preferred features, 107
Previous Edition option, 20
previousKey property, 264, 270, 271
primitive beans, 63–65. *See also* GUI beans;
    invisible beans
println() method, 118, 120–121
private modifiers, 16, 144
Professional VisualAge for Java edition,
    4, 6, 11, 16, 31
progress indicator bars, 13–14, 308, 309, 337
project_resources directory, 33, 212–214
projects, 10, 11, 12–14, 32–34, 212–214,
    216–218
Projects view, 9, 10, 24, 28
promoting JavaBeans, 267, 272
properties, JavaBean, 86, 95–104, 107–111,
    149, 151–154, 167–170, 333, 335, 336
property events, passing of, 110–111
Property icon, 96, 97
property sheets, Layout Managers as, 71
Property SmartGuide, 98, 99
property-to-parameter connections, 270–272
property-to-property connections, 105–111
    circular connection pattern, 328–329, 333
    tight coupling pattern, 330, 331
propertyChange event, 105, 270, 320
PropertyDescriptor class, 98, 99
propertyEditorClass, 99
protected modifiers, 16, 144
public access modifiers, 144
public class methods, 87
public class variables, 86
public modifiers, 16, 91
Publish Project SmartGuide, 217, 218
publishing of projects, 216–217, 218
push buttons, Swing, 336

R

radio buttons, 261–267, 336
RadioButtonManager bean, 261–264
RadioButtonPanel bean, 261–262, 264–267
raised events, 319
RAM requirements for VisualAge, 2–3
read-only text fields, 79
Readable check boxes, 97
readObject() method, 275
refreshListBoxItems() method, 242–243
relational databases, DAB control of, 301–318
Reminder application, 275–298
    RadioButtonManager bean, 261–264
    RadioButtonPanel bean, 261–262, 264–267
    ReminderApp bean, 262, 273–274
    ReminderHashtable bean, 261, 267–272, 282–284
    ReminderPanel bean, 262, 267–272
ReminderApp bean, 262, 273–274
ReminderHashtable bean, 261, 267–272, 282–284
ReminderPanel bean, 262, 267–272
Remote Method Invocation (RMI), 31, 106, 302
removeListener() method, 87
Reorder Connections From window, 286, 287
Replace with option, 20
Repository Explorer window, 9
repository, VisualAge, 4, 9, 11, 206
resizing applets, 75
resource files, 33, 209, 212–214, 215, 221
result property, 170
RMI Access Builder, 302
RMI (Remote Method Invocation), 31, 106, 302
rows, DAB control of, 302–311
Run button, 14
run-time requirements, 5
running juggler applet, 210, 212, 213, 214, 222–224

S

Save and Generate All option, 308
saveCurrentCategory() method, 272
saving applets, 45–46, 57
saving application information, 275–287

Saving Replaces Methods option, 30
schemas, mapping of, 303, 305–308
Scrapbook icons, 124
Scrapbook window, 9, 122–127
Search dialog window, 65
selectInternetAddressListItem() method, 243–244, 245
serialized beans, 275–288
Set Bookmark icon, 24
set methods, 86, 97
setBrowser() method, 294–295
setCheckboxGroup() method, 262
setCurrent() method, 263–264
setDisplayName() method, 98
setExpert() method, 98
setHidden() method, 98
setLayout() method, 73
setShortDescription() method, 98
setText() method, 59, 292–293
Settings window, 15
show() method, 127
showException() method, 191
showHelp() method, 296
signaled events, 319–320
Simple Calculator, 65–67, 109–114
    adding logic to, 68, 88–109
    user interface for, 68–92
size, controlling applet, 72
sliders, Swing toolkit and, 337
SmartGuides
    Add Package, 33, 34, 68, 69
    Add Project, 12, 33, 34, 67, 68, 69
    Create Class/Interface, 36, 37, 70, 90, 230
    Create Method, 282, 284
    Event Listener Methods, 323, 324
    Exceptions, 282–284
    Export, 202–208, 211, 215–217, 287
    Import, 128, 129, 194, 223
    Mapping, 303, 305, 306
    New Event Listener, 323, 324
    New Method Feature, 234, 235, 236
    New Property Feature, 97, 98, 99, 231, 234
    Publish Project, 217, 218
    Versioning Selected Items, 20–21, 23
software, installing VisualAge, 3–8
source code, Java, 32, 45–51, 58–60, 111–113, 144–146, 221, 236–237
    See also debugging tools, JavaBean.
source editor, changing fonts in, 30
source-level debugger, VisualAge, 128–140

Source pane in Debugger window, 136
spacing, Layout Manager control of, 72
spanning grids, 158–159
SQL statements, 315–318
start() method, 47, 48
starting VisualAge for Java, 8
static modifiers, 16
Sticky check box, 75–76, 156
strings, 56, 101–103, 118, 234–236, 237
stub code, 111–113
sub-panels, 155–158. *See also* panels.
subtract() method, 172
Sun BDK Examples project, 210
Sun class libraries, 11
Sun JDK applet viewer tool, 204
superclasses, indicating, 36
Swing toolkit, 332–337
SwingSet sample application, 333–337
Switcher program
  loading interchange files and, 128–132
  source-level debugger and, 132–140
switching GUI beans, 194–195
synchronized modifiers, 16
System bean, 285
System.out.printIn() method, 118, 119,
    120–121

T

Tab GUI beans, 247
Tab stop positions, ordering, 80–83
table view improvements, 337
tables, DAB control of, 302–311
Team edition of VisualAge for Java, 21
terminating programs in debugger, 139
test access classes, 301, 310–311
Test icon, 46
text
  on beans, 44, 151–152, 291–293
  on buttons, 52, 77
  Swing toolkit and, 337
Text Editing page of Workbench, 30
text events, 320
TextArea bean, 260–261, 292
TextField bean, 79, 151–152, 155, 175,
    192–200
this feature, 239–240
Threads pane in Debugger window, 136
threads, visual cues and, 16
throws keyword, 121
tight coupling connection patterns, 330, 331

toggle buttons, 336
toString() method, 56, 118, 237
Towers of Hanoi puzzle applet, 15–23
trace information, 119–121
transient modifiers, 16
tree view in Swing toolkit, 333, 335
try/catch blocks, 87, 121–122, 182
Type for field error, 143–144
Type of Export SmartGuide, 203, 204, 205
types, Java, 86, 97, 103–104, 167, 168

U

Unresolved Problems view, 10, 13, 14, 28
Update button, 227
updateInternetAddress() method, 245–246
user code areas, 59, 73–74
user-generated events, 318–327
User Info button, 227, 254
UserInfoPanel, 254
user interfaces, 39, 40–41, 63–64
Uvm class libraries, 11, 127–128
uvm.tools.debugger package, 127–128

V

Value pane in Debugger window, 136
Variable beans, 237–240
version controls in VisualAge, 13, 20–21
Version window, 20–22, 23
Versioning Selected Items SmartGuide,
    20–21, 23
video files, packaging, 209–211
viewing Java code, 45–51, 58–60, 144–146
views, VisualAge, 9–10, 13, 14, 24, 28, 41,
    42, 47, 58, 332–337
Visible Variables pane in Debugger
    window, 136
visual beans. *See* GUI beans.
Visual Builder. *See* Visual Composition
    Editor.
Visual Composition Editor, 16, 38–41
  bean palette in, 191, 222–225
  connections and, 53–56, 105–109,
    172–176, 194–196
  Layout Managers and, 73–74, 149, 150
  main() method in, 146–147
  regenerating code with, 145–146
  visual design patterns in, 327–332
visual connections. *See* connections.
visual cues, IDE, 16

visual programming patterns, 327–332
    aggregation pattern, 328, 329
    circular pattern, 328–329, 330
    diamond pattern, 331–332
    GUI pattern, 327, 328
    monolithic pattern, 329, 330
    tight coupling pattern, 330, 331. *See also* connections.
VisualAge for Java
    bookmarks in, 24
    code documentation and, 114–115
    debugging code in, 119–128, 136–140
    default JavaBeans in, 39–40
    Enterprise edition, 6, 11, 31, 301–318
    Entry edition, 4, 6–8, 11
    exception handling in, 59, 87, 121–122, 182–191, 319
    hardware requirements for, 1–3
    installation of, 5–8
    online documentation for, 7–8
    Professional edition, 4, 6, 11, 16, 31
    resource files and, 33, 209, 212–214, 221
    software requirements, 3–5
    source code and, 45–51, 58–60
    Swing toolkit improvements of, 332–337
    Team edition of, 21
    version controls in, 13, 20–21

views in, 9–10, 13, 14, 24, 28, 41, 42, 47, 58, 332–337. *See also* IDE, VisualAge; JavaBeans; Visual Composition Editor.
VisualAge for Smalltalk, 215
volatile modifiers, 16
<VSPACE> HTML tag, 221

W

Web browsers
    Java applet security and, 17–18
    Javadoc and, 114–116
    selection by applications, 294–296
Web pages, running applets on, 217–221
weightX GridBag property, 149
weightY GridBag property, 149
widgets, 63–64
<WIDTH> HTML tag, 221
windowClosing events, 274, 282, 285
windowOpened events, 266, 273–274
Windows 3.1, 3–4
Windows NT Version 4.0, 3–4
Windows95, 3–4
Workbench, 8, 9–10, 12, 24, 27–31, 92. *See also* IDE, VisualAge.
Workspace, 11, 64–65
Writable check boxes, 97
writeObject() method, 14, 275

Java™ Development Kit
Version 1.1.x
Binary Code License

This binary code license ("License") contains rights and restrictions associated with use of the accompanying software and documentation ("Software"). Read the License carefully before installing the Software. By installing the Software you agree to the terms and conditions of this License.

1. **Limited License Grant.** Sun grants to you ("Licensee") a non-exclusive, non-transferable limited license to use the Software without fee for evaluation of the Software and for development of Java™ compatible applets and applications. Licensee may make one archival copy of the Software. Licensee may not redistribute the Software in whole or in part, either separately or included with a product. Refer to the Java Runtime Environment Version 1.1 binary code license (http://java.sun.com/products/JDK/1.1/index.html) for the availability of runtime code which may be distributed with Java compatible applets and applications.

2. **Java Platform Interface.** Licensee may not modify the Java Platform Interface ("JPI", identified as classes contained within the "java" package or any subpackages of the "java" package), by creating additional classes within the JPI or otherwise causing the addition to or modification of the classes in the JPI. In the event that Licensee creates any Java-related API and distributes such API to others for applet or application development, Licensee must promptly publish an accurate specification for such API for free use by all developers of Java-based software.

3. **Restrictions.** Software is confidential copyrighted information of Sun and title to all copies is retained by Sun and/or its licensors. Licensee shall not modify, decompile, disassemble, decrypt, extract, or otherwise reverse engineer Software. Software may not be leased, assigned, or sublicensed, in whole or in part. **Software is not designed or intended for use in on-line control of aircraft, air traffic, aircraft navigation or aircraft communications; or in the design, construction, operation or maintenance of any nuclear facility. Licensee warrants that it will not use or redistribute the Software for such purposes.**

4. **Trademarks and Logos.** This License does not authorize Licensee to use any Sun name, trademark or logo. Licensee acknowledges that Sun owns the Java trademark and all Java-related trademarks, logos and icons including the Coffee Cup and Duke ("Java Marks") and agrees to: (i) to comply with the Java Trademark Guidelines at http://java.com/trademarks.html; (ii) not do anything harmful to or inconsistent with Sun's rights in the Java Marks; and (iii) assist Sun in protecting those rights, including assigning to Sun any rights acquired by Licensee in any Java Mark.

5. **Disclaimer of Warranty.** Software is provided "AS IS," without a warranty of any kind. ALL EXPRESS OR IMPLIED REPRESENTATIONS AND WARRANTIES, INCLUDING ANY IMPLIED WARRANTY OF MERCHANTABILITY, FITNESS FOR A PARTICULAR PURPOSE OR NON-INFRINGEMENT, ARE HEREBY EXCLUDED.

6. **Limitation of Liability.** SUN AND ITS LICENSORS SHALL NOT BE LIABLE FOR ANY DAMAGES SUFFERED BY LICENSEE OR ANY THIRD PARTY AS A RESULT OF USING OR DISTRIBUTING SOFTWARE. IN NO EVENT WILL SUN OR ITS LICENSORS BE LIABLE FOR ANY LOST REVENUE, PROFIT OR DATA, OR FOR DIRECT, INDIRECT, SPECIAL, CONSEQUENTIAL, INCIDENTAL OR PUNITIVE DAMAGES, HOWEVER CAUSED AND REGARDLESS OF THE THEORY OF LIABILITY, ARISING OUT OF THE USE OF OR INABILITY TO USE SOFTWARE, EVEN IF SUN HAS BEEN ADVISED OF THE POSSIBILITY OF SUCH DAMAGES.

7. **Termination.** Licensee may terminate this License at any time by destroying all copies of Software. This License will terminate immediately without notice from Sun if Licensee fails to comply with any provision of this License. Upon such termination, Licensee must destroy all copies of Software.

8. **Export Regulations.** Software, including technical data, is subject to U.S. export control laws, including the U.S. Export Administration Act and its associated regulations, and may be subject to export or import regulations in other countries. Licensee agrees to comply strictly with all such regulations and acknowledges that it has the responsibility to obtain licenses to export, re-export, or import Software. Software may not be downloaded, or otherwise exported or re-exported (i) into, or to a national or resident of, Cuba, Iraq, Iran, North Korea, Libya, Sudan, Syria or any country to which the U.S. has embargoed goods; or (ii) to anyone on the U.S. Treasury Department's list of Specially Designated Nations or the U.S. Commerce Department's Table of Denial Orders.

9. **Restricted Rights.** Use, duplication or disclosure by the United States government is subject to the restrictions as set forth in the Rights in Technical Data and Computer Software Clauses in DFARS 252.227-7013(c) (1) (ii) and FAR 52.227-19(c) (2) as applicable.

10. **Governing Law.** Any action related to this License will be governed by California law and controlling U.S. federal law. No choice of law rules of any jurisdiction will apply.

11. **Severability.** If any of the above provisions are held to be in violation of applicable law, void, or unenforceable in any jurisdiction, then such provisions are herewith waived to the extent necessary for the License to be otherwise enforceable in such jurisdiction. However, if in Sun's opinion deletion of any provisions of the License by operation of this paragraph unreasonably compromises the rights or increase the liabilities of Sun or its licensors, Sun reserves the right to terminate the License and refund the fee paid by Licensee, if any, as Licensee's sole and exclusive remedy.